HEALTH, S.
ENVIRO
DICTIONARY

CW01432794

by

Derek A. Grayham

New Edition

ISBN 1 86089 903X

GEE Publishing Ltd
100 Avenue Road
Swiss Cottage
London NW3 3PG
Tel: 020 7393 7400

www.safety-now.co.uk

THE AUTHOR

Derek Grayham is a Registered Safety Practitioner, a Full Corporate Member of the Institution of Occupational Safety and Health and Fellow of the Royal Society of Health and a former member of the National Examination Board in Occupational Safety and Health, the NEBOSH Diploma Behavioural Science Group Co-ordinator and examiner, resigning late in 1982 to live and work for nearly five years in South East Asia as a health and safety consultant and University lecturer.

Very experienced in terms of applied practical health, safety and environmental matters, Derek has been employed in several industries in a large variety of occupations and professions, ranging from the shop floor to boardroom level. In 1979, aged 47, he achieved his first degree, a BA (Hons) in Organisation Studies at the University of Lancaster. He then won a full scholarship from the Department of Occupational Health and Safety at the University of Aston in Birmingham, later being awarded the Bland Payne Scholarship. At the age of 58 he was awarded his Master of Philosophy. In 1998 he was appointed a Visiting Professor in Health and Safety in the Institut Universitaire de Technologie, Universitaire Bordeaux 1, and is English editor of *Hygiène et Sécurité*. He is a NEBOSH course tutor and examiner, a writer, conference speaker (at home and abroad) and researcher on health, safety, environment and related disciplines, and Safety Consultant to several UK companies.

PRINCIPAL COLLABORATOR

Martin Foster MIOSH MIIRSM is a safety practitioner who has travelled widely and has considerable experience in a broad range of industries. After successfully completing his NEBOSH Diploma in 1998, he set up his own Health and Safety Company providing safety training, advice and consultancy services for business and industry. He is a Safety Advisor to several UK companies and an accomplished tutor, trainer and course writer.

COLLABORATORS
(in alphabetical order)

Septi CHAABANE BSc MSc PhD (Co-author French Edition) Associate Professor in Health and Safety in the Department of Health and Safety, University of Bordeaux 1, Tallance, Bordeaux, France. Editor, *Hygiène et Sécurité Préventique*. Member Institut Européen de Formation à la Gestion de l'Environment and Risque Management Groupe Preventique, Bordeaux, France.

Geoff. CLARK Dip.SM MIIRSM MRSH FInst.M Consultant/Trainer, Halcyon Consultancy Services, West Bromwich, West Midlands.

Mark GRAYHAM BSc Senior Analyst and Computer Programmer, Lancashire County Council, Preston, Lancashire.

Juliet GRIFFITH-EDWARDS Tech.SP, Chief Administrator/Safety Advisor, George Dixon (Grant Maintained) School, Bearwood, West Midlands.

Tom MAYCOCK Assistant Health, Safety and Welfare Officer, Sandwell Metropolitan Borough Council, West Midlands.

Tam WYLLIE Health and Safety Advisor, Owens Corning (Building Products) UK Ltd, Queensferry, Flintshire, North Wales.

PREFACE

This is new, updated and revised edition of the popular *Health and Safety Dictionary*, with a greater cover of environmental legislation and an index. It is primarily written as a source of *quick* reference for all those who have a concern for or involvement in health, safety and the environment, especially managers, supervisors, representatives and students on various courses. Complicated language and legal jargon is avoided as much as possible, with references set in a practical context. This edition has nearly doubled the number of entries compared with the first edition, while remaining a convenient size for slipping in a jacket pocket or very small bag.

After nearly half a century of personal involvement with the application of health, safety and environment in business, I (and my colleagues) still find it to be very interesting, even fascinating. We have tried to communicate and share some of our enthusiasm through our style of writing and presentation. The major emphasis throughout this book is on *simplicity* and *clarity*, to provide the target readership with an understanding of the selectively chosen main points of legislation and the many other factors within health, safety and the environment.

It is recommended that the section 'Points about this dictionary' be read before use. Throughout the book, words and terms, which receive further analysis and description within the dictionary text, are in **bold *and* italic**. Words and phrases in plain italic are important, their meaning usually clear in context but not receiving separate entry and discussion. Selected **case law** or **precedents** receive reference, with a brief summary of some cases. Where **case law** is not available – usually because legislation has recently been introduced and therefore 'legal interpretation' is not yet available – the best available *professional opinion* is provided. However, the interpretation, 'amendment', refinement or 'updating' of legislation through case law is a continuing process, carried out by judges in the courts.

Writing a reference dictionary on a multi-discipline science, such as health, safety, welfare and the environment, is necessarily selective. It is as much a question of 'what to put in?' as 'what to leave out?' We need your help to satisfy *your* needs. Therefore, constructive comments and suggestions (via the publisher) from readers concerning text and content are genuinely welcomed. Finally, my collaborators' and the marketing editor of GEE's contribution to this work proved invaluable but ultimately the overall responsibility for the text and selection of references is mine and mine alone. Please bear that in mind should you meet any of us in the future!

Derek Grayham
Rowley Regis
July 2000

v

ACKNOWLEDGEMENTS

Acknowledgements are seldom read but so important. In health and safety networking is part of professional activity. The people who helped in the formulation of this book range from long standing professional colleagues and friends, providing invaluable advice, discussion and/or information on various points, to the students who asked apparently 'simple' but actually very difficult and awkward questions – students sometimes do, don't they? In fact, such questions were very useful, in that they often provoked a re-think or opened up a new perspective.

Others who deserve credit and mention include, in no particular order: Andrew Hale, Professor of Safety Science, Delft TH; Steve Downing, National Training Manager, Lloyds Plant and Safety Training; Roger Clark, Standards Manager, NEBOSH; the anonymous but always very helpful, courteous, efficient and patient staff at the Health and Safety Executive Information Centre, Sheffield (and indeed, throughout the Health and Safety Executive). A special thank you to the staff at the Sandwell Metropolitan Borough Reference Library; the staff at IOSH Headquarters and IOSH reference library; Don Mason, Health, Safety and Welfare Advisor, Sandwell MBC; Richard Bell, Solicitor, Poulson, Cowley and Bell, Redditch; together with literally thousands of students, many hundreds of convention delegates and several clients. Apologies to those overlooked.

POINTS ABOUT THE DICTIONARY

The following will assist when using the dictionary.

i. Only the courts can interpret the law and this is a continuous process of change and development taking account of changes in technology and even societal expectations.

ii. References are occasionally made to *case law*, the context identifies its relevance.

iii. Words and terms made in bold italics have separate entries and description elsewhere in the dictionary.

iv. Words and terms in italics *only* or bold *only* are important but generally considered outside the scope of this work.

v. Selected key points of Acts and Regulations, following a general introduction, are not in section or regulation order but listed alphabetically, e.g. 'Assessments', 'Exceptions', '*Hazards*', 'Special risk' within the text.

vi. Selected important terms and key points in legislation are explained and clarified.

vii. Legislative requirements relating to health, safety and the environment are sometimes found in what could reasonably be considered **non**-health, safety and environmental legislation (i.e. *Consumer Protection Act 1987*). However, all references in this dictionary to non-health and safety law, legal terms and phrases are made because of their health and safety influence, implication and/or application.

viii. References are often made in an entry to the excellent current range of relevant *Health and Safety Executive* (**HSE**) single copy free information booklets and leaflets. When an order is placed with the distributor, *HSE Books*, if they have been updated or revised, the latest issue will be supplied.

ACRONYMS and ABBREVIATIONS

The following list includes common acronyms and abbreviations used in this reference dictionary. A 32-page list of *acronyms and abbreviations used in the HSE* can be obtained from http://www.open.gov.uk.hse/ab98int.htm.

ABI	Association of British Insurers
ACL	Approved Carriage List
ACOP	Approved Code of Practice
AIDs	Acquired Immunodeficiency Syndrome
ALR	Asbestos (Licensing) Regulations
AP(S)R	Asbestos Products (Safety) Regulations
APC	Air Pollution Control
APSR	Asbestos (Prohibitions) (Amendment) Regulations
ASL	Approved Supply List
BATNEEC	best available techniques not entailing excessive cost
BI 510	Approved Accident Book
BNFL	British Nuclear Fuels
BOHS	British Occupational Hygiene Society
BPM	best practical means
BS	British Standards
BSC	British Safety Council
BSI	British Standards Institute
CAA	Clean Air Act
CAAR	Control of Asbestos in the Air Regulations
CAWR	Control of Asbestos at Work Regulations
CBI	Confederation of British Industry
CDC	Chancery Divisional Court
CDGAR	Carriage of Dangerous Goods (Amendment) Regulations
CDGCPLUTPRR	Carriage of Dangerous Goods (Classification, Packaging and Labelling) and Use of Transportable Pressure Receptacles Regulations
CDGRDTR	Carriage of Dangerous Goods by Road (Driver Training) Regulations
CDGRR	Carriage of Dangerous Goods by Road Regulations
CDMR	Construction (Design and Management) Regulations
CE	Commission Européene (used by majority of EU member countries)
CER	Control of Explosives Regulations
CERR	Carriage of Explosives by Road Regulations

CFCs	chlorofluorocarbons
CHIP	Chemicals (Hazard Information and Packaging for Supply) Regulations
CHPR	Construction (Head Protection) Regulations
CHR	Community Homes Regulations
CHSWR	Construction (Health, Safety and Welfare) Regulations
CIAPRWR	Control of Industrial Air Pollution (Registration of Works) Regulations
CIEH	Chartered Institute of Environmental Health
CITB	Construction Industry Training Board
CLER	Contaminated Land Engineering Regulations
CLWR	Control of Lead at Work Regulations
COMAH	Control of Major Hazards Regulations
CORGI	Confederation for the Registration of Gas Installers
COSHH	Control of Substances Hazardous to Health Regulations
CPA	Consumer Protection Act
CPR	Construction Products Regulations
CSR	Confined Space Regulations
DDA	Disability Discrimination Act
DDERR	Disability Discrimination (Employment Relations) Regulations
DoH	Department of Health
DSER	Health and Safety (Display Screen Equipment) Regulations
DSNMSR	Dangerous Substances (Notification and Marking of Sites) Regulations
DSS	Department of Social Security
DTI	Department of Trade and Industry
EA	Environment Agency
Eact	Environment Act
EAT	Employment Appeal Tribunal
EC	European Commission (see CE)
EEC	European Economic Community
EEF	Engineering Employers' Federation
EESR	Electrical Equipment (Safety) Regulations
EIA	Environmental Impact Appraisal
EIS	Environmental Impact Statement
ELCIA	Employers Liability (Compulsory Insurance) Act
EMAS	Employment Medical Advisory Service
EPA	Environmental Protection Act
EPPPSR	Environmental Protection (Prescribed Processes and Substances) Regulations
ER	Elected Representative

ERA	Employment Rights Act
ERDRR	Employment Rights (Disputes Resolution) Act
ETA	Employment Tribunals Act
EU	European Union
FA	Factories Act
FLT	Fork Lift Truck
FPA	Fire Protection Act
FPWR	Fire Precautions (Workplace) Regulations
FSA	Food Safety Act
FSGFHR	Food Safety (General Food Hygiene) Regulations
FSSPSA	Fire Safety and Safety of Places of Sport Act
GNs	Guidance Notes
GPSR	General Product Safety Regulations
GR	Groundwater Regulations
GSIUR	Gas Safety (Installation and Use) Regulations
GSMR	Gas Safety (Management) Regulations
HACCP	Hazard Analysis and Critical Control Points
HAZOP	Hazard and Operability Study
HFL	Highly Flammable Liquids
HFLLLPGR	Highly Flammable Liquids and Liquified Petroleum Gases Regulations
HIV	Human Immunodeficiency Virus
HMIP	Her Majesty's Inspectorate of Pollution
HMSO	Her Majesty's Stationery Office
HRA	Human Rights Act
HSC	Health and Safety Commission
HSCER	Health and Safety (Consultation with Employees) Regulations
HSDSER	Health and Safety (Display Screen Equipment) Regulations
HSE	Health and Safety Executive
HSEAR	Health and Safety (Enforcing Authority) Regulations
HSEiAR	Health and Safety (Emissions into the Atmosphere) Regulations
HSFAR	Health and Safety (First Aid) Regulations
HSIER	Health and Safety Information for Employees Regulations
HSSSR	Health and Safety (Safety Signs and Signals) Regulations
HSTER	Health and Safety (Training for Employment) Regulations
HSWA	Health and Safety at Work etc Act 1974
Hz	Hertz
IEE	Institute of Electrical Engineers
IIR	Ionising Radiations Regulations

ILO	International Labour Organisation
IOSH	Institution of Occupational Safety and Health
IPC	Integrated Pollution Control
IPPC	Integrated Pollution and Prevention Control
ISO	International Standards Organization
LOLER	Lifting Operations and Lifting Equipment Regulations
LPG	Liquid Petroleum Gas
MAF	Minimum Acceptable Flow
MASHMR	Management and Administration of Safety and Health at Mines Regulations
MEL	Maximum Exposure Limit
MHOR	Manual Handling Operations Regulations
MHSWR	Management of Health and Safety at Work Regulations
NCTECR	Notification of Cooling Towers and Evaporative Condensers Regulations
NEBOSH	National Examination Board In Occupational Safety and Health
NIA	Nuclear Installations Act
NICEIC	National Inspection Council for Electrical Installation Contracting
NIDOR	Nuclear Installations (Dangerous Occurrences) Regulations
NIHHSR	Notification of Installations Handling Hazardous Substances Regulations
NIHL	noise induced hearing loss
NNSR	Notification of New Substances Regulations
NSNA	Noise and Statutory Nuisance Act
NWR	Noise at Work Regulations
OES	Occupational Exposure Standard
PPCA	Pollution Prevention and Control Act
PPE	personal protective equipment
PPER	Personal Protective Equipment Regulations
PUWER	Provision and Use of Work Equipment Regulations
RCD	Residual Current Device
RIDDOR	Reporting of Injuries, Diseases and Dangerous Occurrences Regulations
RoSPA	Royal Society for the Prevention of Accidents
RTA	Road Traffic Act
SIA	Statutory Instruments Act
SR	Safety Representative

SS(CP)R 1979	Social Security (Claims and Payments) Regulations 1979
STEL	Short Term Exposure Limit
SWR	Special Waste Regulations
TLV	Threshold Limit Value
TUC	Trades Union Congress
WCAR	Work in Compressed Air Regulations
WHSWR	Workplace (Health, Safety and Welfare) Regulations
WIA	Water Industry Act
WMLR	Waste Management Licensing Regulations
WRA	Water Resources Act
WTR	Working Time Regulations
www	World Wide Web

A

abandoned vehicles on highways or vacant land may be removed and destroyed by the local authority under the *Refuse Disposal (Amenity) Act 1978*.

abatement with regard to health, safety and environmental law is the termination, removal or destruction of a *nuisance*. An example of its use in health, safety and environmental terms is when a *statutory nuisance* as defined in the *Environmental Protection Act 1990* exists, or is likely to occur, then a local authority will serve an abatement notice on:

(a) the person creating the *nuisance*, or
(b) if of a structural nature, on the owner of the premises, or
(c) if the person creating the *nuisance* cannot be traced, on the owner or occupier of the premises.

Contravention of an abatement notice can lead, on *summary conviction*, to a maximum fine of £20,000. In addition, an order for compensation can be made. Appeals against abatement notices must be made to a *Magistrates' Court* within 21 days of service. A commonly used defence is that the *best practicable means* were used to prevent or minimise the *nuisance*. However, beware! In strict legal usage the term *abatement* has a far wider application and use.

abrasion in *occupational health*, is the wearing away of any surface material, such as skin or mucous membrane etc., through rubbing or scraping.

Abrasive Wheels Regulations 1970 (or AWR) were *revoked* in their entirety and replaced on 5 December 1998 by the *Provision and Use of Work Equipment Regulations 1998 (PUWER)*.

abrasive wheel requirements demonstrate the manner in which aside from the prime or superior legislation, e.g. the *Provision and Use of Work Equipment (PUWER)*, 'specialist' legislation can also apply. For example, health hazards from abrasive wheel operations, such as dust, are covered by the *Control of Substances Hazardous to Health (COSHH); noise* by the *Noise at Work Regulations (NWR)*; protective equipment by the *Personal Protective Equipment Regulations (PPER); lighting* by the *Workplace (Health, Safety and Welfare) Regulations (WHSWR)*.

absolute duty effectively means that something **MUST** be done. Two examples of *absolute duty* are (1) the remedy of a *health and safety hazard*, which may

absolute liability

or may not be without taking account of cost, time or trouble and (2) the duty to carry out an assessment required by the *Management of Health and Safety at Work Regulations (MHSWR)* or under **COSHH**.

Absolute duties **cannot** be delegated to *employees*, although an *employer* may appoint an *employee* as a *competent person*, to provide health and safety assistance (**MHSWR**). In addition, an absolute duty is not generally satisfied, for example, through the posting of notices. Failure to carry out an absolute duty almost invariably means the offender faces *absolute liability*. Therefore, the posting of a notice by an *employer* (or by a *competent person*) instructing *employees* to 'take care' would not usually, by itself, satisfy the (absolute) *duty of care* and the *employer* would generally be held liable (*Holmes v Hadfield Ltd [1944] 1 AER 235*). The courts may consider that if a company goes bankrupt through complying with an absolute duty, then so be it (but see *practicable* and *reasonably practicable*). In strict legal terms, absolute duties are those to which there are no corresponding rights.

absolute liability see *liability* and *mens rea*.

absorption means (1) in **occupational health** terms one of the routes of entry into a body, especially through broken or unbroken skin; (2) in terms of **sound**, the ability of a material to absorb (**sound**) energy; (3) in physiological terms, the process by which, e.g. end products of digestion, enter the fluids and cells of an organism and (4) in **radiation** it is the phenomenon by which **radiation** imparts some or all of its *energy* to any material through which it passes.

access has many meanings in health and safety, the term *access* covering 'simple' *access*, e.g. through a door, to the complex, e.g. the use of *access equipment*, such as *ladders*, *stepladders* and *trestles*; *scaffolds*; *tower scaffolds*; *suspended access systems* (e.g. *cradles* and chairs); and *work platforms*.

Access is 'initially' covered by s.2 of the **HSWA** which places a *general duty of care* on *employers* to provide a safe means of *access* and *egress* (exit) to *all* places where *employees* have to work – not merely their 'normal' place of work. In brief, *access* points must be safe, clear of obstruction, well lit and well maintained (e.g. to maintain good *access* by de-icing the *access/egress* in winter).

More duties regarding *access* (and *egress*) are found in various *Regulations*, some quite specific, for example, those in the *Construction (Health Safety and Welfare) Regulations (CHSWR)*, fire legislation and the *Workplace (Health and Safety) Regulations (MHSWR)*.

access equipment see *access*.

accessory for lifting is a term meaning *'lifting tackle'*, introduced by LOLER.

accident is an unplanned, unexpected event that *may* (or may not) cause death, injury, damage or loss (*Fenton v Thorley [1903] AC 443*) The current tendency is towards acknowledging the importance of 'force' and 'release of energy' in the course of an *accident*. However, the **HSE** differentiates between *accident* and *incident*. In **HS(G)65** *Successful Health and Safety Management*, an *accident* includes any undesired circumstances which give rise to ill-health or injury; damage to property, plant, products or the environment; production losses or increased liabilities; an *incident* includes all undesired circumstances and *near misses* which could cause accidents. Most importantly, those injuries, diseases and *dangerous occurrences*, which may or may not have resulted in injury or death that are reportable, are identified in the current **Reporting of Injuries, Diseases and Dangerous Occurrences Regulations (RIDDOR)**.

Accidents have several causes; the **direct** or **immediate** and the more distant or **root causes**, the first of which almost invariably includes both *unsafe acts* and *unsafe conditions*. *Accidents* can occur as a result of a failure in the organisation, a deviation from the 'normal' or 'ideal', which can range from lack of *adequate* supervision, failure to provide (or use) a *safe system of work* or failure to provide *suitable and sufficient* health and safety *training*, information and/or *instruction* to *employees* (including managers and supervisors). *Accidents* are almost invariably traceable to the *act* or *omission* of an individual, for example a designer of machinery, a person who devises a system of work or a shopfloor worker.

All *industrial accidents*, whether resulting in an injury or not, must be entered in an *accident book* and may be reportable to the authorities under **RIDDOR**. They should be investigated, as part of the company *risk assessment* procedure and to establish *qualitative* and *quantitative differences* of *outcomes*. Ideally, *near misses* should also be recorded and investigated. Such action is part of efficient *risk management* and develops effective *accident prevention*.

accident book is a BI 510 or an 'approved book'. It is a requirement of the *HSWA 1974, Social Security (Claims and Payments) Regulations 1979* and *1987*. The entries are *discoverable*. Under the **SSCPR 1987**, *employers* at factory premises, or places with ten or more *employees* (for example, each floor or building on a site where ten or more *employees* are employed) should possess and maintain an Accident Book or an *approved book* held at a convenient and always accessible place.

The person who suffered the accident should make the entry. Someone other than the 'victim' may *act on his/her behalf* (which has a special legal meaning) and make the entry, either following a request from the 'victim' or if an injured person is unable so to do, e.g. through being unconscious. Such entries should be agreed and countersigned, when possible, by the 'victim'.

Entries in the accident book are **NOT** restricted to lost time, known or visible injuries. For example, work related stress symptoms, breakdowns due to stress, or sudden sharp pains in the small of the back, should be reported to the *employer and* recorded in the accident book. Accident books should be kept for three years from the date of the last entry.

Accidents to specified other persons, such as those *which occur to customers in retail premises*, whether or not time off, or medical treatment, is incurred, should also be entered in the Accident Book held by the *'employer'* or occupier of the premises. It is possible that a report may have to be made additionally under the current **RIDDOR.**

The *employer* also has the duty, under the SS(CP)R 1987, to inform the *employee* who suffered an *accident* at work what he/she should do, detailed in the front of the **BI 510** or other 'approved book'. For example, this includes the suggestion that the 'victim', whether or not there is a known injury, applies to the local **Benefits Agency** office for a form **BI 95.** Completion and submission of the **BI 95** (whether or not an injury occurs or lost time is involved) is not a claim for benefit but a request for a **declaration** that the **accident was an industrial one**, which is placed on record and protects the 'victim'. As an example, there may have been a sudden sharp pain in the back, which 'goes away' after an hour or so. Submission of a **BI 95** would generally lead to a *declaration of industrial accident* by an **Insurance Officer** which would be placed on record and assist in any possible future claims for benefit. The obtaining, completion and submission of a **BI 95** can be considered essential.

accident causation is a term used to describe the process leading to an *accident*, which may or may not have resulted in an injury, damage or loss. To establish the many factors which cause an *accident* is a first priority towards prevention. The causes are referred to as *immediate causes* (such as tripping over rubbish on the floor) and *root causes* (basically hidden causes, e.g. bad housekeeping which meant the rubbish was left on the floor).

There have been several models developed to analyse and establish the causes of an *accident*, some of which are referred to in the text, e.g. the systems model of human behaviour by Hale and Hale (qv).

accident data see *accident statistics*.

accident investigation has the prime purpose of establishing how a reoccurrence can be prevented and of learning how to improve *accident* prevention in general within an organisation by investigating *root causes*. It will also assist in lessening the effects and number of *accidents* through the introduction of safeguards, procedures, *training* and information etc. Ideally investigations should be carried out by a team, headed by the relevant manager with, where appropriate, assistance sought from other staff.

The investigation should include consideration of both the *immediate* and *root causes*. Following the investigation, an *accident report* should be drawn up and a copy forwarded to the Senior Manager, appointed *Competent Person*, the *Safety Advisor*, the Manager, the foreperson, the *Safety Representative* or *Elected Representative* of the workplace concerned, to advise them of the findings and should be discussed at *Health and Safety Committee* meetings, in compliance with statutory *and* organisational requirements.

Safety Representatives and *Elected Representatives* have the statutory right to be informed of, involved in, and consulted during, the investigation into *accidents* and incidents that occur in their area of responsibility.

Employees, at all levels, should be informed by the *employer* of the summary findings from the investigation **and** most importantly, informed of any steps taken to prevent a recurrence.

accident prevention is a requirement of **MHSWR Schedule 2**. All action should be primarily a *pro-active*, or pre-*accident* activity. If loss, damage, injury or ill health occurs, then the attempt at *accident* prevention and *pro-active* damage limitation exercise has not been carried out satisfactorily or has failed and must be reviewed. The prime motivators for *accident* prevention are moral, legal and economic, with the involvement and commitment of top management being of key importance.

There is a problem in that an *accident* prevented is seldom recognised or realised, *unless* valid comparisons can be made. Organisations seldom identify the savings to the organisation of following good health, safety and environmental practice or the cost if they do not. For example, how many organisations have established the *actual* cost of an *accident*. The cost arising from loss or damage is far better recognised and documented.

The need, therefore, arises for accurate *accident* records to form an essential component of all-effective *accident* prevention programmes and systems. In the case of new processes and substances, where no records exist, assessments are still a legal requirement. Effective *accident* prevention is a *process*, elements of which receive constant reference throughout this text. In 1956 the *Industrial Safety Sub-committee of the National Joint Advisory Council* identified six principles of *accident* prevention and these are still valid today. However, the current minimum legislative requirements and principles, which **must** be followed and implemented are:

(a) avoiding risks;

(b) evaluating the risks which cannot be avoided;

(c) combating the risks at source;

(d) adapting the work to the individual, especially as regard the design of workplaces, the choice of work equipment and the choice of working and production methods, with a view, in particular, to alleviating monotonous work and work at a predetermined work rate and to reducing their effect on health;

(e) adapting to technical progress;

(f) replacing the dangerous by the non-dangerous or the less-dangerous;

(g) developing a coherent overall prevention policy which covers technology, organisation of work, working conditions, social relationships and the influence of factors relating to the working environment;

(h) giving collective protective measures priority over individual protective measures; and

(i) giving appropriate instructions to *employees*.

The above principles are *additional* to the *employer's* common law duty to provide, *so far as is reasonably practicable*:

(a) a safe place of work;

(b) a safe system of work; safe plant, equipment and appliances;

(c) safe fellow *employees*;

(d) safe and competent supervision;

(e) *adequate and suitable instruction*, information and *training*.

It is emphasised that each of (a) through (e) above, in addition to being common law duties are also *duties* found in the **HSWA** and other legislation.

accident records see *accident reporting* and *accident statistics*.

accident reporting: all *accidents*, work related injuries and ill health (i.e. *stress or depression*) should be reported and recorded in the *accident book* (BI 510) or an 'approved book'). Reference should also be made to **RIDDOR** for the list of diseases, injuries and dangerous occurrences which **must** be reported on an F2508 or F2508A and/or by telephone to the enforcing authority within ten days or as soon as possible.

Accurate, valid and comprehensive **accident** records (and statistics) can assist in identifying **accident** 'black spots' within an undertaking and lead to a reduction in the number of **accidents**. All **accidents** that result in injury, loss or damage, must be investigated as part of truly effective health and **safety management**, following procedures detailed in the company's **Safety Policy Document**.

accident statistics are numerical data organised and presented to show what is significant. However, in **occupational health**, safety and environment usage of the term *accident statistics* (or *accident data*) commonly has a wide meaning and can include their collection, checking 'outside' material and sources, drawing inferences, discussing findings, making conclusions and recommendations.

They are an essential tool in the prevention of **accidents** as part of effective health and safety management. Their collection and 'use' can identify trends, savings and costs of health and safety; assist the process of health and safety monitoring, planning and review of health, safety and environmental programmes and, incidentally, the identification of **training** needs. This requires the careful gathering, recording and analysis of *accurate* **accident** statistics, with **all accidents**, incidents, injuries *and ideally near misses* reported, recorded and investigated (around 85% of **accidents** are not reported (Grayham 1972, 1997)).

When considering, comparing or using **accident** statistics it is useful to recognise or identify which method of measurement and, possibly even more important, any hidden agenda – especially the unintentional – is present or used in gathering, preparing or presenting data and findings. Among the most widely used measures in British industry and by the health and safety authorities to present **accident** data in summary are the **incidence rate**, the **frequency rate** and the **severity rate**.

An example of data being accurate, but leading to inaccurate conclusions through method of presentation or use concerns air travel and its comparative safety. Air travel is often cited as being far safer than travelling by car or rail. Indeed research findings confirm that 'there are 0.03 fatalities per 100 million kilometres flown, compared with 0.10 fatalities per 100 million kilometres for rail travel'. Sometimes it is added that a person is three times more likely to be killed in a rail than an air crash. However, fatality data *based against 100 million passenger journeys* shows that the figure for rail is 2.7, cars 4.5 and planes 55 – or an individual is 12 times more likely to be killed during an air journey than

account for

during a car journey (see Wier *The Tombstone Imperative* 1999). This underlines the need for data, findings and reports to be carefully considered and analysed before use, particularly those sourced from outside the company. Incidentally, the work of the **HSE** is relatively 'value free'.

In the wider context, several studies have suggested there is a consistent relationship or ratio between near misses or non-injury **accidents, accidents** resulting in injury and number of fatalities. For example, in a review of almost one million **accidents** in British industry, Tye and Pearson found for each fatal or serious injury, up to three days' absence for minor injuries, 50 injuries requiring first aid treatment, 80 property damage incidents, 400 non-injury/ damage incidents or near misses (*Management Safety Manual*, British Council 5-star Health and Safety Management System), reported in HS(G)65 1993. The inferential evidence from this and other studies (e.g. **Heinrich**) suggests that preventing non-injury **accidents** would have a ripple effect up the hierarchy. In grossly over simple terms, nil non-injury **accidents** would equal nil fatalities.

However, such a simplistic conclusion, while useful to illustrate the point, is difficult to apply in practice. Such an approach must take account of differences in work environment, work equipment, **training**, human factors, causes and therefore the different preventive measures applied. Furthermore, there needs to be sufficient numbers of **accidents**, injuries, damages and near misses to construct a triangle. Irrespective of numbers of **employees** or level of risk, an effective health and safety culture and safety management may prevent such numbers accumulating to provide a large enough data base – after all, it is obvious but worth re-emphasising, the **accident** prevented cannot be recorded, although possibly inferred through reference to accurate past statistics.

In summary, good and effective health and safety management and **accident** preventive measures utilise the findings from a variety of sources and techniques. These include the findings from the legally required risk assessments, the conclusions and findings of **accident** investigations, together with the collection and analysis of *accurate* **accident** statistics which contribute to a reduction in the number of **accidents**, loss and damage.

account for (*examination term*) requires an answer to the questions 'why', 'where', 'when', 'what on the way' and 'how' something came about.

ACOP see *Approved Code of Practice*.

acoustic trauma, sometimes referred to as *acute* acoustic trauma, is when a single, relatively intense *noise* exposure is followed by a change in hearing threshold. *Tinnitus* almost invariably follows an *acute* exposure, sometimes temporary but it can be permanent. If the single *noise* exposure is very intensive, then permanent hearing *threshold shift* can result.

The following symptoms can also occur; pain in the ears, tickling sensation, vertigo, *tinnitus,* hearing loss or lessening of *communication* skills.

acquired immunodeficiency syndrome (AIDS) is a disease caused by a *retrovirus* called T-lymphotropic virus type III (HTLV-III). It is spread through sexual contact, contact with body fluids of an infected individual, the use of unclean needles and through (infected) blood transfusions and is found throughout the world. Its spread can be minimised by the practice of 'safe sex', avoiding contact with the body fluids of an infected individual, screening blood donors and monitoring blood supplies. It should be noted that the spread of AIDS at work is most unlikely (however, please see *first aid*).

Unlike **hepatitis B,** AIDS is *not* a reportable disease under the *Reporting of Injuries, Diseases and Dangerous Occurrences Regulations 1995* or RIDDOR. However, an *employer* who knows that an *employee* is suffering from AIDS would be subject to the requirement of the **HSWA 1974** to ensure, so far as is reasonably practicable, the work environment to be without risk to *employees'* health. It should be noted, however, that no *case law* reference was found.

actinide is the group name for the series of elements of atomic numbers 89-104. Some occur naturally (i.e. thorium and *uranium*) but most are the product of nuclear reaction (i.e. *plutonium* and neptunium). *Nuclear waste* containing actinides continues to release radiation for very many years, creating storage and disposal problems for the nuclear industry.

action levels are established levels or measurements of, e.g., sound, concentration of dust, at which point certain actions must be taken or carried out.

As an example with regard to *noise,* under the *Noise at Work Regulations 1989* 85 dB(A) is termed the 'first *action level'*. At that level, *employers* have the duty to identify the group(s) and number(s) of *employees* exposed, inform them of the level of *noise,* inform their *employees* of the risk to their hearing, install suitable *control measures as the first option* and supply (free of charge) suitable hearing protection to their *employees* **on request,** until such time that a further *noise* assessment confirms that the *noise* level has returned to below 85 dB(A).

90dB(A) is termed the 'second *action level'*. At that level the *employer* **must** install, implement and monitor *suitable and adequate control measures.* NB

acts (human)

Hearing protection is **NOT** a *control measure* and can only be used as a last resort. It **must** be supplied by the *employer* and **must** be worn by all *employees* working in *or passing through* the affected area. The various specific legislative measures should be consulted.

acts (human) are generally recognised observable patterns of behaviour, considered acceptable or unacceptable by reference to many influencing variables, including those from culture, upbringing, education, knowledge and understanding, religion, societal expectations, legislative requirements, etc. What is an acceptable act (or behaviour) in one society or situation may be unacceptable in another.

Heinrich stated that **all** *accidents* are due either to *unsafe conditions* or to *unsafe acts*. For example, a machine may be dangerous to clean – this is the result of human deficiency (the designer) creating *unsafe conditions*, compounded by the *employer* purchasing and installing an unsafe machine (*unsafe conditions and unsafe act*) and the operator carrying out an *unsafe act.*

Acts (of Parliament) are *statutes,* documents drawn up by legislators and involving discussion with many professionals. Acts are introduced to Parliament as Bills. They are discussed in both Houses of Parliament and are 'accepted' by a simple majority. After receiving Royal Assent, Acts then form part of the written law of the land, usually setting out a framework of principles or objectives. Arising from or associated with Acts may be specific *Regulations* and/or *Orders (in Council)*. In very simple terms, Acts in modern safety legislation generally describe 'what must be achieved'.

acute (in *occupational health* terms) is a term meaning sudden, severe and *of short duration*. The 'opposite' (antonym) is *chronic.*

acute dose is a quantity of anything administered in one dose which may cause an adverse reaction.

acute exposure is a short-term exposure to a hazardous substance.

acute health effect or reaction may result *within a short period* following a single exposure to a toxin or micro-organism. The acute health effect can be contrasted with the *chronic health effect.*

acute toxicity relates to the acute effects to some part of the body (e.g. skin or liver) resulting from a single dose of, or exposure to, a poisonous substance.

adequate and suitable in health and safety terms is what is considered to be *suitable and sufficient* for the purpose, e.g. to enable *employees, so far as is reasonably practicable*, to identify and avoid a particular risk to their health and safety. However, what is considered *suitable* or *adequate* in each particular circumstance may ultimately be decided by the courts.

Administration of Justice Act 1982 is concerned with various aspects of damage and loss following personal injury, including industrial injuries. There is a large body of *case law* associated with this Act.

aerobic organisms are those which live or are only active in the presence of oxygen in the atmosphere.

agriculture is covered by general and specific health, safety and environmental legislation, 'headed' by the *Health and Safety at Work etc Act* and the *Management of Health and Safety at Work Regulations*. In addition, there is agricultural sector specific legislation.

It should be noted that much of agriculture health and safety legislation is quite old and in the process of being extensively updated, *revoked* and *repealed*. Therefore it is useful to establish the current position through contacting the *Regional Administrator* at the appropriate Regional Office of the National Farmers' Union or the London Headquarters, Tel: 020 7331 7200, web site: www.nfu.org.uk.

AIDS see *acquired immunodeficiency syndrome*.

Air Pollution Control (or APC) is administered by the local authority, under the *Environmental Protection Act 1990* s. 4(3) and applies to 'less polluting' Part B types of processes, with the purpose of preventing or minimising pollution of the environment due to emissions into the air.

See also *Integrated Pollution Control*.

air quality standards follow the national strategy developed by **DETR** in 1997, updated January 2000. The *Air Quality (England) Regulations 2000* (and the Scotland Regulations), together with **EPA 1990**, place a *duty* on *local authorities* to review and assess air quality in their area, as part of National Air Quality Strategy. See *The Air Quality Strategy for England, Scotland Wales and Northern Ireland* (January 2000).

air sampling is a *measurement technique*, which establishes air quality and levels of contaminant. The techniques used include *direct monitoring, dust sampling, and grab sampling, humidity monitoring, personal sampling* and *static sampling*.

alveoli

The use of technical equipment, often electronic and sometimes very sophisticated, highly technical equipment and equally pertinently, the *interpretation* of the results, demands professional *training* and qualifications. The use of more simple equipment (e.g. basic *grab sampling* devices) requires *adequate* and *suitable* training. Such basic equipment, while effective in identifying the presence of some hazards, is not reliable as sole evidence e.g., when designing *control measures.*

alveoli are minute sacks in the lung, arranged similarly to bunches of grapes, where the exchange of oxygen and carbon dioxide takes place. Through the walls of the sacks carbon dioxide leaves the blood and the blood takes on oxygen.

amphibole is any of a group of complex silicate minerals with crystal-like structures that contain calcium, sodium, magnesium, aluminium and iron ions or a combination of them. *Asbestos* is an example of such a mineral.

anaerobic bacteria are organisms *only* able to survive in the absence of oxygen (obligates), e.g. bacteria that cause food poisoning. Others can live either in the presence or absence of oxygen (facultative).

analyse (*examination term*) means examine minutely the constitution or make-up of something.

analysis in environmental, health and safety (and *examination*) terms, is the process of determining and completely 'breaking down', inspecting, testing and/ or explaining the component parts of, e.g. a health and safety programme, a substance, a task, etc.

anthrax is an *acute* infective *notifiable* disease caused by the anthrax bacillus, communicated from animals alive or dead (e.g. via skin, fur etc.) to human beings. Symptoms include cutaneous malignant pustules (blister like spots) and infection in the lungs, intestines and nervous system. The anthrax bacillus can live for decades in the soil, dead animal hair (fairly extensively used for some time in the past as a binding agent in wall plaster) or skin. The anthrax bacillus is a direct *zoonose*. Anthrax is a *notifiable disease* (it is also known as *woolsorters disease.*

anthropometrics is the measurement and recording of the size and proportions of the human body. The derived data are used, as examples, in the design of personal protective equipment and in *ergonomic* factors associated with machinery and workplaces.

antigenic substances include, for example, pollen and house dust-mite faeces, which can be found in homes, hospitals and hotels. These substances are among the most common linked to increased sensitivity in asthmatics.

Anti-Pollution Works Regulations 1999, introduced under the WRA, gives the *Environment Agency* the power to issue a *works notice* to the person responsible for a site or premises *threatening* to pollute the water environment and to take preventative action. The *works notice* should identify what measures need to be taken by the *responsible person*, and why it was served.

appeals (in *industrial injury* benefit terms) are made by claimants who are dissatisfied by decisions of an *Insurance Officer* in respect of a claim.

See also *review*.

appeals against a decision by a lower court, *civil, criminal, magistrates' court* or a tribunal are almost invariably heard in a higher court and, with limited exceptions, cannot be made of right. One exception to the general rule is found with health and safety, e.g. appeals against initial decisions by *enforcement officers* (e.g. *improvement notice*) are heard at an *employment tribunal* and **are** of right.

application of (European and British Health and Safety) Directives within the UK is one of the functions of the *Health and Safety Commission* (HSC). On receipt of the Directive, the HSC draw up a *consultative document* for comments from concerned bodies and individuals. After approximately four months (to allow for consultation), a draft set of *Regulations* is submitted to the appropriate Secretary of State. The proposed *Regulations* are 'laid' before Parliament (for forty days). If there is no request from a Member of the House to debate the *Regulations* before the assembled Houses of Parliament, the proposed *Regulations* become part of health and safety legislation in Great Britain, except for those parts specifically identified as excluded or covered elsewhere (e.g., legislation may declare that Scotland or Northern Ireland is excluded from cover).

appointed person in relation to health and safety is used in association with several legislative demands. Two examples of appointed persons are: firstly, *first aider*, who is a person who is appointed *by an employer*, to provide strictly first line first aid. (**NB** *appointed persons* are **not** *first aiders*); secondly, a **Safety Representative**, a recognised trade union member who has been *appointed by and notified in writing by the* **trade union** *to their member's* **employer** as a Safety Representative for a specified area.

Approved Carriage List provides for the classification of dangerous goods

Approved Code of Practice

and substances, in conjunction with relevant legislation. The classification must be shown on a package label and present the following information:

(i)   classification code;
(ii)   packing group;
(iii) subsidiary hazard code (or in the case of goods *not* named individually in the approved carriage list, 'subsidiary hazards');
(iv) shipping names;
(v)   UN number;
(vi) appropriate danger sign; and
(vii) subsidiary hazards sign (if appropriate).

Approved Code of Practice (ACOP) gives practical guidance and best practice as to how to comply with the law (**Health and Safety at Work Act etc. 1974 (HSWA)** Section 53(1)). The *approval* of a Code of Practice is given to the HSC following extensive consultation. The **HSWA** Section 16(2) requires the HSC to (a) consult any body that may be appropriate in the opinion of the HSC; (b) consult with those bodies required by the **HSWA** Section 16; and (c) obtain the consent of the Secretary of State, prior to the approval of a Code of Practice.

An **ACOP** describes what is considered to be *reasonably practicable*, the minimum sufficient to satisfy legal requirements, although alternative methods to those stated in the **ACOP** can be used (Section 16), provided their use achieves the same standard. Therefore, it is *not a statutory duty* to follow what is laid out in an **ACOP**. Nevertheless, changes to **ACOP**s are increasingly being used, in effect, to change **Regulations** because they have a function *similar* to **Regulations** (**HSWA** Section 16). Failure to comply with an **ACOP** does not, in itself, normally lead to court action. However, if under the **HSWA** ss 2-7 or any **Regulations** made under the **HSWA** there are criminal proceedings for **breach of statutory duty**, proof of a failure to comply with an **ACOP** is taken as further evidence of guilt. A defence is to demonstrate that the **ACOP** was complied with in some other way, which was equally effective.

The Highway Code (an **ACOP**) can be used to demonstrate the application and meaning of an **ACOP**. Failure to comply with the Highway Code invariably means that a breach of the Road Traffic Act (RTA) has occurred. The offender is therefore charged with breach of a section of the RTA, not *primarily* with breach of the Highway Code.

Approved Lists in simple terms are lists of various 'things' which have been approved by the HSC. Two examples are (1) the L57 which presents information approved for the classification, packaging and labelling of dangerous goods for carriage by road and rail and (2) the *Approved Supply List,* which should be used in conjunction with the regularly updated and revised **EH40.**

Approved Supply List identifies both *approved* and *banned* substances and is amended in accord with changes in or additions to the official list. The ASL should be used in conjunction with **EH40** and various applicable legislation (e.g. **COSHH**).

arising out of and in the course of insured employment is a requirement, which must be satisfied by a claimant to obtain industrially-based benefit. This requirement dates back to the *Workman's Compensation Act 1897.* An *accident,* which arises in the course of *employment,* is assumed to arise *out* of it, unless proven to the contrary.

In essence, no fault liability applies, therefore even if the **accident** was the consequence of an *employee* acting contrary to the **HSWA** s.7 (i.e. *employees* have the duty to take care of themselves and others), it does not prevent an *employee* applying for and even obtaining benefit, subject to the decision of an *adjudicating officer.* The *adjudicating officer* is independent of, but usually located in, a local **Benefits Agency** Office and provides a **decision** on various applications, not restricted to claims for benefit.

arsine is a highly dangerous gas generated suddenly and without irritant warning when metal ores or metals such as *zinc* (or lead or cadmium) *containing impurities* of arsenic come into contact with acid. Arsine is colourless and virtually odourless when chemically pure. The welding of galvanised metals, which can include the use of *zinc,* is a typical example where arsine may be released.

A major **toxic** effect of arsine is massive intra-vascular haemolysis. An acute reaction to arsine poisoning is nephropathy. In addition the onset of arsine poisoning can lead to fatal consequences following the development of other illnesses, e.g. greater than normal amounts of potassium in the blood (hyperkalemia), leading to renal failure.

articles, for use at work include any plant designed for use or operation 'by persons at work *and* any article designed for use as a component in any such plant'. (**HSWA** s.53(1))

Manufacturers, designers, importers or suppliers under the **HSWA** s.6 and other health and safety legislation, have a duty 'to ensure, *so far as is reasonably practicable,* that any *article* used at work is so designed and constructed that it will be safe and without risks to health at all times when it is being set, used, cleaned and maintained by a person at work'.

15

asbestos

Employers have the duty to ensure articles used at work are tested and/or examined as required by any relevant statutory provisions, with records maintained as appropriate. Adequate information, revised as necessary, must be provided to involved *employees* and, *so far as is reasonably practicable*, updated following revisions. (*HSWA* s.6)

asbestos is a natural mineral comprised of silicate fibre, differentiated as serpentine or amphibole. Fibres are indestructible at temperatures up to 800oC. Serpentine asbestos is termed chrysotile (commonly known as *white asbestos*); amphibole asbestos includes crocidolite (*blue asbestos*), amosite (*brown asbestos*) and anthophyllite. However, identifying solely by colour is **not** recommended, as in use it can be a mix. The 'white', 'blue' and 'brown' are the most used. Asbestos was frequently used in the past as insulation because of its heat resistant properties, e.g., in ships, buildings, on pipes and brake shoes. There are many *Regulations* (and prohibitions) associated with the use and removal of asbestos and the EU is moving towards a complete ban on its use.

Asbestos has long been known internationally as a cause of various lung diseases, although the UK was slow among the industrial nations to adopt adequate control measures. The major diseases associated with asbestos include *asbestosis*, lung cancer and *mesothelioma* (a specific cancer of the lining of the lung). These diseases may only appear up to 40 years after the initial exposure to asbestos fibres. The target organs include the lungs, pleura (lining of the thorax and enveloping the lungs), peritoneum (lining of abdomen), larynx and gastrointestinal tract.

Control and preventive measures range from complete *isolation* and enclosure of the area affected to full suited *respiratory protection* of individual workers.

Asbestos at Work Regulations see various specific asbestos *Regulations*, especially the *Control of Asbestos at Work Regulations 1987* as amended by the *Control of Asbestos at Work (Amendment) Regulations 1992.*

asbestos disposal see *disposal of hazardous waste.*

Asbestos (Licensing) Regulations 1987 (as amended) require **anyone** who works with *asbestos* insulation, *including* insulation board and coatings to apply for and be granted a licence from the **Health and Safety Executive (HSE)** which must be obtained at least 14 days **before** commencing such work. There are strictly limited exemptions, which must be granted *before* commencing the work, e.g. an *employer* using his/her own *employees* is doing the work on his/her own premises, or the work consists solely of air monitoring or collecting samples. *Employees* of firms working with asbestos insulation and coatings must be given regular medical examinations.

Failure to comply can lead to heavy fines, such as the £60,000 (plus £5,000 costs) fine against Rover Cars in May 2000. It is recommended that those who require a licence obtain from *HSE Books* copies of the associated guidance notes HSG189/1 (stripping techniques) and HSG189/2 (asbestos cement and asbestos insulation, coatings and insulation board), obtainable from *HSE Books* by those who require an asbestos licence.

Asbestos Products (Safety) Regulations 1985 identify the labels that **must** be affixed to products containing asbestos and prohibit the supply of products containing crocidolite or amosite.

Asbestos (Prohibitions) (Amendment) Regulations 1998 prohibit the importation and *supply* of amphibole and *use* or *supply* of chrysotile asbestos.

asbestosis is a chronic lung inflammation caused by inhalation of asbestos fibres. Initially those afflicted suffer coughing, shortness of breath and some chest pain, after some time clubbing of the toes and/or fingers occurs, followed by bronchitis, pneumoconiosis and/or heart problems. Asbestosis, similar to *silicosis*, may continue to progress after removal from exposure. Smoking seriously exacerbates asbestosis.

assaults (on employees/staff) see *violence to staff*.

assessment is a legal *duty* placed on all *employers* and means, in health, safety and environmental terms, the measurement and evaluation of 'something' (e.g. 'risk') by a *competent person* including consideration of what action is required and of the possible consequences of failing to take action.

Association of British Insurers (ABI), 51 Gresham Street, London EC2V 7HQ, Tel: 020 7600 3333, is an insurance industry based information centre.

asthma (occupational or industrial) is a multi-factorial pulmonary disease. Through genetic factors, some people are more likely than others to develop the disease. Asthma can be triggered by exposure to and/or contact with a sensitising agent (e.g. *antigenic substances* found in the workplace*) or even by an abnormal response to stressors. The symptoms include a shortness of breath and a lack of concentration at critical points in tasks, e.g. when driving or operating machinery.

There is considered to be a link between increased airway sensitivity and ozone (produced e.g. by photocopiers). As a precaution, *employers* who are aware of their *employees'* asthmatic condition should check their reported asthmatic attacks against the periods of extended use of photocopiers in their vicinity. If an *employee* is known to suffer from occupational or industrial asthma the *employer* has an **extra duty of care**. If it is impossible to remove the *employee* from a particular workplace or task, then the *employer* has to consider carefully what next to do; *dismissal*, as the last resort, may be adjudged unfair.

Occupational or industrial asthma is a prescribed disease and reportable under *RIDDOR*.

at work is defined in the **HSWA 1974** as being work carried out in 'the course of *employment'*. However, s. 52(2)(a) of the **HSWA 1974** declares '*Regulations* made … may (alter) the meaning of **work** or **at work**. These alterations can be confusing, e.g. Reg. 19 of **COSHH 1999** stated 'the meaning of work shall be extended to include any activity involving the consignment, storage or use of any of the biological agents listed in Part 1 Schedule 3 and the meaning of "at work" shall be extended accordingly.' An *accident* is not recorded as an *industrial accident* (irrespective as to whether or not an injury occurs) unless it can be shown that the person was **at work**.

atom is the smallest unit of an element that retains the characteristics of that element and can take part in chemical reaction. It consists of a central core, or nucleus, which comprises two types of stable particles – *protons* (positively charged) and *neutrons* (electrically neutral). Protons and neutrons occur in an atom in equal numbers, therefore atoms are electrically neutral.

attitude is a psychological construct; an exact definition is hard to provide, since it depends on a variety of factors, including the domain of reference and 'school' of psychology. An attitude is founded in a *belief*. In basic terms, visualise an iceberg, which has seven-eighths of its volume below the water. An attitude is represented by the one-eighth above the water, with a *belief* figuratively the remaining seven-eighths of the whole. An attitude can be analysed by breaking it down into three components:

Cognitive, consisting of the *beliefs* which a person holds with respect to an attitude object (e.g. health and safety). For example, an individual may think that the application of health and safety in the workplace is only possible through the use of strict discipline, e.g. 'wear safety goggles or you're fired'. The belief relating to the application of health and safety through use of discipline make up the *cognitive component* of that person's attitude.

Affective, consisting of the feelings a person has towards a particular issue which can differ considerably between individuals. There may be conflicting attitudes concerning the effectiveness of discipline or *training*, e.g. an individual worker may not see the need to wear eye protection. The reasons will vary; if it is through failure to understand the danger or consequences, *training* may be the most effective remedy; if it is a 'macho' reaction, then constant supervision (discipline) may be required. The affective component of attitudes can be the most deep-rooted and highly resistant to change.

Behavioural, consisting of the visible (observed) reaction of an individual to an attitude object. If someone has a negative attitude to health and safety, then that person is likely to ignore safety instructions or procedures and that will be observable. Such persons may also express this view to their peers very strongly, trying to pressurise others to follow *their* negative behaviour.

Two other important terms are (i) **evaluative,** which refers to a positive or negative attitude and (ii) **conative,** identifying the disposition of an individual for action.

Attitudes exist in a matrix of relationships with other attitudes, for example, if an individual values personal safety very highly, then that person's attitude towards health and safety reflects this concern.

attitude changes is a term and concept the application of which is of prime importance and relevance in health and safety. In simple terms, an *attitude* is the observable or visible part of a *belief*; therefore to effect a long-term change in *attitude* requires a fundamental long-term change in the underlying *belief* held by individuals. For health and safety, the change process includes the provision of information and *training*. However, its success (or failure) depends on many influencing factors, most importantly the strength of feelings of an individual (or possibly associated group members) on an issue.

As with all psychological terms the definition and application of techniques of attitude change partly depends on which theoretical 'school' of psychology is followed by the professional concerned. The problem is further compounded by the fact that attempts at attitude change result in *positive* or *negative* changes. Furthermore, in practice what is considered to be positive or negative ultimately may be subjectively derived.

The attempt to change workers' negative attitude to a positive attitude to health and safety at work is to be actively encouraged. Nevertheless, if the change in attitude is thought to lead to a reduction in levels of production, the same change may be seen by some as negative. Changes may take time to apply,

audible sound

but measurement of the overall cost benefits to the company over a period e.g. through reducing absence following injury and/or the cost of replacing or reorganising staffing, is seldom recorded or possibly delayed in receiving full recognition.

audible sound is that between the frequencies of 20-20,000 hertz and can be heard by persons with normal hearing.

audiometry is the measurement of the *acuity* (sharpness, perception) of hearing at various frequencies of sound waves.

audit (safety) see *safety audit*.

autotransformer is a *transformer* where electric current is passed through a single winding on a laminated core, with the coil tapped to give the desired voltage(s).

B

back injuries account for approximately one-third of all *manual handling* injuries, according to the **HSE.** They are usually the result of failing to lift correctly, possibly through lack of training. However, it is not only lifting which can cause back injuries, prolonged sitting and awkward posture also contribute to back pain and/or injury.

Preventive measures include *training* in manual handling, which is a legal requirement of the *Manual Handling Operations Regulations 1992* (and the **HSWA).** *Ergonomics* should be used and applied in the design of jobs and the workplace, taking account of the capability of the worker.

NB *All* back injuries, including that sharp pain in the back (e.g. which can happen when seated at a desk and reaching for a pen), which *may* or *may not* result at the time as a recognised actual injury or cause of lost time, should be entered in the *accident book*. The 'victim' should obtain from the *Benefits Agency,* complete and return a **BI 95** to apply for a *Declaration of Industrial Accident.*

bacteria are very simple single-celled organisms, without chlorophyll and lacking a distinct nuclear membrane. Sometimes the letter 'b.' is used as a prefix instead of the word *bacteria* (e.g. *b. cerus*). They reproduce through a process called *binary fission*. At optimum conditions (i.e. with food, warmth and moisture) they can grow and multiply by dividing into two. In food hygiene, *pathogenic* and spoilage bacteria are of prime concern.

Pathogenic bacteria are those that cause food poisoning through growing, multiplying and producing *toxins*; some have the ability to form *spores*. Very few types of *pathogenic bacteria* actually cause food poisoning, but contaminated food can look, smell and taste perfectly normal, leading to unexpected *acute* or **chronic** ill effects. Most *pathogenic* bacteria are killed through thorough cooking at temperatures in excess of 82°C.

Spoilage bacteria grow on foodstuffs altering colour and taste and, sometimes, smell. They do not, in themselves, induce food poisoning but will create an ideal medium for the growth of *pathogenic* bacteria. Safe disposal is recommended for foodstuffs affected by spoilage bacteria.

bacteria cerus, also called *b. cerus*, is an aerobic spore former. It produces two entiroxins which can lead to vomiting or diarrhoea and multiplies in cooked vegetables or meat dishes left at room temperature. Control is by proper cooking of food and rapid cooling in refrigerators.

bactericide

bactericide is a substance that kills bacteria.

balance of probabilities see *standard of proof*.

BATNEEC means using the 'best available techniques not entailing *excessive cost*', see *Environmental Protection Act 1990* (EPA) s.7. The meaning of *techniques* in connection with **BATNEEC** extends far beyond current technology and equipment in use; it also takes account of design, qualifications of person(s) involved, etc.

battery hazards are largely associated with use of electrical batteries and most particularly during charging. As examples (followed by control or preventive measures):

(i)   Charging batteries generates hydrogen gas, providing fire or explosion risks. It should be carried out in a well-ventilated area, free of sources of ignition and with suitable warning signs.

(ii)   Battery acid, highly corrosive in nature, can be spilled in the charging area or while removing batteries. Effective handling procedures should be devised and suitable *personal protective equipment* provided, together with first aid equipment, e.g. eyewash.

(iii)   Batteries are often very heavy and awkward to lift and move, with slipped discs or sprains possible if *manual handling* is used. The *manual handling* of batteries **must** be avoided, *mechanical aids* provided wherever possible. In addition, all personnel must receive formal *manual handling* training.

(iv)   Fire or explosions due to electrical shorting are a potential hazard in the charging bay. Electric shorts are due to *unsafe acts* or *unsafe conditions*. Mechanical and electrical equipment must be suitably and adequately maintained, and, sometimes to satisfy legislative duties, regularly inspected and tested.

(v)   Tools and terminals should be suitably insulated, precautions taken against connections being 'overloaded' through overcharging.

(vi)   The charging area must prominently display suitable warning signs.

(vii)   A first aider or under certain specified circumstances an appointed person should be readily available, with suitable first emergency equipment signed and accessible (e.g. eye wash).

(viii)   All personnel working in or near the charging area must be informed of the hazards, control and preventative measures in place and provided with adequate and *suitable instruction and training*.

(ix)   A *safe system of work* must be in place.

behavioural psychology (US – *behavioral*) considers that should psychology be a true science then it must study *observable* behaviour. Behaviourists therefore define psychology as the science of behaviour and they see unobservable behaviour, such as consciousness, as properly being part of philosophy. Nevertheless, behavioural psychology can prove to be a cheap and effective means of improving and continuing improvement in health and safety. An example follows (see *psychology*).

Ivan Pavlov (1849-1936) was a behaviourist who won the Nobel Prize in 1904 for his work on digestion, and utilised the study of *stimulus* and *response* in the best-known research. He found that, after time, hearing the footsteps (*stimulus*) of their regular food handlers, dogs would salivate (*response*), as they would in response to a ringing bell sounded immediately before feeding. This phenomenon is called a **conditioned reflex;** thus positive stimulation can achieve a desired response, without using verbal **communication.**

A very simple application of this technique in health and safety terms is when managers and forepersons ALWAYS wear safety glasses in designated areas, they thereby consistently remind staff through example to wear safety glasses (*stimulus*), reinforcing verbal instructions and increasing the likelihood that safety glasses will be worn by all staff in that area (*response*). The reverse is also possible, if forepersons and especially managers 'do not bother' to wear safety glasses (*stimulus*) in a designated area, possibly because they are only 'passing through', then the *response* from the staff is often 'they don't wear safety glasses, why should I?' Many very effective behavioural and psychological techniques are as simple in design and application as this example.

behavioural science see *behavioural psychology.*

bel is the amount of energy in the form of sound transmitted to one square inch of the ear.

See also *decibel.*

belief is the underlying 'component' of an *attitude*. A change in a belief will more permanently change an *attitude* (behaviour or opinion). In very basic terms, a belief is the invisible foundation of an attitude which is visible through behaviour (as an analogy, a belief is the submerged seven-eighths of an iceberg). To achieve *long term* positive change in health and safety behaviour, fundamental negative or erroneous held beliefs *must* be changed. **Group norms** can be established which reflect pervasive, sometimes negative, health and safety beliefs visible as *attitudes.*

benchmarking

benchmarking is a planned process of *safety management* whereby organisations compare and contrast their health and safety processes and performances with others, discovering strengths and weaknesses and taking action to resolve any problems identified. *HSE* leaflet INDG301 *Health and safety benchmarking: improving together* is a useful publication (single copies free).

benzene is a colourless, flammable, toxic, aromatic hydrocarbon, which has an acute narcotic effect on individuals and is an irritant to the skin and mucous membranes. Benzene typically is a constituent of some solvents used in the printing industry and in furniture polish. The main route of entry to the body is through inhalation. At exposure to 20,000 parts per million (ppm) death occurs in five to ten minutes, usually through asphyxiation or cardiac collapse; initial symptoms include headaches, nausea, staggering gait and convulsions. High levels of exposure may impair fertility in women.

best practicable means (BPM) allows economic and technological factors to be taken account of, e.g. in particular when applying air pollution controls. It should be noted that the 'best practical means' does **not** necessarily mean the best possible.

best practice, in essence, is the best commercial practice existing and commonly used at a particular time and circumstances, e.g. to control air pollution.

beyond all reasonable doubt see *standard of proof*.

BI 76A or BI 76B are forms sent *from* the *Benefits Agency*/DSS to an *employer*, requesting certain details about an *accident* or disease *arising out of or in the course of employment*.

BI 95 is a form obtained from the *Benefits Agency* and supposedly, the Post Office or local Job Centre. However, research has shown that many Job Centre and Post Office staff (including their management) are not aware that they are a supply point for the BI 95 (Grayham, 1997).

When *industrial accident* details are entered in an *accident book* the *employer* is required to inform the *employee* that he/she should obtain, complete **and** send to the *Benefits Agency*, a BI 95 in respect of the recorded *accident*. This duty applies whether or not an injury, treatment or absence is involved and is additional to the requirements of **RIDDOR**.

On completion of the BI 95 by the 'victim', it must be sent to the local office of the *Benefits Agency* to apply for a *declaration of an industrial accident*, whether or not a known injury occurred or industrial injury benefit was claimed. The *Benefits Agency* sends a **BI 76** to the *employer* to confirm the incident and obtain further details.

The obtaining of the *declaration of industrial accident* places in the personal file of the 'victim' a record of the incident, that otherwise may later be considered to have produced a non-industrially induced pre-existing condition. Pre-existing conditions are cumulatively added and, without declaration and presumed to be non-industrial, deducted from any percentage disablement award. So-called *common law* claims also may be adversely affected. Simply making an entry in an *accident book* is generally insufficient. Firstly, an *accident book* is only required to be kept for three years after the last entry. Secondly, **RIDDOR** may or may not have been activated. Therefore, even if an *Occupational Health Physician, Nurse* or GP was involved *at the time of the accident* and no treatment recorded, it may still prove difficult to prove an *industrial accident* had occurred.

A simple explanation may assist in understanding. Let us assume that, whilst *at work*, an *employee* reaches for something and feels a sudden sharp pain in the back. After ten minutes or so the pain 'goes away'. **No** treatment or sick absence was involved, but unknown to the 'victim' a nodule may form on the spine. Nevertheless it is important the (non-treatment) incident is entered in the *accident book* and a BI 95 obtained, completed and returned to the *Benefits Agency* and a *Declaration of Industrial Accident* (not injury) obtained. If this is not done and later a crippling back injury occurs during the course of *employment*, resulting in a claim for benefit, the claim may be significantly reduced or no benefit paid, because of a non-recorded or reported *pre-existing condition*. Such pre-existing conditions (e.g. nodules on the spine) are *presumed* to be of non-industrial origin unless there is evidence to the contrary. The *declaration of industrial accident* follows submission of a BI 95. In short, no BI 95 means no *declaration of industrial accident and can mean no benefit*.

BI 100A or BI 100B are forms which can be obtained from the *Benefits Agency/* DSS, a Post Office or Job Centre, by claimants disabled by an injury from an *industrial accident* (BI 100A) or industrial disease (BI 100B). Claims should normally be made not less than six months after the *accident* to avoid loss of benefit. The usual maximum period for which benefit will be backdated is three months. The completion of a **BI95** and the subsequent *declaration of industrial accident* can be crucial in the event of a claimant attempting to make a claim.

binding precedent basically is when decisions *on similar facts* concerning a case bind all lower courts (and the court where the decision was made) to follow the precedent. The exception is the House of Lords which can change any otherwise binding precedent, including its own. **Decisions** of the **Court of Justice of the European Communities** establish a binding precedent in the UK on the interpretation of EC legislation.

See also **case law** and **precedent**.

bioaccumulation is the process whereby non-biodegradable chemicals or (toxic) metals either slowly decay or are absorbed more rapidly than they are excreted and therefore accumulate in the body.

See also **carbamates**.

biodegradation is the breakdown in the environment by natural decay of most natural materials and products manufactured from organic substances. There are factors that can mitigate against complete or even partial biodegradation: firstly, for example, crude oil *does* biodegrade but the large quantities, which may flood an area after a disaster, will overwhelm the micro-organisms, which normally break down the oil; secondly, modern products, such as plastics, remain as solid waste or, as with insecticides, accumulate in the environment, frequently as **toxins**.

biohazards see **biological hazards**.

biological agents are **micro-organisms**, cell cultures or **human endoparasites** (including those genetically modified) which may cause infection, allergy, toxicity, or generally constitute a health hazard. Similar to hazardous substances, the listing and classification of biological agents is by reference to the **HSC** Categorisation of biological hazards and categories of containment, revised annually. Biological agents which have no listed classification, the manufacturer or **employer** must make a provisional classification, through placing the agent in one of four groups (see below), 'having regard to the nature of the agent and the properties of which he may reasonably be aware' (Sch. 9 Para. 3-4). If there is doubt as to which of any two groups the biological agent should be allocated, it should be assigned to the higher of the two.

The groups are those:

(i)   unlikely to cause human disease;
(ii) can cause human disease and may be a hazard to **employees**; unlikely to spread to the community and there is usually effective prophylaxis (preventive treatment) or other treatment available;
(iii) can cause serious disease, may be a serious hazard to **employees**; it

may spread to the community, but there is usually effective prophylaxis or treatment available;

(iv) causes serious disease and is a serious hazard to *employees*; it is likely to spread to the community and there is usually **no** effective prophylaxis or treatment available.

biological hazards are those which can cause diseases or pose a threat to the environment. They arise from *bacteria* (e.g. *salmonella, listeria*); *viruses* (e.g. *hepatitis, flu, leptospirosis or Weills disease, HIV*) and *micro-organisms* such as some moulds and/or fungi (e.g. hay, cheese).

The control measures to reduce the risk of infection from biological hazards include natural or applied methods, preferably elimination or substitution of the biological hazard; the use of natural predators, parasites or diseases to control populations of organisms; cleaning; disinfecting; water treatment programme (and monitoring); proofing; vermin control; company procedures. Organisation and arrangements must be clearly explained in the *safety policy* document (confirmed by *employees* as being understood) with suitable and adequate *training* and the maintenance of high standards of personal hygiene; immunisation (if appropriate), health monitoring and, *only as a last resort, adequate and suitable* personal protective equipment. Typical biological agents cause, or are, *hepatitis, leptospirosis* and *Weills Disease.*

bionics is the science of applying data about the functioning of biological systems to the solution of engineering problems.

biophysics is the application of physical principles and methods to biological problems.

Black List is compiled and published by the European Commission identifying dangerous pollutants (currently around 125) commonly discharged into the water environment.

See also *Red List.*

black lung disease is the commonly used name for the disease *pneumoconiosis* that develops, for example, in the lungs of *coal miners.*

See also *silicosis.*

bosun's chair see *suspended access systems.*

botulism is severe 'poisoning' of, e.g., human beings as a result of ingesting *toxins* from contaminated food. The *toxins* are not communicable. Symptoms include blurred or double vision, paralysis, vomiting, diarrhoea and possibly death. It takes some 12-36 hours for the symptoms to appear. Control methods include careful food processing and disposal of contaminated food.

breach of statutory duty is where a *duty*, described or defined by *statute* and imposed on someone or some body, is not complied with. The offender is then subject to criminal charges and, on conviction, penalties *as defined in that statute*.

British Council is an independent, non-political organisation that promotes Britain abroad. The British Council is represented in 230 cities and towns in 109 countries, runs over 200 libraries, 95 teaching centres and 29 resource centres around the world. It was founded in 1934 and awarded a royal charter in 1940. Its total income, including Foreign and Commonwealth Office grants, is in excess of £400 *million*. Amongst other activities, the British Council funds travel and accommodation for courses, together with travel and accommodation for lecturers and tutors, liaising with foreign governments and bodies. The British Council (deservedly) has established a very high international reputation.

Included in its brief is promoting and expanding knowledge and understanding of health and safety, especially in the less developed and developing countries. Examinations abroad (e.g. for health and safety and other British qualifications) are frequently held in British Council premises, invigilated by its staff.

British Nuclear Fuels Limited, commonly referred to as *BNFL,* was formed in 1971 from the Production Group of the UK Atomic Energy Authority (UKAEA). With headquarters in Britain, BNFL also operates offices in the US, Japan, South Korea and China. The company is involved in everything concerned with nuclear fuel, manufacture, reprocessing, waste management, supply and decommissioning of nuclear facilities. In addition, BNFL carries out nuclear research and development and reprocessing at their plant in Sellafield, Cumberland.

British Occupational Hygiene Society, Suite 2, Georgian House, Great Northern Road, Derby DE1 1LT, Tel: 01332 298101, is a standard setting monitoring body for occupational hygiene.

British Safety Council (BSC) was formed in 1957 and operates as a Registered Charity. Similar to *RoSPA*, it is involved in all aspects of health and safety, not restricted to the occupational. The BSC is amongst the leading publicists of safety and its contribution has often proved invaluable. For example, the BSC, and in particular the late James Tye were among the earliest proponents of Total Loss Control and Risk Management, arguably two of the most effective techniques of health and safety management. The journals and literature produced by the BSC are clear, concise and useful.

The BSC runs courses for home and overseas students at various levels, from awareness to diplomas, with many students/candidates coming from overseas. Successful completion of the BSC Diploma course is one of the entry qualifications for full Membership of the International Institute of Risk and Safety Management (IIRSM). Publications produced by the BSC include Safety Management magazine, Health and Safety at Work Newsletter, Safety Manager's Newsletter and monthly Safety Guides. The address of the BSC is National Safety Centre, Chancellor's Road, London WC1A 1DU, Tel: 020 7741 1231/2371.

British Standards Institute (BSI) has a major role in establishing standards, which may or may not have been 'harmonised' with European standards. If these standards are followed, they contribute to ensuring safe systems of, for example, equipment, machinery design and guarding, (safety) management, work and plantetc. The BSI is a member of the *International Organisation for Standardisation* (ISO) and the *International Electrotechnical Commission* (IEC). Address: BSI, Head Office, 389 Chiswick High Road, London W4 4AL, Tel: Customer Services 020 8996 9001; Information Centre 020 8996 7111; web site hrrp://www.bsi.org.uk/bsi/.

Strictly speaking, complying with a British Standard in itself *does not* mean that legal requirements have been satisfied, although the converse applies, i.e. failing to follow a British Standard invariably means that legal requirements have **not** been complied with unless practices have been adopted which satisfy the courts.

See also **Codes of Practice** and **Guidance Notes**.

bronchial tube is a sub-division of a *bronchus* within a lung.

See also *bronchus* and *respiratory system*.

bronchus is a passageway conveying air to and *within* the lungs.

See also *bronchial tube* and *respiratory system*.

BS is a British Standard devised by the **British Standards Institute**. Increasingly that of *EN* follows the acronym *BS* (shown as **BS EN**).

BSI

BSI see *British Standards Institute.*

BS EN is a *British Standard* that, in simple terms, has been checked, approved and accepted to be compatible with EC *Regulations.*

BS 7750 is an environmental management system developed by the British Standards Institute. Its objective is to comply with applicable legislation *and to have a commitment to continual improvement.*

BS 8800 : 1996 is a *Guide to Occupational Health and Safety Systems,* 'based on the general principles of good management and designed to enable the integration of *occupational health* and safety management (OH&S) within an overall management system'.

The standards (or Guides) within the BS 8800 broadly follow those provided in *HSE HS(G)65 Successful Health and Safety Management* and integrate with the international health and safety Quality Management system, **(BS EN) ISO 9000** and the international environmental Quality Management system **(BS EN) ISO 14001.**

See *risk management* and *total quality management.*

BS EN ISO 14000 is an environmental management system developed within the EU by the *International Standards Organisation.* Its objective is to assist compliance with applicable legislation and most importantly to improve environmental management.

buffering agent is an alkaline or basic material which can reduce or neutralise acidity. Lime exemplifies the use and application of a typical natural buffering agent; limestone can help to reduce impact on the environment of acid rain; lime either added to fossil fuel or to the content of gas scrubbers contributes to the reduction of the acidity of emissions; natural lime added to acidic soil reduces its acidity, improves its quality and generally increases its productivity.

building operations are defined 'within the meaning assigned to that phrase by Regulation 2(1) of the *Construction (Design and Management) Regulations 1994 (as amended)*'.

Building Regulations 1991 (and 1984) are concerned with the design and *construction* of buildings. In summary, the *Building Regulations* include: requirements regarding the escape from buildings in case of fire; inhibiting internal and external fire spread; providing good facilities for fire-fighters and their equipment; location of gas appliances and *access* and *egress*. In broad terms, buildings must be safely constructed; not built on toxic ground; with provision and maintenance of safe *access* and *egress*, (and other facilities) made available for *employees* and visitors, including those disabled persons who have difficulty in walking or use a wheelchair, or have impaired hearing or sight, together with suggestions as to how requirements may be met regarding stairs, handrails, stair/platform lifts, and location and accessibility of WCs.

The *Regulations* are enforced by the local authority and provide strict *civil liability*, with limited *liability* at *common law* possible (e.g. for personal injury). *Case law* has determined that local authority enforcement officers have no compulsion to check a building during or after *construction* or alteration to see if the *Building Regulations* are being or have been complied with (*Richardson v West Lindsey District Council and others [1990] AER 296*). The onus is on the contractor to comply.

bullying in the workplace is recognised as a work related problem, contributing to unnecessary and avoidable stress. The bullying takes many forms and is by one member of staff of another, or *employer* of members of staff, irrrespective of age or position. It is covered by the legal duty for *employers*, under the *HSWA* ss.2, 40 and 53 (and other legislation) to ensure, *so far as is reasonably practicable*, the health, safety and welfare at work of their *employees* and the duty on *employees*, under *HSWA* ss.7 and s.8, not to put their colleagues in danger or ill health through their actions and/or activities at work. In addition, *employers* have a *vicarious liability* – that is, they can be held liable for the actions of their *employees*. Breach of these duties could lay offenders open to criminal prosecution by the **HSE** under the **HSWA**.

There is a very useful **TUC** booklet, *Bullied at Work: don't suffer in silence: your guide to tackling workplace bullying* (HS070) obtainable direct from **TUC** headquarters. Single copies are free, *provided* an SAE is included with the order.

burden of proof is the need to prove a fact or facts in dispute. The applicable standards are different in civil and criminal law.

Civil law requires proof of *commission* of an act, or offending by *omission*, *based on the balance of probabilities*, i.e. a person is considered *more likely than not to be guilty* of an offence.

Criminal law requires proof that a person *beyond reasonable doubt* committed an offence or guilty act.

However, for offences covered by the **HSWA**, s.40 states the *prosecutor* only has to prove:

(a) a *breach of* **Regulations** took place;
(b) the *accused was responsible* for the breach.

If the above facts have been proven under health and safety legislation, the accused has to prove innocence, the prosecutor does not have to prove guilt. Finally, for example, if as a consequence of (a) and (b) above occurring someone was injured, then a convicted offender may be found liable for compensation.

Under **HSWA** s.40, to prove innocence the accused has to show **beyond all reasonable doubt** that to do what was required by health and safety legislation:

(i)   was not **practicable**; or
(ii)   was not **reasonably practicable**; or
(iii) there was **no better means** than those used by the accused to 'discharge' the duty (i.e. satisfy the legal requirements/duty).

butane is either of two *isomeric* flammable gaseous alkanes usually obtained from petroleum or natural gas and used as fuels. In grossly simple terms, isomers are 'things' which are similar.

C

cadmium is a soft, silver-white metal used, for example, in the production of some batteries, plastics and synthetics, etc. It is hazardous to the respiratory system, kidneys and bones. Symptoms include pneumonitis, pulmonary edema, renal damage and death.

caissons see *cofferdams and caissons*.

cancer is any malignant cellular tumour, encompassing a group of neoplastic diseases in which there is a transformation of normal body cells into malignant ones. Environmental, hereditary and biological factors influence the development of cancer.

See also **CHIP 1994** and **COSHH 1999**.

carbamates are chemical compounds from carbamic acid (NH2COOH) and used, for example, as insecticides, fungicides and herbicides. Their *advantages* include the fact that they are not stored in the body tissue of animals (a process termed *bio-accumulation*) and they do not remain long in the soil. Their disadvantages include the fact that their *toxicity* for humans and other animals is variable and they are highly toxic for bees and fish. **Sevin** – a commercial insecticide – is a typical example of a widely used carbamate.

carbon dioxide is a colourless, odourless gas at normal temperatures and is a natural constituent of air, exhaled by humans and 'inhaled' by plants. Industrial uses include cooling and refrigeration; as a neutralising agent in textile preparation; treatment of leather and use in fire extinguishers because it is heavier than air and does not support combustion. Hazards from carbon dioxide include those to the lungs, skin and cardiovascular system and it is toxic by inhalation and following contact. Symptoms of exposure include headaches, dizziness, malaise, high blood pressure, pulse increase and, at high concentrations, asphyxia convulsions.

carbon monoxide is a colourless, virtually odourless, *very* toxic gas produced through the incomplete combustion of substances containing carbon, such as coal, oil, petrol and natural gas. Carbon monoxide can cause severe ill-health symptoms or death to individuals exposed at levels of 100-100,000 parts per million (ppm). It is toxic by inhalation and contact with liquid. Symptoms following exposure include headache, nausea, dizziness, hallucinations, angina and fainting.

carcinogen is a substance or preparation 'which, if inhaled or ingested or penetrating the skin, may induce cancer or increase its incidence' (cited in H7 Part II *Special Waste Regulations 1996*).

In terms of *occupational cancer*, a carcinogen is an agent (either physical, chemical or viral) which has the ability to produce malignant tumours, e.g. cancerous cells formed by a carcinogen attacking the mechanism which controls the reproduction of normal cells. It should be noted that it could be impossible to differentiate between occupational and non-occupational cancers.

Development of measurable clinical effects of cancer may take place many years after the first exposure and there may not be any early warning of adverse effects. Therefore, the *mandatory* assessments should identify the nature and extent of the risk and should ensure the information obtained is used to plan effective control measures and necessary precautions, which must be communicated to all concerned *employees*.

Every effort must be made to eliminate the use of carcinogenic substances in favour of a safer alternative, otherwise totally enclosed systems **must** be the first choice of necessary control measures. *Personal Protective Equipment* as the only or first line of protection is not a satisfactory option.

care, duty of see *duty of care*.

Care Homes see *Community Homes Regulations, Nursing Homes and Mental Nursing Homes* and *Residential Care Homes*.

carpal tunnel syndrome arises from compression of the median nerve in the carpal tunnel, resulting in a burning or tingling sensation in the fingers, hand, even extending up to the elbow. It is often the consequence of long-term or repetitive excessive wrist movements. If provably associated with *employment*, it is an automatic compensatory (prescribed) 'disease' (DSS/*Benefits Agency* leaflet NI 2).

Carriage of Dangerous Goods (Amendment) Regulations 1999 have amended ten *Regulations*, as noted in relevant entries. Selected changes from the 1999 amendment included: exemptions for goods carried in an emergency (to protect the environment); those which are part of machinery or equipment; new training requirements for drivers (including *theory* and practice) **and** for *employees* who have responsibilities associated with the carriage of dangerous goods.

Carriage of Dangerous Goods by Rail Regulations 1996 (amended) as its title implies, is concerned with precautions regarding the carriage of *dangerous goods* by rail.

Employees' duties are: not to overfill a tank container or wagon; not to load, stow or unload dangerous goods so as to create a significant health risk; to prevent unauthorised *access*; to prevent significant risk of fire or explosion.

Information displayed on 'containers, tank containers, tank wagons and wagons' is specified in Reg. 14 and Schedule 5 of the *Regulations*.

Operators may allow dangerous goods to be carried in bulk, unless the letter 'Y' appears in column 8 of the *Approved Carriage List (ACL)*; wagons must be closed, open *and* sheeted or with a moveable roof; large containers must be closed or open *and* sheeted.

Tank container or tank wagon operators should not allow dangerous goods to be carried in them, unless the letter 'Y' appears in column 7 of the **ACL**. Operators of containers etc. should not allow dangerous goods to be carried in them *unless* the containers, tank containers or tank wagons are suitable for such carriage and have been adequately maintained; and the dangerous goods must be classified, packaged and labelled in accordance with the *Carriage of Dangerous Goods (Classification, Packaging and Labelling) and Use of Transportable Pressure Receptacles Regulations 1996*.

Train operators are required: not to allow containers to be used, unless they are suitably and adequately maintained; to keep the record of Carriage Information for at least three months after the journey has been completed; to ensure suitable warning signs are displayed as appropriate; to provide crew members with adequate *instruction*, information and *training*; and to draw up and (if necessary) give effect to safety systems and procedures in the event of an emergency arising from the carriage of dangerous goods.

Carriage of Dangerous Goods by Road (Driver Training) Regulations 1996 include requirements for drivers of vehicles:

carrying dangerous goods, to receive 'adequate' *training* and instructions;

Drivers of road tankers with a capacity of:

    (i)   more than 1000 litres and/or;

    (ii) tank containers with more than 3000 litres (apart from explosives, radioactive material and goods in transport category 4);

(iii) together with certain other categories for vehicles with a 'permissible maximum weight exceeding 3.5 tonnes'

must hold *valid* **vocational *training*** certificates, issued by the Secretary of State (incidentally the Certificates were originally required by the earlier, 1992 Regulations).

Such driver vocational *training* certificates must be carried in the vehicle during the 'period of carriage' and held ready for possible inspection by a police officer or goods examiner.

Carriage of Dangerous Goods by Road Regulations 1996 place requirements on operators *and consignors* concerned with the transportation of dangerous goods. The **Regulations** also place duties on designers, manufacturers, importers, suppliers, repairers and testers regarding the **construction**, maintenance, repair of tanks and containers used to transport dangerous goods.

Competent *person* over the age of 18 must supervise parked or broken down vehicles. When vehicles are parked, normally they must be isolated and the vehicle properly secured.

Designers, manufacturers, importers, suppliers and repairers must comply with:

(i) *Approved Vehicle Requirements*; and
(ii) *Approved Tank Requirements*.

Drivers' duties include: not to carry any passengers, other than crew members; and to ensure transport documentation is carried on the vehicle, readily available and produced on request to an authorised person.

Emergency equipment must be adequate for the purpose, e.g. suitable fire extinguishers must be provided on vehicles.

Information, which must be displayed, on panels affixed to vehicles is specified in the **Regulations**, e.g. regarding orange coloured panels, with the UN number and emergency action code, telephone number, danger sign and subsidiary hazard signs, and hazard warning panel.

Operators of tanks or vehicles must comply with the **Approved Carriage List**.

Carriage of Dangerous Goods (Classification, Packaging and

Labelling) and Use of Transportable Pressure Receptacles Regulations 1996 (as amended 1999) cover dangerous goods, dangerous substances and transportable receptacles intended for dangerous substances (e.g. asbestos) or goods (e.g. gas) transported by road and rail.

Classification of dangerous goods is by reference to the revised relevant *Approved Carriage List*; the *Approved Requirements and Test Methods for Classification and Packaging Goods for Carriage*; and the *Approved Requirements for Transportable Pressure Receptacles*.

Dangerous goods packaging must display the following particulars:

(a) designation of goods;
(b) UN number;
(c) subsidiary hazards signs (if any).

Exemptions include, for example, those of more than $3m^3$ in size do not have to meet these requirements or those noted as exempted in the *Approved Carriage List*.

Particulars must be plain to see and easy to read, clearly and indelibly marked on the package or on a label securely fixed to the package and be in English *or the language of the recipient state*.

Packages 'must be suitable', i.e.:

(i)   prevent the escape of contents;
(ii)   not liable to damage by the contents;
(iii) with closures capable of repeated use;
(iv)   of a design tested by an approved testing laboratory and clearly marked accordingly.

Packages which come within CHIP2 have separate requirements for substances and/or preparations in a single package/receptacle but must display specified information or particulars on the outside of the package according to type or weight.

Particulars which must be shown described on the packages, include:

(i)   designation of the goods; and
(ii)   (v), (vi) and (vii) above (Reg. 8 and 11).

Viscous substances of certain types are exempt from classification as flammable liquids, e.g. substances not having toxic or corrosive qualities, or substances which have a flash point equal to or greater than 23ºC.

Selected points from the *Regulations* concerning *transportable pressure containers* include:

Classification which requires that dangerous goods are classified, packaged and labelled in accord with that classification. The *Regulations* apply to all the more common classes of dangerous goods. The armed forces are exempt from these *Regulations*.

Exceptions include (a) pressure systems in aircraft; (b) portable fire extinguishers with working pressure below 25 bar at 60 weighing no more than 23 kilograms; (c) a road tanker or tank container to which the *Carriage of Dangerous Goods by Road Regulations 1996* apply (2 Sch).

Marking of transportable pressure containers must (a) be carried out by a competent authority or approved person; (b) where required by the Approved Requirements, the receptacle must be examined and tested to certify it conforms with the *Regulations*; (c) the periodic examinations required are carried out when due (Reg. 14).

Transportable pressure containers must (a) be safe and suitable for the purpose and (b) comply with the Approved Requirements (Reg. 12(1)).

Carriage of Explosives by Road Regulations 1996 are largely concerned with the duties of operators *and consignors* regarding the carriage of explosives by road and outline the duties of drivers and labelling of tankers and vehicles carrying packaged explosives. NB *Packaging* of explosives is covered by the *Packaging of Explosives for Carriage Regulations 1991*.

The duties cover: the types of explosives which may or may not be carried; information requirements; the need to record routes when more than five tonnes of explosives is carried and to follow such an agreed route; to ensure emergency requirements are in place and carried out; operators *and drivers* to ensure that vehicles are signed in accord with the *Regulations*, etc.

case law is largely established through a **binding precedent** from an earlier case, which has to be followed *unless* the 'present case' can be 'distinguished' (differs) from the case under consideration. *Case law* is quite distinct from *statute law* and yet, in simple terms, assists in interpreting meanings, application of legislation and clarification.

Basically, the higher the court the more binding the precedent. A strength of this system is that in effect it enables law to be practical and up to date; a weakness is that until judges consider an issue and provide a *binding precedent*, interpretation of legislation can remain uncertain. Finally, *case law* can lead to a plethora of cases, which have to be considered – currently there are over 1,000 volumes of law reports and over 400,000 cases to be considered in association with legislation.

case stated is a statement of facts in a case submitted (e.g. by *magistrates* or a *tribunal*), for the opinion of a higher court, such as the *Divisional Court*, on a point of law or *jurisdiction*. Any person who was a party to the proceedings or is aggrieved by the decision can request a court or tribunal to 'state a case'. If a court or tribunal wrongly refuses the request it can be compelled to do so by order of *mandamus* (in this context, we command the hearing of an appeal). The application must identify the point of law on which the opinion is sought.

cash benefits are derived from implementing and applying high standards of health and safety, and often much greater than the cost. Unfortunately, the true costs (and savings) of applying health and safety are seldom *accurately* considered, calculated or measured.

Research has shown that up to 85% of *accidents*, which resulted in an injury, are not reported and accurate costing of *accidents* and damage is not carried out (Grayham, 1978, 1988, 1998). The HSE and other authoritative studies have had similar findings. Thus gross inaccuracies in records are compounded by failure to take account of all costs, for example, a simple cut finger has been found to cost an *employer* some £250! Other costs involve damage to plant and machinery. Effective health and safety management, such as *risk management*, assists. It is authoritatively agreed that areas which require consideration to establish health and safety costs and benefits include:

(i) First aid costs, such as;
   a) *training*;
   b) first aid equipment, such as first aid boxes, eye wash equipment and fittings, replacement items; displayed signs for first aid points;
   c) where in attendance, cost of medical staff (OH Nurse, etc);
   d) where provided, first aid room and equipment;
(ii) variable costs, such as time spent by 'victim' in getting attention;
(iii) disrupted production costs, e.g. lost production of 'victim', persons stopping work to look after 'victim' to pausing while 'victim' passes;

(iv) cost of sick absence and payments;

(v) cost of replacement staff;

(vi) cost of actual paperwork, e.g. forms and books;

(vii) cost of completing records and other paperwork;

(viii) indirect costs, e.g. rise in National Health Insurance rates due to large number of sick absences;

(ix) direct costs, rise in liability and other insurance charges.

Taking the examples provided in (i) to (vii) above, it is suggested that efficiency can be improved and savings made through applying the following (but remember, each company or organisation has its own objectives and criteria). This *aide memoire* includes:

(i) (a) considering whether or not it is cheaper and/or better to train own staff as trainers for certain courses or areas of health and safety. If calling on outside providers, carefully select provider, if possible obtaining references from known persons. Ensure course content satisfies your particular needs, beware of simple 'cover changes' on standard courses if specialist requirements; however, accept constructive criticism of elements in your health and safety programme or techniques.

(i) (b) seeking competitive tenders;

(i) (c) good quality OH staff saving money and contributing to effective health and safety;

(i) (d) taking the advice of all concerned when purchasing plant and machinery, or the introduction of new systems of work, including *employees*/operators and safety professionals;

(i) (e) choosing secondhand equipment which may be perfectly satisfactory, seek advice if necessary;

(ii) information, **training** and the location of first aiders and equipment relevant in saving wasted time;

(iii) good prevention measures, e.g. **training**, regular maintenance;

(iv) multi-task trained staff, high quality production control methods and staff;

(v) ensuring purchasing system efficient;

(vi) not allowing departments to run riot – do they *really* need their own form? Be ruthless: check for (unnecessary) duplication of forms *and entries*, reduce 'empire building' to a minimum; use networked computers wherever possible so that entries can be made by individuals on proformas in the workplace, rather than individuals going to forms;

(vii) investigating, itemising and considering the many indirect costs, all of which add in the long term to costs to the company;

(viii) itemising and considering the direct costs. Reducing these can produce an immediate cash benefit.

The above lists are not exhaustive, but indicate the wide range of matters which should be considered. There are several problems for the safety professional. When measures are effective, the *accident* (cost) prevented cannot be recorded – it didn't happen! At best, there is a reduction in the actual number of *accident*s, damage and injuries, provided records in the past were reasonably accurate (even if not properly costed). However, if a more efficient *accident* and damage reporting system is introduced it is inevitable that *initially* it will appear that there is an increase in *accidents*, injuries and incidents of damage – a consequence can be that the safety professional (and health and safety) is held responsible for the increase by some staff and *employers*, the fact that records are at last accurate being overlooked.

To assist small and medium sized businesses, the **HSE** are required to calculate estimated costs of applying health and safety legislation. Contact **HSE Books** for further information: **HSE** HSG96 *The Costs of Accidents at Work;* **HSE** INDG113L *Your firm's injury records and how to use them* and **HSE** INDG208 *The Cost of Accidents – A guide for small firms* are useful.

caustic chemicals are corrosive alkaline solutions, which burn exposed flesh and completely or partially destroy other organic materials. Examples are sodium hydroxide (caustic soda) and potassium hydroxide.

cell is the fundamental structural and functional unit of living organisms.

celothelioma see *asbestos, asbestosis* and *mesothelioma.*

Celsius temperature scale see *centigrade temperature scale.*

centigrade temperature scale provides for the freezing point of water at *standard atmospheric pressure* at approximately 0°C, with boiling point approximately 100°C. The Celsius scale (from a lay person's viewpoint) is basically the same as centigrade.

challenging of EU Directives and legislation can be done under *Article 173* of the **Treaty of Rome**, within two months of issue using the grounds that they are *ultra vires* (unconstitutional).

See also *application of Directives within the UK.*

Chancery Divisional Court (CDC) is a division of the *High Court of Justice* consisting of the Lord Chancellor, a Vice Chancellor and other *puisne judges* (judges of the **High Court**). Its *jurisdiction* includes companies, administration of estates and execution of trusts. The CDC sits in London and at eight provincial centres. A single judge of the Division may hear appeals, e.g. those made by the Commissioner of Inland Revenue.

change management see *management of change.*

Chartered Institute of Environmental Health (CIEH), Chadwick Court, 15 Hatfield's, London SE1 8DJ, Tel: 020 7928 6006, is the standard setting, monitoring and membership body of Environmental Health Officers.

chemicals, routes of entry into the body by see *routes of entry.*

Chemicals (Hazard Information and Packaging for Supply) Regulations 1994 (or CHIP 1994), these are *Regulations* that are often updated or altered and it is essentially advisable to check the current situation, e.g. via the **HSE Information Line**, and obtain from **HSE Books** the (current) pamphlet INDG 186 *Read the label: how to find out if chemicals are dangerous* (single copies free). The amendments include those of **CHIP 1997, CHIP 1998** and **CHIP 1999**. CHIP requires *suppliers* to classify, label and package dangerous chemicals appropriately and provide *safety data sheets* for each item or preparation. References to relevant amendments are included in this entry. Selected points from the *Regulations* and the amendments are listed below.

Coverage of any substance that is dangerous for supply. The *Regulations* make it an offence to supply any substance or preparation **unless** it has been classified.

Exemptions from CHIP include specified preparations, e.g. cosmetics, medicinal products, pesticides etc.; specified substances and preparations containing pathogenic micro-organisms and radioactive substances (see CHIP Reg. 3).

Classification must be carried out by the manufacturer, importer or supplier, as laid out in the *Regulations* and the *L63 Approved guide to the classification and labelling of substances and preparations dangerous for supply.* All labels must include an appropriate symbol.

Displayed *information. Regulations* 9 and 10, together with Schedule 6, detail what information and other certain circumstances should be displayed on labels. The label must be securely fixed on the outside of the package **and** on the containers of dangerous substances, for use at work. The label must clearly present the following summarised information for dangerous substances: indication(s) of danger and danger symbols (see below); risk phrases as shown in Part III of the *Approved Supply List*, e.g. 'may cause cancer' or 'highly flammable'.

Enforcement authorities for these *Regulations* will be *either* the Health and Safety Executive, the Royal Pharmaceutical Society or the local Weights and Measures Authority (Reg. 16(2)).

Labels or indelible marking must be used, clear to read and understand, written in English in the UK or the language of any EU destination country (non-EU countries may have their own requirements, with appropriate hazard symbols on the label (Reg. 11)). The label size is determined by capacity of package, ranging from 3 litres or under to be at 522 mm x 74 mm, to 500 litres at 148 mm x 210 mm. The hazard label on the supply labels is defined in Schedule 2 of CHIP and must be:

(i) printed in black on an orange yellow background;
(ii) at least one-tenth of the label area; and
(iii) not less than 100 mm squared side length.

See *Restricted to professional user* below.

Packaging. CHIP requires dangerous substances to be suitably packaged, i.e. not split, not affected by the contents, replaceable closures repeatedly to operate safely (Reg. 8). Regulation 10 lists certain preparations, which have particular labelling requirements.

Preparations must display on the outside of the package and on each container the following information: many are as for substances above, and additionally; the constituents which make it dangerous for supply; indications of danger and symbols; any preparation containing a substance (one per cent or in excess) which has not been fully tested under the *Notification of New Substances Regulations* 1993, to have the words 'Caution – this substance has not been fully tested' included on the label.

Record keeping. Anyone who classifies a dangerous substance which is not on the *Approved Supply List* (see Reg. 5) must keep a record of the way the classification was arrived at for at least three years **after** the *substance was last supplied*. These records are to be available for inspection by the authorities (Reg. 13).

Replaceable lids. Regulation 12 requires for all substances dangerous for supply which are in containers with a replaceable lid, that such a lid conforms to BS EN 28317/1993 *Specification for packaging resistant to opening by children* and that preparations dangerous for supply must **NOT** be in packaging that is attractive to children.

Restricted to professional user. Certain Category 1 and 2 substances, that are *carcinogenic, mutagenic* and **toxic**, must be labelled '*Restricted to professional user*'. These are referred to and listed in the **Regulations** as amended.

Safety data sheets (commonly called 'hazard data sheets') **must** be provided *free* of charge, **by the supplier** for all classified substances intended for use at work at or before the time of first purchase, in the *language of the recipient*, and *updated* as and when necessary (Reg. 6). Safety data sheets **must** include the following: identification of the substance or preparation; identification of hazards; first aid measures required; handling and storage details; exposure controls and personal protection required; physical and chemical properties; toxicological information; disposal considerations; transport information; other regulatory information. **NB.DO NOT** use safety data sheets as the *only* source of information when carrying out the **COSHH** assessment duty.

Warning symbols *must* **be displayed** on package or container labels. The signs (as part of a multi-component sign) must be fixed to road vehicles and railway carriages carrying hazardous substances or preparations in bulk, as well those packaged according to the **CHIP Regulations** and associated schedules. A useful **HSE** pamphlet is INDG181 *The complete idiot's guide to CHIP 2: a guide to the* **CHIP Regulations**, single copies free, obtainable from **HSE Books.**

Incidentally, if reading health and safety material originating in the USA, beware! CHIP in US health and safety terms usually means *Chemical Hazardous Information Profile* and records information listed on the US **Material Safety Data Sheets** which have limited similarity to the UK **Safety Data Sheets.**

child employee definitions depend on context and legislation. In *employment* terms, a *child employee* is someone of compulsory school age (between five and 16 years of age) who undertakes paid work.

It is **illegal** to employ any child under 14 years of age, or any child during school hours – which is considered to be between 0700 and 1900 hours – or for more than two hours *on a school day*, to lift, carry, or move anything that is likely to cause injury to the child, or to employ a child for more than two hours on a Sunday.

Local authorities (in particular the Education Department) generally enforce *Regulations* concerning child *employment* and may make their own additional provisions in the form of by-laws, especially for children *13 years* or over employed in *light work*. Such by-laws must be *confirmed* by the Secretary of State for Health.

CHIP see *Chemicals (Hazard Information and Packaging for Supply) Regulations 1994.*

chlorine is a heavy, greenish-yellow gas with a pungent, irritating odour. It is used in the manufacture of solvents, antifreeze and/or anti-knock compounds, resins, pesticides, etc. Chlorine is toxic following inhalation, ingestion or contact. Symptoms include irritation of the eye, nose or throat, bronchitis and pulmonary edema (abnormal accumulation of fluid causing a swelling of tissues).

chromium is a hard metallic element used in the metallurgical, refractory and chemical industries and found in a variety of products, including toners for photocopiers, water treatment and magnetic tapes. Chromium or its compounds are used in the manufacture of stainless steel, for plating, the dyeing industry and leather tanning. Hazards (for the same *dose*) appear to be age-related and symptoms associated with chromium include asthma, skin eruptions, dizziness, bronchospasms, respiratory system cancers and death.

chronic (in *occupational health*) is a term meaning *of a long duration*. The 'opposite' is *acute*.

chronic exposure is exposure to a hazardous substance for a very long period, e.g. 365 days or more.

chronic health effect or reaction produces a permanent adverse health effect, e.g. following exposure to any of the four major *hazards*. It can be the result of repeated or continuous exposure to a *hazardous substance* over a long period of time or frequently reoccur as a result of exposure to a toxin, e.g. occupational dermatitis, or development of a non-occupational disease, e.g. diabetes mellitus.

chronic toxicity produces adverse chronic health effects resulting from repeated doses of, or exposures to, a substance, usually over a relatively long period.

chrysotiles are a white-green hydrated magnesium silicate and a fibrous form of *asbestos*.

cilia

See also *asbestos*.

cilia are very short, hair-like cells which through eyelash-like movement produce a current in higher organisms (e.g. see *ear*) or locomotion (provide movement) in some simple (unicellular) organisms.

circadian rhythm (also known as *solar day rhythm, diel rhythm* or *diurnal rhythm*), refers to the fact that physiological and psychological functions almost invariably describe a rhythmic behaviour during a 24-hour cycle, i.e. a human's function level oscillates between high and low levels over each 24-hour period. In addition, persons regularly deprived of time cues, such as light, move to living on a 25.2-hour day/night schedule.

It has been found that shift workers can be adversely affected by the alteration to their circadian rhythms, especially **night workers**. For example, experiments in the US have found that train drivers on night shifts made more errors than those working days (Hildbrandt et al '12 and 24 hour rhythms in error frequency of locomotive drivers and the influence of tiredness' in *International Journal of Chronobiology 1974 2; 175-180*).

circuits in electrical installations are categorised in the following groups:

(i)   circuits (excepting fire alarm or emergency lighting circuits) operating at a low voltage and supplied direct from a mains electrical supply;

(ii)   circuits for tele*communications* (e.g. data transmission, intruder alarm or sound distribution) supplied at an extra low voltage, *excluding* fire alarm and emergency lighting circuits;

(iii)   fire alarm and emergency lighting circuits.

civil court is one that exercises *jurisdiction* in civil rather than criminal cases. In England, **Magistrates' Courts** have both criminal and limited civil *jurisdiction*, largely confined to matrimonial proceedings.

civil law is non-criminal law and largely concerned with recompense, financial or otherwise, e.g. an apology.

civil liability see *liability*.

claimant is someone, in simple terms, who, for example, makes a claim for an entitlement from the **Benefits Agency** or a person who takes action against someone or a company in a court.

classification of fires see *fire classification*.

Clean Air Act 1993 (CAA) prohibits, with six categories exempted (as prescribed in the *Clean Air (Emission of Dark Smoke) (Exemptions) Regulations 1969*), the emission of *dark smoke* (defined by reference to the **Ringlemann Smoke Chart** *Section 3*, but ultimately determined for offenders by the **Courts**) from a chimney of any building, or premises which are used for industrial or trade purposes, or any industrial plant. Other selected CAA provisions include:

(a) new furnaces must, *so far as is reasonably practicable*, be smokeless (Section 4);
(b) the height of chimneys of furnaces must be approved, in certain cases, by the local authority (Sections 14 and 15);
(c) there are limits on the emission of grit and dust from the chimneys of furnaces;
(d) smoke control areas can be established by local authorities (Section 18);
(e) the occupier of the premises *and* any other person who causes or permits the emission is considered guilty of an offence;
(f) convicted offenders on **summary conviction** can be subject to a fine of up to £20,000 for each offence.

Part 1 of the **Environmental Protection Act 1990** excludes certain premises cover from CAA Parts I to III. CAA Part IV replaces Part IV *Control of Pollution Act 1974* giving the Secretary of State powers to make air pollution **Regulations**.

NB Private householders can be subject to provisions of the CAA.

clean air legislation was originally introduced to reduce atmospheric pollution. Initially directed at the visible – smoke and soot – it has come to include controls over invisible pollutants, such as sulphur dioxide or oxides of nitrogen.

Most clean air legislation, as with health and safety legislation generally, is reactive, following public outcry, less often pro-active. For example, in the UK the first comprehensive *Clean Air Act* came into effect in 1956, following public concern over the effects of the London smog of 1952. As a comparison, the US State of California has had air quality legislative requirements since the 1940s.

coalescence is the process by which small water droplets suspended in the air combine to make larger droplets.

cochlea is the spiral shaped structure, looking somewhat like a snail, that forms part of the inner *ear* and is an essential organ of hearing.

Codes of Practice

Codes of Practice provide practical guidance or best commercial practice, which is recommended usually by a trade group, trade association or manufacturer. If the recommended practices are followed health and safety legislation should be satisfied. **NB** Not as high a 'standing' as an *Approved Code of Practice*.

cofferdams and caissons are watertight enclosures (confined spaces), somewhat like an upside-down mug, constructed and located in water or water-laden locations, such as swampland. They are constantly pumped dry, sometimes fed with pressurised air, used for constructing bridge piers, etc. *Permits to Work* apply.

collective agreement, in broad terms, means an agreement between members of an *'independent' trade union*, (or collectivity of trades unions) recognised by an *employer* for the purpose of *collective bargaining*.

See also *workplace*.

combustion, in basic terms, is a chemical reaction in which a substance combines with oxygen (free or as a compound) to release energy in the form of heat and light, most frequently during burning.

comment on (*examination term*) requires a person (e.g. an examinee) to give *justified* opinions on an issue or statement, together with opinions of others, compared and contrasted.

committees generally consist of a group of people, meeting for some special purpose, such as a *Safety Committee*. A seminal work on the operation of committees is Lord Citrine's *ABC of Chairmanship* (henceforth *ABC*). The role of a Chairperson is to summarise and guide discussion and ensure the business is progressed, with the Committee rules and procedures observed. Citrine states a Chairperson must not put forward personal views or opinions on a subject under discussion but, if wishing to make a contribution, should temporarily vacate the chair.

In many cases, such as a Health and *Safety Committee*, the meetings are usually on a regular basis, with additional meetings arranged as required or demanded by circumstance. Minutes must be taken and publicised to all concerned in or affected by its decisions, with action (including time schedules for its completion) detailed. Applicable legislation for Health and Safety Committees includes the *Health and Safety (Communication with Employees) Regulations 1997*, the *Safety Representatives and Safety Committee Regulations 1977* and the *Workplace (Health, Safety and Welfare) Regulations*.

common law (or judge made law) has developed over many hundreds of years, in particular the three centuries immediately following the Norman Conquest in 1066. It was the Normans who set out to establish a national system of law.

However, modern common law was introduced largely due to the efforts of Henry II. In the late twelfth century he sent out Royal representatives to carry out judicial duties. They based their judgments (or decisions) on universal rules, as opposed to the then current variety of decisions based on local custom and practice. The Assize of Clarendon (1166) and the following decade laid the basis whereby royal representatives went out on a *regular* basis, their journeys being termed a *circuit*. The representatives became known as wandering justices (*justiciae errantes*) and took over the work of local courts. The aim was to ensure a common system of law throughout the land: hence the term '*common law*'. In addition, at Westminster a *Court of Common Pleas* (loosely, an **appeal court**) was established in the twelfth century although since 1880 it has been merged with the *Queen's Bench Division*.

This was the foundation of modern common law and the principles still apply some 800 years later. The **decisions** of **courts** and **judges** still establish what is called **judicial precedent** – simply put, decisions taken in the higher **courts** take precedent over (or bind) decisions made in lower **courts** (see also **case law**).

Where or when a decision *must* be followed, it is called a *binding precedent*, where it *may* be followed it is called a *persuasive precedent*. The difference to courts is how a judge identifies the precedent distinction. This is frequently made in an introductory statement, e.g. if the judge says 'If I were called upon to decide ... I should be inclined to say ...' then what follows is a *persuasive* precedent. Through these precedents common law is flexible, constantly evolving and alive.

However, where there are conflicts between **statute** and **common law**, **statute** takes precedent because Parliament is legally sovereign.

Two weaknesses of the provisions of common law, particularly with regard to **environmental law**, is that (i) they have largely been concerned with the protection of private property, rather than those of the community and (ii) they depend on the entering of litigation by someone who has the legal entitlement to sue. These weaknesses have been noted and increasingly **statute** law is supplementing common law provisions.

Common law duties, in effect, are separate from health and safety legislative duties. However, in simple terms, one frequently duplicates the other. For example, the common law duties of an *employer* are to provide and maintain:

(a) a *safe place of work*, with safe means of *access* and *egress*;
(b) safe appliances, equipment and plant for doing the work;
(c) a *safe system of work*;
(d) competent and safety-aware personnel.

Each of the above (a) to (d) are repeated and effectively reinforced in UK health and safety legislation. Partly due to this 'dual' responsibility (from common law and health and safety legislation) placed on *employers*, those who transgress can face a *double-barrelled action*. A relevant *case law* decision is *Kilgollan v William Cooke and Co Ltd [1956] AER 294* whereby an *employee* sued for damages from the *employer simultaneously* but *separately* on the grounds of *negligence* and *breach of a statutory duty* by the *employer*.

An *employer* has two principal defences against charges of breach of common law; *volenti non fit injuria* (simply, a person knew the risk but still continued the activity) and *contributory negligence* (a person contributed to his/her own misfortune). The former defence rarely succeeds and therefore is less often used now than in the past.

common parts are usefully defined in Reg. 2(1) of the *Health and Safety (Enforcing Authority) Regulations 1998* as 'those parts of premises used in common by, or for providing common services to or common facilities for, the occupiers of the premises'. The person or body who holds responsibility for the *maintenance* of the common parts generally has legal responsibility for health and safety in that area (e.g. see *occupiers liability* and testing of electrical installations).

communication is the process of transferring knowledge and understanding from one person to another, wherever possible obtaining confirmation (*feedback*) that the transfer has been successfully completed. Understandable health and safety *communication* is a legal *duty* placed on *employers*. Therefore, in the application of *effective* health and safety policies, programmes and procedures the importance of understanding the process of *communication* cannot be over-emphasised.

In *behavioural science* or *psychological* terms someone, called the *transmitter*, *encodes* (puts together), in *open codes* (which everyone can understand) or *closed codes* (which only those 'in the know' can understand) a *message*. The *transmitter* decides on the *target* person or group, *transmits* the message in the form of a *signal* through a *channel*. which may be *oral*, *verbal*, *written* or *visual*.

The *receiver* of the message *decodes* the signal and reacts according to the perception of the message. However, the message or signal may be *interfered with* by *noise* during transmission and not understood by the receiver. In such cases the receiver, if possible or able, may provide *feedback*, asking questions to clarify the message, and the whole process may be repeated. Furthermore, in some cases the **communication** may not be intentional or known to be happening by the sender – e.g., through the use of body language, inflection or tone of speech.

The prime points that must be considered (followed by examples) when making a **communication** include:

(i)   what is it for? (social or business)
(ii) who is it for? (the highly educated or the virtually illiterate)
(iii) what type is it? (instructional, asking for advice/information, sales)
(iv) which transmission medium would be best to use and most effective? (telephone, written, face to face, individual or group)
(v)   where is the **communication** going to take place? (on notice boards in a busy area, in letters/memos opened by the target individual or a synopsis read before a committee and interpreted by one individual)
(vi) will the **communication** be *encoded* in an '*open code*' (so that anyone would understand it, such as the word/sign/message 'danger') or can it be in *closed code*? A *closed code* will restrict the numbers of people who will understand it. (If the *transmission* refers to a certain process in a certain factory or workplace, only workers involved in that process or working at that factory may fully understand the transmitted message).

Each of the above points may be part of an automatic process during our daily **communication**s. However, some **communication**s (such as those for health and safety) would benefit from very careful thought, planning and preparation before transmission. We can – and do – automatically take such steps on non-health and safety occasions. Think of the way we carefully prepare what we are going to say when we want something from our partner!It is necessary to take similar care regarding health and safety **communication**s.

Because they greatly influence the effectiveness of the **communication**, even the location of **notice boards** is part of the **communication** process, almost as much as the written or visual information displayed on those boards. Barriers to successful **communication** can inadvertently be raised, making **communication** impossible. For example, the picture of a pretty but scantily clad woman can be a turn-off for the majority of a workforce largely composed of Muslims as practising Muslims usually consider such posters disrespectful (see *notice boards*).

Effective *communication* helps prevent *accidents*, injuries, incidents, damage or loss. The **MHSWR** places a *duty* on *employers* to provide *comprehensible instruction*, information and *training*, which means that all health and safety *communications* and *training* must be clearly understood by individual 'receivers' to avoid non-compliance with legislation.

Community Homes Regulations 1972 require, amongst other matters, regular fire practice to be carried out and extensive consultation with the fire authorities.

compare (*examination term*) means to identify the differences (contrasts) and similarities between two or more items, issues or statements. Sometimes written in questions as '*compare and contrast ...*'.

compensation is monetary payment for loss or damage, typically awarded via the courts following a *civil law* action and/or *common law* claim. Most of the different 'types' of compensation are covered by insurance, e.g. *industrial injuries* by the compulsory *Employers' Liability Insurance*. State Industrial Injury Benefit is also covered by compulsory (National Health) Insurance, but strictly speaking is not 'compensation'.

competent authority, in health and safety terms, refers to those *enforcement authorities* that either jointly or separately work to enforce (and frequently advise on) health and safety legislation. The relevant *competent authority* is usually identified in a *statute* or *regulation*. Do **NOT** confuse with *competent person*.

competent person (or persons) **must** be appointed by an *employer* to assist them with carrying out their health and safety duties and obligations. By preference such appointments should be made from their *employees*, or as a second choice alternative suitable consultants from outside the organisation may be appointed, **MHSWR** Reg. 7. In addition, the accompanying 1999 amended **ACOP** requires such appointments to be included 'among the health and safety arrangements recorded' under **MHSWR** Reg. 4(2).

In summary the definition of competent person varies according to the statutory (and other) specifically defined requirements. There is no *one precedent* or legislative definition that covers all the different situations, tasks or requirements. The *employer* **must** ensure that their appointed person has sufficient time and resources allocated to carry out their duties. If something 'goes wrong' it is likely the *employer* will generally be held accountable for the activities of their appointed competent person.

Discussion based on legislation demonstrates two of the problems faced when appointing a competent person:

(i) in the **MHSWR** a *competent person* is a person '*who has sufficient training and experience OR knowledge and other qualities to enable . . . (them) . . . properly to assist . . . (the employer)* in securing compliance with the necessary legal requirements'. **MHSWR ACOP** 39 adds that who is considered a '*competent person*' depends on the situation and '*does not necessarily depend on the possession of particular skills or qualifications*' declaring, 'Simple situations may require only: (a) an understanding of relevant current best practice; (b) an awareness of the limitations of one's own experience and knowledge';

(ii) by reference to **COSHH Regulations** a competent person is defined as someone who has 'an appreciation of occupational hygiene principles', 'the range of control measures' available and needed, and 'an understanding of the point of each Regulation and what it involves'. For example, 'where respiratory protective equipment is being used, someone with a sound knowledge of occupational hygiene principles, as well as the procedures and practices should be involved' (**HSE**, 1990 p 33).

As an example, a highly qualified and experienced chemistry teacher may not be regarded as a competent person to carry out a risk assessment in an educational establishment laboratory simply because they have knowledge of chemistry, or because they are qualified chemistry teachers with years of experience. Unless such persons have *adequate* and *sufficient* health and safety *training*, knowledge or understanding, e.g. of relevant legislation, *regularly updated* they may not be considered a *competent person*. Similar caveats apply to those in other fields who otherwise are considered technically 'competent' for conducting a risk assessment; professional knowledge, experience or qualifications in any discipline, by themselves, are often insufficient, without the essential health and safety training.

Finally, an *employer* **must**: (i) consult with *employees* regarding the competent person's appointment; (ii) provide *adequate and suitable training* in health and safety for the appointed staff member competent person; (iii) ensure the competent person has sufficient time (and resources) allocated to carry out these duties effectively; and (iv) make sure that any external professional or body appointed is indeed competent (e.g., check *claimed* qualifications, *training* and possibly obtain references).

compound

compound in technical terms, is a substance containing two or more elements united by chemical bonds. Two key facts concerning compounds are:

(a) Elements lose their individual properties when they form a compound. For example, salt is formed by the combination of a highly reactive metal (sodium) and a poisonous gas (chlorine) but displays none of these characteristics; and

(b) Certain compounds contain a fixed proportion of elements and a constant set of properties. For example, water always has two hydrogen atoms and one oxygen atom and always freezes at zero centigrade.

comprehensible health and safety information (and *instruction* and *training*) for all *employees* is a *mandatory* requirement under several Acts and *Regulations*, especially the **MHSWR, HSWA, PUWER, COSHH** and the *Asbestos Regulations*.

It is the *employer's* **duty to ensure** *relevant* health and safety information etc. is understandable, taking account of **literacy** levels, language or learning difficulties of members of the workforce. *Relevant* is that which is necessary concerning risks faced by workers (or students) in their work environment and in the task which an individual carries out.

conduction, technically speaking, is the transmission of thermal energy directly through matter from places or objects of higher temperature to those of lower temperature. For conduction to take place, the objects must be in direct contact. Conduction can be controlled and useful – the free flow of an electrical current through a suitable conductor – or potentially dangerous or destructive – the overheating caused through the flow of electricity along a high-resistant, *unsuitable* conductor.

See also *sources of ignition*.

Confined Spaces Regulations 1997 (or CSR) came into force on 28 January 1998. The definition of a **confined space** is 'any place, including any chamber, tank, pit, pipe, sewer, flue, well or *any other similar place*, in which, by virtue of its enclosed nature, there arises a foreseeable *specified risk*' (Reg. 1(2)). **NB** It is possible for somewhere to be a confined space only during a certain work activity, depending on the presence of a reasonably foreseeable risk of serious injury, e.g. a room during spray painting; an open vat; enclosures during asbestos removal; excavations; and interiors of **machines, plant** or vehicles;

Selected principal requirements from the **Regulations** include:

Assessments that are suitable and sufficient must be carried out of all confined spaces:

(i) to 'identify the measures needed so that work in confined spaces can be avoided' (Reg. 2 GN 21)
(ii) and 'if, in the light of the risks identified, it cannot be considered reasonably practicable to carry out the work without entering the confined space, then it is necessary to determine the measures need to be taken to secure a safe system for working within the confined space in accordance with regulation 4(2)'. (Reg. 2 GN21)
(iii) Recording of the *significant findings* of *significant risks* must be made if five or more are employed. Insignificant risks can be ignored. (Reg.2 GN 20)

Construction of confined spaces, *so far as is reasonably practicable*, should be safe and without risks to health. (**HSWA** s.6; **CDMR** Reg. 13; **CSR** Reg. 4 GN 31-34 also BS 5502 and BS 8005).

Design of confined spaces, *so far as is reasonably practicable*, should be safe and without risks to health. (**HSWA** s.6; **CDMR** Reg. 13; **CSR** Reg. 4 GN 31-34 also BS 5502 and BS 8005)

Emergency arrangements, suitable and sufficient, **must** be in place **before** any person enters a confined space and these include, where the need for resuscitation is 'a likely consequence of a relevant specified risk', the provision and maintenance of suitable resuscitation equipment. (Reg. 5, **ACOPs** and GNs 80-92)

Employers' **duties** under these *Regulations* include ensuring their *employees* and the *self-employed* under their control comply. (Reg. 3 **ACOP** 18)

Exceptions include normal ship-board activities carried out solely by a ship's crew under the direction of the master; any place below ground in a mine; any diving operation covered by the *Diving Operations at Work. Regulations 1981* (Reg. 2)

Hazards include flammable substances and oxygen enrichment; oxygen deficiency; toxic gas, fume or vapour; ingress or presence of liquids; solid materials which can flow (e.g. flour, sugar, sand). (Reg. 1 GN 9)

Permit to work is the usual *safe system of work* for *confined spaces,* but if the risks are very low, with simple work, the *permit to work* system may not be required.

Personal protective equipment is the last resort, after other control methods have been considered and/or tried. Reg. 4 and 7 of the **PPER** are the 'dominant' legislation over the **CSR** and detail the *personal protective equipment* statutory requirements for persons working in confined spaces.

Safe working in confined spaces is largely determined by the findings from the assessment and includes supervision, *competent person*, testing, monitoring, suitable equipment, ventilation, etc. (Reg.4 ACOP/GN 35-79)

Training **must** be provided, of *adequate and suitable* standards. (*HSWA* S (2)(2) (c) and CSP Appendix 1, **ACOP/GN**s 92 and 113-116) For example, those 'likely to be involved in any emergency should be trained for that purpose', **ACOP** 92 lists the minimum *training* requirements.

Work equipment used in confined spaces is defined and covered by the 'dominant' legislation. **PUWER** (Reg. 5) Basically *work equipment*, when used correctly, should not affect the health and safety of any person. (**CSR ACOP** 31)

Construction (Design and Management) Regulations 1994 or

CDMR came into force on 31 March 1995 generally to implement, with minor exceptions, Directive 92/57/EEC. The coverage of the **CDMR** and its **ACOP** (**L54**) includes:

(a) *construction* work involving demolition at all times and non-notifiable *construction* work where five or more persons are on site at any one time;

(b) notifiable *construction* work, which will last more than 30 days or involve more than 500 person days of work;

(c) design work, *irrespective* of the duration of the work or the number of persons involved.

Therefore, the **CDMR** only applies to *construction* sites where the work is *notifiable* AND where five or more people are employed at any one time, otherwise the **CHSWR** apply. Selected key points from the **CDMR** include:

Advice must be provided to, collected and distributed by, the Principal Contractor, who must establish a suitable mechanism in place for discussing and conveying such advice to all *employees* (Reg. 18).

Appointment of duty holders must be notified in writing to the appropriate enforcing authority (Reg. 4).

Construction (Design and Management) Regulations 1994

Client is '. . . any person for whom a project is carried out, whether it is carried out by another person or carried out in house . . . ' and appoints 'competent people' such as the planning supervisor, designer and principal contractor (**Reg. 4**); ensures that no *construction* phases starts without a health and safety plan (**Reg. 10**); ensures that a health and safety file is maintained and available for inspection (**Reg. 12**).

Contractors (and the *self-employed*) **must** co-operate with the principal contractor; comply with applicable rules in the health and safety plan; ensure their *employees* (i) know the names of the planning supervisor *and* the principle contractor; (ii) know the contents of the health and safety plan relevant to their activity (**Reg. 19**).

Designer is 'any person who prepares a design or arranges for any person under his/her control to prepare a design relating to a structure or part of a structure' and must have an awareness of health and safety legislation and risk assessment methods, taking account of health and safety matters in materials used and methods of *construction*, providing such details and information to the other duty holders (**Reg. 6 and 13**).

Duty holders are appointed by the *client* (or client's agent), who must satisfy themselves, so far as is reasonably practicable, that the appointed persons are competent in health and safety. The duty holders and their responsibilities are the client, designer, planning supervisor, principal contractor.

Exempted are (but see paragraphs (a) to (c) above):

Domestic premises, unless part of the premises is used for business (**NB** Developers of housing estates or similar have certain duties under the CDMR);

Premises where the local authority is the enforcing authority, i.e. offices, shops and where only minor *construction* work is being carried out.

File (health and safety) must be prepared and maintained by the planning supervisor, with the co-operation of the other duty holders and handed to the client at the end of the *construction* project (Reg. 14). The file should detail the health and safety aspects arising from design, materials used in *construction* and in the case of future alteration, conversions or additions prevent any health and safety problems during subsequent alterations.

Plan (health and safety) must be prepared initially under the aegis of the client and the Planning Supervisor (**Reg. 10**). However, once *construction* work has started, keeping the plan up-to-date then becomes the duty of the Principal Contractor (**Reg. 15(4)**). The health and safety plan must contain:

(i) a general description of the *construction* work;
(ii) the time within which the project is intended to be completed;
(iii) that the planning supervisor and the designer are competent and that adequate resources (for health and safety) will be allocated;
(iv) information that the contractor needs in order to keep the safety plan up-to-date.

Planning supervisor is appointed *as soon as possible* after there is commitment to the project by the client and co-ordinates the health and safety aspects of project design and planning, ensuring that . . . the principles of prevention and protection are applied by everyone connected with the planning process (**Reg. 6**). The planning supervisor will draw up a health and safety plan, in consultation with other appointed duty holders and prepare a health and safety file (**Reg.14**).

Principal contractor is appointed by the client, or client's agent, and must conform to the health and safety plan, employ competent personnel, have adequate resources (financial and human), technical and managerial approach capable of dealing with health and safety risks and comply with the relevant statutory provisions (**Reg. 6**).

Purpose of the CDMR is to ensure effective direction and co-operation of health and safety matters takes place throughout the duration of a *construction* project and a health and safety file containing specified details is handed on to the eventual owner of the *construction*. The CDMR is intended to ensure that health and safety on *construction* sites is well managed and that health and safety aspects of materials are taken into account.

Training (and information) – the Principal Contractor must ensure that all *employees* on sites must be adequately trained, instructed and informed on the risks to their health and safety and in safe systems of work, leading to a reduction in *accidents*, incidents and loss (Reg. 17) by all contractors to their *employees*, and ensured by the Principal Contractor as required by *Regulations* 8 and 11(2)(b) of the **MHSWR**.

The defence against prosecution by *employers* or *self-employed* for breach of the **CDMR** is that they can show that they made all reasonable enquiries and believed that the **CDMR** did not apply to the work or that they had been given.

Construction (Head Protection) Regulations 1989 place duties on *employers* (or persons in control of *construction* sites), the *self-employed* and *employees* concerning the provision and wearing of head protection on *construction* sites where head injury is reasonably foreseeable. Selected key points include:

> *Employers* **must provide head protection** to every *employee* (and ensure its being worn) while working on building or *construction* operations (Reg. 3). **Exemptions:** Sikhs *wearing turbans* are exempted from the wearing of head protection; Sikhs not wearing turbans must wear head protection.

> *Employers* **must provide maintenance training** to every *employee* issued with *suitable* head protection. The head protection must be maintained or replaced as per manufacturers instructions (Reg. 3).

> **Persons in control** have the duty to ensure, *so far as is reasonably practicable,* that their *employees* wear the head protection provided (Reg. 4(2)); identify the areas when and where head protection should be worn and provide adequate supervision. Persons in control include main contractor; managing contractor; contractor *bringing in subcontractors*; contract manager; site manager; subcontractor; managers (including forepersons and supervisors); engineers and surveyors; clients and architects with control over persons at work.

> **Storage facilities** for the head protection must be provided, to enable it to be kept safe, cool, dry and out of direct sunlight.

> *Visitors* are an 'in-between' case. The Head Protection **Regulations** do not cover visitors but the **HSWA** does and *employers* have a general duty of care. In the event of a head injury to a *visitor* an *employer* could be held liable, therefore the prudent *employer* will take the necessary precautions.

Other legislation, such as the *Personal Protective Equipment Regulations 1992* can overlap and/or take precedence as dominant legislation over the *Construction (Head Protection) Regulations.*

Construction (Health, Safety and Welfare) Regulations 1996
(CHSWR) apply at *all* '*construction* sites,' from the smallest to the largest, where the '*principal work activity being carried out is construction work*'. The

CHSWR consist of a large number of *Regulations*, followed by Schedulesthat require careful reading. It is always necessary to check the Regulation against the Schedule that applies. In very simple terms the CHSW *Regulations* outline what must or should be done, the Schedules provide greater detail.

The following are selected extensive key terms or points, in alphabetical order:

Carriage of dangerous goods connected with *construction* activity, an amendment of **CDMR** Reg. 2(1), means Reg. 7 of CHIP 2 is replaced by Reg. 5 of the **CDGRR(CPL)R** (Schedule 10(9) **CHSWR**).

Coffer dams and caissons must be constructed, installed, altered or dismantled under the supervision of a *competent person*. They must be of suitable design and *construction*, which includes strength, purpose, maintenance (Reg. 13).

Construction **site** is where any alteration, renovation, fitting out, conversion, etc., including '*installation, commissioning, maintenance, repair or removal of mechanical, electrical . . . or similar services which are normally fixed within or to a structure*' is being carried out on a site-**only** actual 'place of work' where *construction* work is being carried out is covered by the **CHSWR**.

Doors and gates: provided the doors and gates are **not** part of mobile plant and equipment, Regulation 16 requires, where necessary, for the prevention of risk of injury from 'any door, gate or hatch' that it 'must incorporate (or be fitted with) suitable safety devices'.

Electricity on site must be rendered safe, power cables isolated where possible and/or practicable; a residual duty (Reg. 44) from the *Construction (General Provisions) Regulations 1961* is that all practicable precautions must be taken to prevent injury and risk, e.g. signs and barriers erected.

Emergency procedures: *Regulations* 18, 19, 20 and 21 are concerned with 'Fire Prevention, Emergency Routes, Exits and Procedures' and 'fire detection and fire-fighting' are comparatively new. They expand on the general requirements in the **HSWA** and the *Construction, Design and Management Regulations 1994*.

Excavations: Regulation 12 requires that all practicable steps must be taken: to ensure that excavations do not collapse accidentally; to ensure they are sufficiently supported so that persons are not trapped or buried by a fall or dislodged material; to prevent persons falling into the excavation; that underground services are identified and that of risk of injury from such services is prevented.

Explosives require *suitable and sufficient* steps to be taken to ensure no one is exposed to risk of injury from their use (Reg. 11).

Falling through fragile material: Regulation 7 requires *employers* to take *suitable and sufficient* measures to prevent their *employees* 'falling (two metres or more) through fragile material'; these include 'affixing' of '*prominent* warning notices ... at the *approach* to the place where the material is located', e.g. inside the last door giving *access* or *egress* to a roof made of fragile materials.

Fire and explosions: sufficient steps must be taken to prevent fires, explosion or risk of asphyxiation (Reg.18). Regulation 21 requires suitable and sufficient fire fighting equipment, fire alarms and fire detectors. The fire fighting equipment (Reg. 21) must be properly maintained, examined, tested, and easily accessible, with the locations 'suitably signed'. In summary, emergency procedures must be known to all on site (not just *employees*) and *employees* are to be instructed on site fire prevention measures.

Goal setting: in application the *Regulations* are somewhat 'looser' than those replaced, with fewer measurements than before, and allow *employers* greater autonomy to decide what is 'reasonably practicable' under the circumstances.

Good order sites must be kept in 'good order', e.g. good housekeeping, perimeters suitably bounded and signed.

Guard-rails, barriers, toe boards and 'other similar means of protection' must be of suitable and sufficient strength and rigidity for the purpose intended, secured to prevent the possibility of displacement.

Inspection of 'places of work': Schedule 7 and 8 cover these areas. Schedule 7 (Reg. 29(1)) outlines the 'places of work' requiring inspection and when made (e.g. before any working platform is used for the first time) and, together with supported excavations, cofferdam or caissons, inspected at the beginning of each shift. Inspections must be recorded.

Ladders: Schedule 5 explains the requirements of Regulation 6(6):

Construction (Health, Safety and Welfare) Regulations 1996

Access or egress by ladders is **not** allowed as means of *access* to or *egress* from a place of work, *unless* it is reasonable to do so having regard to the nature and duration of the work and the risk to the safety and health of the person using the ladder. (Reg. 6(5))

Erected ladders **must be** on a stable, level and firm surface, 'be suitable and of sufficient strength for the purpose or purposes for which it is being used', ladders three metres or more in height must be secure 'to the extent that it is practicable to do so', 'be so erected as to ensure it does not become displaced' and where tying is not possible, a person **must** be positioned at the foot of the ladder.

Handhold of a 'suitable' nature can be provided *or* the ladder extended to a 'sufficient height' above a level to give safe *access* and a safe handhold.

Hazardous substances used in any aspect of *construction* are covered by the current superior legislation, **COSHH.**

Ladders are NOT to be used as a *place of work, unless* it is reasonable to do so having regard to the nature and duration of the work and the risk to the safety and health of the person using the ladder. (Reg. 6(5))

Ladders running vertically nine metres or more require a safe landing or rest platform to be (must) provided 'at suitable intervals'.

Ladders, if they are three metres or over in height, must be safety erected, secured or where that is not practicable, footed by someone at the bottom of the ladder to prevent it slipping or falling.

Lighting on *construction* sites must be *suitable and sufficient*, safe and with emergency lighting where needed to ensure safety. (Reg. 25)

Place of work, under the **CHSWR** (Reg. 2(1)) is any place used by any person for the purpose of *construction* work, or anything connected with *construction* work. For example, installation of a new overhead travelling crane could be covered by the **CHSWR** (or possibly the **CDMR**) because the main activity is '*construction* work'. Similarly, the fixing of trunking for the carrying of cables would be covered by the **CHSWR** – both opinions pending *case law.*

Plant and equipment was covered by **CHSWR** Reg. 27 but this was revoked by the *Provision and Use of Work Equipment Regulations 1998.*

Construction (Health, Safety and Welfare) Regulations 1996

Protection of children and the requirement to prevent them being injured, *even though they may be trespassing*, is found in the *Occupiers' Liability Acts* and must be taken into account when leaving company vehicles on a *construction* site.

Records following inspections can be on a form supplied by the **employer** or in a computer record (the F91 is now redundant) and **must** include:

(i)   name and address of the person on whose behalf the inspection was carried out;

(ii)   location of place of work inspected;

(iii)   description of place of work (or part of) inspected (including plant, equipment and materials);

(iv)   date and time of inspection;

(v)   details of any matter that could give rise to the health and safety of *any person*;

(vi)   details of any action taken as a consequence of paragraph 5;

(vii) details of any further action considered necessary;

(viii) name and position of person making report.

Safe place of work, including safe *access* and *egress*, must be provided, *so far as is reasonably practicable*. Every workplace must be suitable and have sufficient working space for those who work there. *Suitable and sufficient* steps must be taken to prevent *access, so far as is reasonably practicable*, to any place that is dangerous if accessed.

Safety equipment: Schedule 4 explains Regulation 6(3)(d), requiring 'equipment' of suitable and sufficient strength to arrest the fall of *any* person at work to be provided, with suitable and sufficient steps taken to ensure, so far as is **practicable** (a higher level than 'reasonably practicable') in the event of a fall, 'the equipment itself (must) not cause injury to that person'.

Schedules associated with the **CHSWR must** be read in conjunction with the *Regulations*, examples have been provided above and below.

Supporting *structures* must be of suitable and sufficient strength for the intended purpose: main guard-rails must be at least 910 mm above the edge from which a person is likely to fall; there must not be more than 470 mm between the walking surface and any guard-rail, toe-board or barrier (which invariably means two boards or barriers for the 910 mm requirement); guard-rails etc. must be placed, so far as is reasonably practicable, to prevent the fall of any objects, person or material from a place of work.

Construction (Health, Safety and Welfare) Regulations 1996

Temperature and weather protection (Reg. 24 and Schedule 6 'Welfare'): basically 'suitable and sufficient steps should be taken' that, *so far as is reasonably practicable*, the temperature *at any indoor place of work* is 'reasonable having regard for the purpose for which that place is used'. This includes workplaces, changing rooms or facilities and places for eating food (which must include facilities for non-smokers). Sedentary work will require the provision of higher temperatures than highly physical activities. See also **Workplace Regulations** which, although **not** applying on *construction sites*, can apply in off-site premises.

Traffic routes must be able to be used by vehicles **and** pedestrians without danger to each other, e.g. through separation. Gates used by pedestrians and loading bays are also covered by these **Regulations** (Reg. 15).

Working platforms include any platform used as a place of work or a means of *access* to or *egress* from a place of work and, according to Reg. 2(1), can be a:

(i)   scaffold;
(ii)   suspended scaffold;
(iii) cradle;
(iv)   mobile platform;
(v)   trestle;
(vi)   gangway;
(vii) run;
(viii) gantry;
(ix)   stairway;
(x)   crawling ladder.

Working platforms must be safe, stable, rigid, at least 600 mm wide to allow free movement and passage; without gaps; prevent, so far as is reasonably practicable, tripping or slipping; provided with suitable and sufficient handholds to prevent slipping or falling from the platform; must not be overloaded; on supporting structures sufficiently strong, stably erected on sufficiently strong and stable surfaces.

Vehicles on site: Regulation 17 of the **CHSWR** refers to the movement of vehicles on site, including the requirement to prevent the *unintended* movement of vehicles i.e., to prevent trespassers from starting and moving site vehicles (Reg. 17(1)).

Other duties: some of the specific duties placed on *employees* with regard to welfare facilities under the **CHSWR** are either new or more tightly defined than previously. Notably, in the case of a (signed) supply of drinking water (Schedule 6(10)), *employers* must *also* provide 'a sufficient number of cups or other drinking vessels, unless the water is supplied from a jet where persons can drink easily'. (Schedule 6(11)).

It is strongly re-emphasised that **CHSW** *Regulations,* **CHSWR** Schedules and **ACOPs MUST be read together** to know what is required and how it can be done.

Construction Industry Training Board (CITB) is the training board for the industry. Initial contact is with the head office: CITB Bircham Newton, Kings Lynn, Norfolk PE31 6RH. Tel: 01485 577577; website www.citb.org.uk; email. resource@citb.org.uk.

Construction Products Regulations 1991 (as amended 1994) require all products used in *construction works* and *works of engineering construction* to be suitable and **CE marked.** In summary, *construction* products should be: safe in case of fire and during use; *noise* protected; *energy efficient*; hygienic; healthy and environmental friendly.

construction site is any place where the main work activity is *construction work*. According to Reg. 2 of the *Construction (Health, Safety and Welfare) Regulations 1996* in summary, a *construction* site is where any alteration, renovation, fitting out, conversion, etc., including '*installation, commissioning, maintenance, repair or removal of mechanical, electrical ... or similar services which are normally fixed within or to a structure*' is being carried out.

construction work (and/or *building operations***)** is variously defined, in part depending on the 'controlling' legislation, e.g. **CDMR.** In the **CDMR** *construction work* effectively means the carrying out of any building, civil engineering or engineering construction work but excluding the exploration for, or extraction of, mineral resources or activities preparatory to this.

The **CDMR** covers 38 elements, all under the heading of *construction work*, while the **Construction (Health, Safety and Welfare) Regulations 1996** makes its own contribution. The 'safest way' to establish the definition of construction work or building operations is to extract from and relate them to the work in hand and thereby locate such definitions in the relevant statutory provisions, starting with the **HSWA**.

Many of the steps identified regarding health and safety process and practice in the *demolition* entry also apply to *construction* sites.

Construction work covers virtually everything carried out on a *construction site*

constructive dismissal

from the clearance of a site before commencing construction, everything connected with the construction, through to formal removal of everything connected with the work (see Regulation 2 **C(HSW)R**).

constructive dismissal see *dismissal.*

consultation, in health, safety and environmental terms, is the *legal duty* under the *Health and Safety (Consultation with Employees) Regulations 1996* for *employers* to **listen to and take account of** the views of their *employees* over matters of health and safety *before* any decisions or action is taken. This should not be confused with the *legal duty* for *employers* to provide *adequate and sufficient information, instruction and training.* Examples include *before:*

(i)   introducing any new measure at the workplace, affecting health, safety and the environment;

(ii)   making arrangements for the appointment of *competent persons* to help the *employer;*

(iii)   providing health, safety and environmental information which the *employer* is required to supply; and

(iv)   the planning and organisation of health and safety *training* and health and safety implications of the introduction (*or planning*) of new technology.

There is also a legal requirement (derived from an EU Directive) for all 'governments' to consult with interested parties prior to introducing changes to existing, or introducing new, health and safety legislation. In the UK this requirement is usually satisfied through the use of *consultative documents.*

consultative documents, commonly called *discussion documents*, are issued to allow for discussion on health safety and/or environmental matters by a governmentdepartment (e.g. **HSE, HSC** or **DTI**) and/or interested parties *before* legislation or a **Code of Practice** is issued. The *discussion documents* are free and are obtained from **HSE Books** or via the *internet* website http//www.open.gov.uk/**HSE/HSE**home.htm.

Evidence suggests that many organisations or trade and other groups *or individuals* who will be affected by various changes to, and new, health and safety legislative proposals are often unaware of these consultative documents or of their importance. They therefore miss this opportunity to influence legislation *before* its introduction.

Consumer Protection Act 1987, or CPA, in relation to health and safety and *product liability*, provides *strict liability* in respect of the supply of unsafe products that could cause injury or death to a consumer or damage to property. The term 'products' includes those that form components of a whole product or raw materials but **excludes** those supplied for commercial activity. However, if a person purchases a product for personal use but later does some paid work and is injured while using that product, that person is covered by the *General Product Safety Regulations 1994* (GPSR). The cover of the **CPA** and **GPSR** includes second-hand and reconditioned products.

Water, gas and electricity (except for interruptions in the supply) are included as 'substances'.

Contaminated Land (England) Regulations 2000, or CLER, arise from the **EPA 1990, Part IIA**, which in summary defines contaminated land as 'land which appears to the local authority to be in such a condition, by reason of substances in, on or under the land, that significant harm is being caused, or that there is a significant possibility of harm being caused or that pollution of controlled waters (defined in the **WRA 1991**) and covering virtually all natural surface or underground water) is being or likely to be caused'. There is a **DETR** *statutory Guide to the Regulations* (ISBN 0 1175354 44 3) which is not merely useful, but essential, reading for those concerned (see the website www.environment.detr.gov.uk/contaminated/land/index.htm). It is however, far too long and involved to discuss in this text. The **EPA** entry covers the main details.

Once land is identified as 'contaminated' the enforcing authority has a *statutory duty* to demand remediation from the responsible person, issuing a *remediation notice* after up to three months' consultation with the responsible person and/or the occupier of the contaminated land. Incidentally, general health and safety legislation (especially the **HSWA**) also applies to *contaminated land* and particularly regarding its effects on persons other than *employees*. Scotland and Wales are covered separately, to take account of their different legislative structure, parliament and assembly.

contract is a legally binding agreement, arising as a result of an offer *and* an acceptance, although in strict legal terms several other requirements are involved before a contract can be fully legally binding. As a health and safety example, duties placed on *employers* and *employees* by the **HSWA** do not constitute a contract in themselves; however, the requirement to comply with the duties identified in the **HSWA** can form *part* of a *contract of employment*.

contract of employment is a written legal agreement between an *employer* and an *employee*. To satisfy the *Employment Rights Act 1996* a written contract

contractors' duties

of *employment* must be given to all *employees* within two months of the commencement of *employment* (existing *employees* **must** be given a copy on request or following substantial changes in the terms and conditions of existing contracts).

The written *principal statement* given to *employees* must include as a minimum:

(i) the names of the *employer* and the *employee*;
(ii) the date when the *employment* began and the period of *employment*;
(iii) the scale and rate of remuneration, pay intervals and its method of calculation;
(iv) terms and conditions relating to hours of work and holiday entitlement (see **Working Time Regulations**) and public holiday entitlement;
(v) the job title *and description* of job content;
(vi) the *employee's* place of work.

In addition, provided they are given within the two-month deadline, the following *employment* particulars can be documented by instalments:

(a) whether the *employment* is permanent or for a fixed term;
(b) details of **collective agreements** affecting *employment*;
(c) details of any requirements regarding work outside the UK.

No statutory rights or cover can be taken away by an *employer*; as an example, health and safety legislation cannot be diluted or removed, e.g. an *employer's* prime *duty of care* cannot be abrogated to an *employee*. The County or High Court may enforce contract terms through an injunction or a claim for damages.

contractors' duties regarding health and safety are essentially ones of co-operation, *communication* and compliance, within **construction** legislation – sometimes overlaid by dominant or superior legislation. The following is based on **construction** as an example, but regardless of the type of work being carried out, or the place where the work is being carried out, similar points can be made regarding Health, Safety and Environmental legislative requirements which are inter-active and made up of superior and inferior legislation.

During construction there are often many subcontractors carrying out work. **Communication** between all concerned regarding health and safety matters is a legal requirement. It is possibly useful (for the purpose of this example) to think of each subcontractor as an *employee*, with the principal contractor as an *employer*. The subcontractor must be consulted on health and safety matters, all information concerning health and safety must be exchanged, passed on and discussed. In addition, the *MHSWR (as amended)* requires *employers* on multi-occupancy sites to exchange information on health and safety matters.

contributory negligence, very simply, is the extent someone (e.g. a 'plaintiff') can be shown to be partly to blame for 'what happened'. For example, if a passenger and/or driver suffers facial injuries following a car accident but they were not wearing safety belts which might have prevented all or some of the injuries, then the driver and/or passenger were 'guilty' of contributory negligence (see also *negligence* and *dismissal*).

A *case law* health and safety example where contributory negligence was considered a factor is that of *Bux v Slough Metals Ltd (1974) 1 AER 262* where the *employer* provided safety goggles but the *employee* did not wear them, despite being instructed so to do. The *employer* was found *contributorily negligent* because adequate supervision was not provided to ensure the safety goggles were worn by his *employee.*

However, contributory negligence is not restricted to the apparently obvious; the case of *Barclays Bank v Fairclough Building Ltd (No 2) [1995] AER 289* is a useful illustration. Barclays Bank contracted Fairclough to carry out maintenance work, including asbestos roofing; Fairclough subcontracted in to 'A' who in turn subcontracted the work to 'B'. Neither 'A' or 'B' was experienced in cleaning asbestos roofs. 'B' used a high-pressure hose, producing an asbestos contaminated slurry to enter buildings which, when dried, meant asbestos fibres contaminated the air. A prohibition notice was issued which resulted in remedial work costing £4,000,000. Barclays Bank obtained judgment against Fairclough; 'A' paid £1,250,000 to Fairclough. Following this 'A' took action against 'B', where it was ruled that (i) neither 'A' nor 'B' followed *HSE* guidelines and did not take reasonable care when cleaning the asbestos roof; (ii) when cleaning asbestos roofs with hoses care must be taken not to contaminate the surrounding area, therefore 'B' was *liable* to 'A'; (iii) because of (i) 'B's liability was reduced by 50% to 'reflect the extent of 'A's contributory negligence.

In some repetitive work activities, monotony or boredom can cause a worker *inadvertently* to lose concentration and suffer an injury. These seemingly inadvertent events can be considered *foreseeable*, and in such cases, inadvertence is **not** considered to be contributory negligence. To satisfy the requirements for establishing contributory negligence the person must be shown to have been reckless or deliberate in such actions (in which case, if at

control limits

work, the person would also have been acting in breach of s.7 of the *HSWA*).

control limits are those which indicate the LOWEST *tolerable* level of exposure technically and economically (reasonably) practicable to achieve. Control limits must **not** be confused with so-called *safe levels of exposure* and have replaced *Threshold Limit Values* (*TLVs*) which identified the HIGHEST tolerable level of exposure. Control limits (and health, safety and environmental standards) are continuously being updated (*Qualcast Ltd v Haynes [1959] 2 AER 38*) and failure to reduce exposure to the minimum reasonably practicable can result in prosecution or other action.

control measures are introduced or installed to reduce to the minimum the possibility of *harm* to persons, plant and property. Control measures should be considered in the following order of priority:

(i) **Eliminate or substitute** the tool, *work equipment, workstation, (hazardous) substance, system of work.*

(ii) **Engineering controls** to be installed at source of contamination, e.g. welding and *local exhaust ventilation.*

(iii) **Isolate** the equipment or task.

(iv) **Design and use** of *safe systems of work.*

(v) **Personal Protective Equipment** – assess requirements and provide suitable and sufficient PPE, ensuring it is worn.

(vi) **Training must** be provided, e.g. users of PPE **must** be trained in its use and maintenance.

A useful acronym is **ERICPD**, which means: Eliminate or substitute; Reduce time of exposure; Isolate; Control; Personal Protective Equipment; Discipline.

As an example, the control measures that may be used to eliminate or reduce dust in the workplace include: prohibit the activity; change the process; substitute; isolate; segregate from other areas; enclose process; local exhaust ventilation; and provide suitable personal protective equipment.

Control of Asbestos at Work Regulations 1987 (amended) cover all types of work and workplaces where asbestos is made, used or handled, and wherever there is a possibility of exposure to asbestos. It is useful to see the reference to *case law* concerning *asbestos* and *contributory negligence.*

Assessments are an absolute duty, with findings recorded and copies kept (together with a plan of work) and the *employer* must ensure, *so far as is*

Control of Asbestos at Work Regulations 1987 (amended)

reasonably practicable, that the work follows the plan. The assessment must identify the type of asbestos involved, establish the extent of the exposure, specify the steps that will be taken to prevent or reduce exposure to the lowest level reasonably practicable. The assessment must be monitored, reviewed regularly and if there is a significant change in the working conditions or if the assessment seems invalid, repeated.

Designated areas must cover those where exposure at or above the '*action level'* is likely to be exceeded, e.g. strict no smoking, eating and/or drinking controls should operate in such designated areas or zones.

Duty of *employers* is to prevent the cumulative exposure of their *employees* to asbestos over a twelve-week period, summing above the *action level,* which varies according to the type of asbestos and may be updated or altered at short notice. **Reg. 2 1987 Regulations** and **Schedule 1992 amendment**: Briefly the cumulative exposure:

(i) for chrysotile (white asbestos) 96 fibre-hours per millilitre of air;
(ii) any other form of asbestos *including* crocidolite (blue) or amosite (brown) either alone or with chrysotile, 48 fibre-hours per millilitre of air, or separate exposures over a twelve-week period a proportional number of fibre-hours per millilitre of air.

In addition, *employers* have a duty to clarify the extent of the application of the **Regulations** making it clear that *all workers who are liable* to be exposed to asbestos are covered.

Health records of all *employees* exposed to asbestos above *action levels* must be kept for at least 40 years.

Health surveillance (medical examination during working hours) is to be carried out by the *employer* on *employees* every two years, with a copy of the examination held by *employer* for four years and the *employee* provided with a copy.

Laboratories, which carry out asbestos-related analysis work must be accredited to industry standard EN45001.

Notification to the enforcing authority must be made at least 14 days before commencement of the work.

Personal protective equipment must reduce exposure to the minimum *reasonably practicable*, be properly used, maintained, cleaned and disposed of in suitably marked containers.

Control of Asbestos in the Air Regulations 1990

Prevention of exposure may not be *reasonably practicable* in cost/benefit terms, in which case *employers* should reduce the exposure of their *employees* to the lowest level reasonably practicable, by means *other than* through the use of *respiratory protective equipment*. When the lowest level reasonably practicable has been achieved, only then can *respiratory protective equipment* be used.

Respiratory zones should be designated where the airborne concentration is likely to exceed the *control limit*. All other *employees* should be excluded from designated areas or zones.

Working with asbestos: contractors are òn notice' to the effect that there are serious health hazards associated with working with asbestos.

Written plan must be prepared prior to the work starting and kept for two years after completion of the work.

Control of Asbestos in the Air Regulations 1990 should be considered particularly with the *Health and Safety (Emissions into the Atmosphere) Regulations 1983* and its 1989 amendment. The purpose of the Regulations is to prevent or reduce environmental pollution by asbestos. Convicted offenders face fines not exceeding Level 4 in the *standard scale*. The Regulations include:

(i) **Controls to prevent atmospheric pollution** from asbestos where demolition of buildings, installations, *structures* or the working of products take place.

(ii) **Limits** on the discharge of asbestos into the atmosphere during its use and requirement of regular measurements from plants where the *Regulations* apply.

Control of Explosives Regulations 1991 provide for the:

Barring of anyone with a criminal record from obtaining or possessing a valid explosives certificate.

Enforcement Agency for these Regulations to be the police.

Exemption from the 1991 *Regulations* of *small* quantities of specified explosives that may be kept for private use.

Exemptions to other certain requirements of the *Explosives Act 1875* which is still the prime Statute, although amended by the 1991 *Regulations* (except for Schedule 1 explosives).

Limit on quantity of explosives stored in a specified place; requirement to keep up-to-date records of the explosives and their source for at least three years and to report the loss of any of the explosives.

Control of Industrial Air Pollution (Registration of Works) Regulations 1989 require some scheduled processes not to be operated until a registration certificate has been issued by HM Inspectorate of Pollution. Public *access* is possible on payment of a fee to the register of scheduled processes.

Control of Lead at Work Regulations 1998 revoked and re-enacted, with modifications, the 1980 Regulations and include the requirement that *employers* must ensure 'the protection of workers from the risks related to exposure to metallic lead and its ionic compounds at work'.

The *Regulations* and its accompanying **ACOP** should be consulted; for example, they provide a number of different blood and suspension levels and *action levels* identified in the *Regulations* should not be exceeded.

Salient requirements and points from the 1998 *Regulations* include:

Action level in these *Regulations*, unless the context otherwise requires, 'means a blood-lead concentration of (Reg. 2(1)):

(a) in respect of a woman of reproductive capacity 25 μg/dl;
(b) in respect of a young person 40 μg/dl;
(c) in respect of any other *employee* 50μg/dl'.

Assessments, suitable and sufficient, **must** be conducted by *employers* 'on any work which is liable to expose any *employees* to lead' (Reg. 5).

Blood-lead concentration levels vary widely (e.g. according to individual, age, sex and process) and are extensively detailed in the *Regulations* (Reg. 2).

Controls must be provided, *so far as is reasonably practicable*, where significant risk of exposure to lead is found, with personal protective equipment the last option (Reg. 6). Maintenance, examination and testing of control measures must be carried out by *employers* on any control measure that they have supplied (Reg. 8).

Employers should prevent eating, drinking and smoking, so far as is *reasonably practicable*, in any area likely to be contaminated by lead (Reg. 7(1)).

Control of Major Accident Hazards Regulations 1999

Employees must be informed of the findings from the risk assessment, air sampling, monitoring and their (individual) health surveillance (Regs 5, 9 and 10).

Expectant and new mothers are separately covered regarding work with lead by Regs 13A and 13B of the amended **MHSWR**. Their tasks and work environment should be subject to a 'new' or review risk assessment as soon as the *employer* is informed by the *employee* (her duty) of her pregnancy.

Information, instruction and training, at a suitable and sufficient level, must be provided to *employees* and any person (*whether or not an employee*) 'who carries out any work in connection with the *employers'* duties under these *Regulations*', by *employers* in necessary preventative and control measures; the results of monitoring and health surveillance (without identifying individuals); and an explanation of the significance of the information provided (Reg. 11).

Employers must provide suitable personal protective equipment (PPE) to their *employees* who are liable to exposure from airborne lead (Reg. 6(6)(a) and 6(6)(b)). The **PPER** are the *superior legislation* for **PPE**.

Women of reproductive capacity are prohibited from carrying out certain activities detailed in Schedule 1 (Reg. 4 (2)). See *women and health and safety*.

Young persons (a person who has not reached the age of 18 and is not a woman of reproductive capacity) are prohibited from carrying out certain activities detailed in Schedule 1 of the *Regulations* (Reg. 4 (2)).

Control of Major Accident Hazards Regulations 1999 (or COMAH) define a *major accident* as an occurrence that:

(i) results from uncontrolled developments (sudden, unexpected, unplanned) in the course of the operation of establishments to which COMAH applies;

(ii) leads to serious danger to people or to the environment, on- or off-site; and

(iii) involves one or more dangerous substances defined in the Regulations.

COMAH has the following scope and application:

(a) 'application depends solely on the presence or anticipated presence of threshold quantities of dangerous substances, including dangerous substances which might be generated in the course of an accident due to loss of control of an industrial chemical process, with no differentiation between storage and processing;

(b) the list of substances attracting the **Regulations** relies on fewer named chemicals (than for the earlier Control of Industrial Major Hazards Regulations 1984) and more on generic classes of dangerous substances';

(c) **COMAH Regulations** apply to both explosive and chemical hazards at nuclear installations.

Selected requirements from the **COMAH Regulations** include:

Accident prevention policies shall be prepared and kept by every operator setting out its policy with regard to major accidents. This policy shall be referred to as a *major accident prevention policy document* (Reg. 5).

Emergency plans prepared under **CIMAH** shall generally be kept up to date as if those **Regulations** had not been revoked (Part 7, Reg. 22).

Information to the competent authority shall be provided by the operator on request or following a major accident at the establishment (in addition to the operator notifying the enforcement authority (Reg. 15).

Information to the public shall be provided (without having to ask for it) by the operator, following consultation with the local authority. This information concerns safety measures which the public should adopt, and the way the public is likely to be affected in the event of a major accident at the establishment. The information should be reviewed every five years or following any modifications (see Schedule 6 Reg. 14(2) and 23(2)).

Inspections and investigations of establishments and control measures adopted shall be arranged by the competent authority.

Named or dangerous substances to which the **COMAH Regulations** apply are provided in Schedule 1 of **COMAH**.

Notification shall be sent prior to the start of construction and start of operation (and in the event of any increase in the quantity of dangerous substances or significant change in nature of dangerous substances, processes or closure of an installation in the establishment) by the operator to the competent authority (Reg. 6).

Off-site emergency plans shall be prepared for the establishment *by the* *local authority*, in accord with Part 1 and Part 3 of Schedule 5 of COMAH, using the information provided by the operator (Reg. 10).

On-site emergency plan shall be prepared *by the operator* for existing establishments covered by the 1984 **Regulations**, by 3 February 2001 and for *any other* existing establishment by 3 February 2002. In all other cases, the emergency plan shall be prepared by the operator before the establishment starts to operate (Reg. 9). The emergency plan shall be implemented following a major accident or an uncontrolled event (Reg. 12).

Safety report shall be sent by the operator to the competent authority prior to the start of construction and operation (the construction and/or operation cannot start until the competent authority has, in effect, given its approval) and every five years or following recognition of new facts or technical knowledge concerning safety becomes available (Reg. 7).

COMAH also places duties on the *competent authority, local authorities*, as well as *employers and operators,* including the following:

(a) '*general duties* on all operators subject to the **Regulations** to notify the *competent authority* (CA) of their activities, to take all measures necessary for the prevention and mitigation of major accidents, to prepare a major accident prevention policy, and report *major accidents*;

(b) *top-tier duties* on operators of sites where the quantities of dangerous substances exceed the higher thresholds. These operators must, in addition to the duties in paragraph (a) above, submit safety reports, prepare and test emergency plans and provide information to the public.'

The *competent authority* must:

(a) 'communicate the conclusions of safety report assessments to operators;

(b) prohibit activities if there are serious deficiencies in measures for prevention and mitigation of major accidents;

(c) have in place land-use planning policies;

(d) have inspection systems and programmes, carry out inspections and investigate accidents;

Control of Substances Hazardous to Health Regulations 1999

(e) designate certain sites as domino effects establishments.'

Finally, *local authorities* have duties 'to prepare and test off-site emergency plans'.

There are strict land-use controls, due to extending and modifying the existing *Hazardous Substances Consent* system, encouraging 'developers to submit applications for *Hazardous Substances Consent* and *Planning Permission* together so as to minimise duplication of effort'.

Control of Substances Hazardous to Health Regulations 1999

(COSHH) are the latest to revoke and replace all previous **COSHH** *Regulations*, except for **COSHH 1994**, which the 1999 *Regulations* re-enact, with minor modifications.. In addition, the current extensive number of **ACOPs** which accompany **COSHH** are of particular importance and the current position should be carefully checked (reference to selected **ACOPs** are included). The objective of **COSHH** is to protect persons at work against risks to their health arising from substances hazardous to their health, with specified exceptions (e.g. lead and asbestos, which has its own *superior legislation*) (Reg. 5). **COSHH** currently covers biological agents and carcinogens, this may change, so it is advisable to check the current situation.

Throughout the **COSHH** *Regulations* the term 'shall' is used, which effectively means '**must**'. The following offers a selective alphabetical review of **COSHH** requirements, together with appropriate definitions from the *Regulations*:

> **Assessments must** be carried out by the *employer* 'on any work which is liable to expose any *employee* to any substance hazardous to health and of the steps that need to be taken to meet the requirements' of **COSHH** (e.g. control measures). The assessment must be regularly monitored and reviewed. A new assessment **must** be carried out immediately ' . . . it is no longer valid, or there has been a significant change in the work' (Reg. 6).

> See also **COSHH** *assessments and risk assessments*.

> **Biological agents** are defined at Reg. 2(1) and Schedule 3s as:

> 'any micro-organism, cell culture, or human *endoparasite*, including any which have been genetically modified, which may cause any infection, allergy, toxicity or otherwise create a hazard to human health'.

> **Carcinogens** are defined at Reg. 2.1 and Schedule 1 as:

(a) 'any substance or preparation which is classified in accordance with the classification provided for by Regulation 5 of the *Chemicals (Hazard Information and Packaging for Supply) Regulations 1994* as being in the category of danger, carcinogenic (category 1) or carcinogenic (category 2) whether or not the substance or preparation would be required to be classified under those *Regulations*; or

(b) any substance or preparation:
 (i) listed in Schedule 1; or
 (ii) arising from a process specified in Schedule 1 which is a substance hazardous to health'.

Control measures, of an adequate nature (listed) must be provided if preventive measures cannot be installed (Reg. 7). *Employers* who provide any control measure, **PPE** or other thing or facility in connection with these *Regulations* must take reasonable steps to ensure that it is properly used or applied, as the case may be (Reg. 8(1)).

Defence following contravention of *Regulations* include proving that all reasonable precautions were taken and due diligence exercised (Reg. 16).

Dominant or superior legislation as always applies, e.g. personal protective equipment has to satisfy the *Personal Protective Equipment Regulations 1992 as well as* any special COSHH requirements (Reg. 7(5).

Dust is covered by **COSHH** Reg. 2 when present at a concentration in air of greater than:

(i)   10 mg/m3 as a time weighted average over an eight-hour period of inhalable dust; or
(ii) 4 mg/m3 as a time weighted average over an eight-hour period of respirable dust.

Duties under these *Regulations* apply to *employees*, *employers* and, except with regard to *Regulations* 10 and 11, to the *self-employed*. Non-*employees*, i.e. visitors, are also covered by these *Regulations* if they are on the premises where work is being carried out (Reg. 3, Reg. 7, and Reg. 8).

Employees must make 'full and proper use of any control measure, personal protective equipment or other thing or facility provided', store the equipment in the place provided for it and immediately report any defects (Reg. 8(2)).

Engineering controls must be regularly examined and tested, with records as listed in Reg. 9, Schedule 4.

Control of Substances Hazardous to Health Regulations 1999

Exemptions to COSHH include normal ship-board activities, masters and their crew (Reg. 3(3)).

Fumigation provisions apply and are detailed in Part 1 Schedule 8, Part II Schedule 8 and Reg. 13, Schedule 8.

Health records, of a type and content approved by the *Health and Safety Executive*, shall be maintained for relevant *employee*(s), and records or a copy kept for at least 40 years *from the date of the last entry* in it. A company ceasing trading should notify the HSE *in writing* and the health records should be offered to the Executive.

Health surveillance is required if any *employee* is exposed to substances specified in Schedule 6.

Information, instruction and training must be provided by *employers* for persons who may be exposed to substances hazardous to health. The *employee* must know the risks to health created by exposure and precautions to be taken, together with results of monitoring and *collective* results of any health surveillance which has been carried out (Reg. 12).

Local exhaust ventilation plant should be examined and tested at least every 14 months; plant used in a process specified in Schedule 4 should be examined and tested in accord with requirements specified in that Schedule (Reg. 9).

Maintenance, examination and test of *employers'* provided control measures to ensure they are working efficiently and to comply with legislative requirements (Reg. 9(2), Schedule 4).

Maximum Exposure Limit or MEL is defined in the current EH40 and, in effect, used in conjunction with COSHH *Regulations*. The MEL limits must never be exceeded.

Monitoring exposure at the workplace must be carried out by an *employer*, either every 12 months or, for substances or processes listed in Schedule 5, at the time specified in that Schedule, e.g. vinyl chloride monomer must be monitored continuously. A 'suitable' record must be kept of any monitoring, if personal to identifiable *employees* the record must be kept for 40 years, 'in any other case, for at least five years' (Reg. 10 and Schedule 5).

Occupational Exposure Standard or OES is defined in Regulation 2(1). The controlled level of exposure should be held below the OES which, together with the associated substances or process, are listed in the **EH40 Occupational Exposure Limits**. An OES is the maximum *concentration* of an airborne substance to which **employees** may be exposed to through inhalation. However, if an OES is exceeded it must be brought down below the standard as soon as possible.

Penalties for breach of COSHH: *employers* or *employees* who breach the COSHH **Regulations**, face onsummary conviction the same penalties as those who breach the HSWA s.2-6–£20,000 and/or imprisonment for up to six months in a **Magistrates' Court** or unlimited fines and up to two years imprisonment in the higher courts.

Personal protective equipment supplied in accord with the demands of the **Regulations** must comply with the requirements of the **Personal Protective Equipment Regulations 1992** 'which is applicable to that item of personal protective equipment'. (Reg. 7 (5)).

Prevention or control of exposure to substances hazardous to health.

Respirable dust is that which is airborne material capable of penetrating to the gas exchange region of the lung (Reg. 2(1)).

Substances hazardous to health mean any substance (Reg. 2(1)) (including any preparation) which is:

(a) listed in Part 1 of the approved supply list as dangerous;
(b) a substance for which the **Health and Safety Commission** has approved a maximum exposure limit or an occupational exposure standard;
(c) a biological agent;
(d) substantial amounts of airborne dust;
(e) a substance, not being a substance mentioned in sub-paragraphs (a) to (d) above, which creates a hazard to the health of any person which is comparable with the hazards created by the substances mentioned in those sub-paragraphs.

Biological agents have special provisions located in Schedule 3 of **COSHH 1999** and these (alphabetically) include:

Assessments must be carried out by any *employer* who intends to carry on any work which is liable to expose *employees* to any biological agent and these shall take account of the Group that agent is classified in when carrying out the assessment (Para. 4).

Control of Substances Hazardous to Health Regulations 1999

Control of exposure to a biological agent: when it is not otherwise reasonably practicable to prevent that exposure, then a number of steps **must** be taken as detailed in Para. 6, e.g. number of *employees* exposed or likely to be exposed to the biological agent must be minimised; where appropriate, making available effective vaccines for *employees* who are not immune to the biological agent to which they have been exposed.

Employees must report to their *employer* or *employee* appointed by their *employer* with specified health and safety responsibilities any accident or incident that may have resulted in the release of a biological agent that could cause severe human disease.

Employers must keep a list of *employees* who have been exposed to Group 3 or 4 biological agents. The list must be kept for at least ten years following the last entry.

Information for *employees* provided by the *employer* must include written instructions at the workplace, appropriate notices displayed, full details of any incident or accident involving biological agents, including cause and preventive measures taken or to be taken to rectify the situation or prevent re-occurrence.

Non-approved and non-classified biological agents will be provisionally classified by the *employer* according to their level of risk of infection. If in doubt, the *employer* shall assign the higher classification of the two, as follows:

(a) Group 1 – unlikely to cause human disease;
(b) Group 2 – can cause human disease and may be a hazard to *employees*, but is unlikely to spread to the community and there is usually an effective prophylaxis (preventive treatment) or treatment available;
(c) Group 3 – can cause severe human disease and may be a serious hazard to *employees*, it may spread to the community, but there is usually effective prophylaxis or treatment available;
(d) Group 4 – causes severe human disease and is a serious hazard to *employees*, it is likely to spread to the community and there is usually no effective prophylaxis or treatment available.

Notification of consignment of biological agents must be made in writing at least 30 days beforehand to the *HSE* by the *employer*, whether or not the premises are under the control of the *employer*, *unless* the consignment is for the purpose of analysis, for disposal or is in a human patient being transported for treatment.

Notification of the use of biological agents must be made to the Health and Safety Executive at least 30 days prior to storage or use and under certain other specified circumstances.

Personal protective equipment, when provided to comply with the *Regulations*, must be properly stored in a well-defined place; checked and cleaned; repaired or replaced if defective, before further use. Contaminated personal protective equipment must be removed on leaving the work area and kept apart from non-contaminated clothing and equipment. It is the *employer's* duty to ensure that contaminated clothing and equipment is decontaminated or destroyed.

Special control measures are in place for laboratories, health care (human), health care (veterinarian), animal rooms and specified industrial processes.

Superior legislation concerning hazardous substances (including carcinogens and biological agents) is the COSHH *Regulations*, but there is other particularly relevant legislation, such as **CHIP**.

controlled waters are defined in the **WRA** s.104 and include all relevant territorial waters, coastal waters, inland and ground waters; they are subject to legislation.

convection, technically speaking, is the vertical transfer of heat through a liquid or gas by the movement of that liquid or gas. Possibly one of the best-known examples of convection are atmospheric thermals, which demonstrates most of the components of convection. Thermals (air heated by *conduction* from the world land surface) rise, cool and fall.

coolant is a fluid or gas used to extract heat from a source and thereby cause cooling. For example, water circulating in an internal combustion engine removes the heat from the engine block and may transfer the heat to the atmosphere via the radiator and possibly the use of a fan for airflow through the radiator. Alternatively, the circulation of gas (or liquid sodium) may cool nuclear reactors. Failure of a coolant can lead to serious, if not disastrous consequences.

corporate killing has been proposed by the Home Secretary to be a specific offence covering corporations in an unnamed new Bill. The four offences would be *corporate killing; reckless killing; killing by gross carelessness*; and *killing when the intention was to cause only minor injuries*, if it can be proved that 'a management failure' is the cause, *or one of the causes*, of one or more deaths. It would no longer be necessary to identify or name someone senior in the organisation. Proposed penalties for convicted offenders include imprisoment for life, unlimited fines and/or company directors being struck off and not allowed to become directors again, or for a period. There are criticisms of the proposals, e.g. how is it decided which director should be held accountable or criminally liable.

corrosive substances and preparations are those which may destroy living tissues on contact, e.g. hydrochloric acid or ammonia liquid.

COSHH see *Control of Substances Hazardous to Health Regulations 1999.*

COSHH assessments MUST be carried out by a *competent person* who is *appointed by the employer* (see Reg. 12(3)). A competent person to carry out the COSHH assessment, according to the booklet *COSHH Assessments* (**HSE,** 1990), is someone who has 'an appreciation of *occupational hygiene* principles', 'the range of *control measures'* available and needed, and 'an understanding of the point of each Regulation and what it involves'.

It is necessary to obtain information concerning the hazards (harmful effects) of substances. This requires *reliable* information and advice, initially (a legal requirement) from manufacturers, suppliers or importers. If an *employer* imports directly from sources outside the UK, the *employer* assumes the duties of an importer, *in addition* to the duties of an *employer.* Assessments may require atmospheric sampling and measurement, particularly where substances involved have an occupational exposure limit (**ACOP** 20).

cost benefit analysis is a practical way of assessing the desirability of projects through an enumeration and evaluation of *all known* costs and benefits.

cost of accidents and damage incidents see *cash benefits.*

county courts are the main civil courts established by the *County Courts Act* 1846, with the area of each court's *jurisdiction* not necessarily corresponding with local government boundaries (e.g. county or metropolitan borough boundaries). Their statutory *jurisdiction* includes actions concerning contract and tort, within specified limits. The county courts sit once a month, before Supreme Court or Circuit Judges, or *recorders.* Trial by jury is possible but exceptional. Appeals on matters of law, evidence or fact are almost invariably to the *Court of Appeal* or, exceptionally, to the *High Court* (e.g. for bankruptcy).

course of employment is commonly termed 'in the course of his (sic) *employment'* and is a reference to the scope of a person's *employment.* For

83

example, if an accidental injury occurs within the scope of *employment*, and the activity is authorised by the *employer or necessarily incidental to something that the employee did*, then the accidental injury arose out of the course of such *employment*. The test of 'in the course of employment' is one that must be satisfied, e.g. before any claim for **Industrial Injury Benefit** can be successful.

Court of Justice of the European Communities was established under the Treaty of Rome to ensure that the interpretation and application of Treaty law is observed. Its make-up includes a judge from each member state, appointed for six-year periods, assisted by six *Advocates General*, who advise through making *reasoned oral submissions*, before judgement is given by the Court. Procedures are generally inquisitorial (unlike in the UK where procedures are adversarial). The Court can annul **Council** or **Commission** acts if they are based on lack of competence, misuse of powers, infringement of the treaty or of an essential procedural requirement. The decisions of the Court are binding and currently *there is no appeal against them*.

The Court has the power, at the request of a court of any member state, to give a ruling on any point of Community law on which that court requires clarification. The Court can hear cases brought by individuals, through an involved process culminating in a Court of First Instance *attached* to the Court. On *ALL* matters of Community law, courts of the UK defer to relevant decisions of the Court of Justice, which is therefore the highest court *for* health and safety in the UK.

court of the first instance is a court in which any proceedings are begun (initiated) or any court in which a case is tried, but not a court in which a case is heard on appeal.

courts *in the UK* are established by the State and conduct their procedure in accordance with the rules of natural justice. Their procedure includes public hearing, reception of oral evidence, hearing of argument, oral examination and cross-examination of witnesses. The courts have before them at least two parties, one of whom may be the Crown, and arrive at a decision concerned with legal rights. The highest court *in the UK* for health and safety is the House of Lords. However, the highest court for health and safety *in the UK* is the European Court.

cradles see *suspended access system*.

crane signallers see *signallers*.

cranes see the *Lifting Operations and Lifting Equipment Regulations 1998*.

criminal courts are those who deal with criminal rather than civil cases. In England all criminal cases are initiated in the **Magistrates' Court**. *Summary offences* and some *indictable offences* (those triable either way) are also initially tried in **Magistrates' Courts**, with the more serious indictable offences committed to the **Crown Court** for trial by judge and jury.

criminal law is concerned with punishment and penalties, e.g. fines or imprisonment for *convicted* offenders who breach or fail to comply with certain health and safety legislative requirements, such as the **Health and Safety at Work etc. Act, 1974**.

criminal liability see *liability*.

criminal negligence, in very simple terms, occurs when someone unreasonably (negligently) or knowingly breaches the law, sometimes causing an injury. It is higher than 'ordinary' negligence. (i.e. 'greater' than ordinary negligence). In order to establish a criminal offence, e.g. following death through an *industrial accident*, the degree of negligence required to prove the crime of manslaughter is higher than that sufficient to prove civil liability.

critical mass is the minimum mass of fissionable material required to sustain a chain reaction in, for example, a nuclear reactor. Below critical mass, too many neutrons escape without splitting the additional atoms for the reaction to be self-sustaining.

Crown Court(s) were created by the Courts Act 1971 as part of the Supreme Court and as a superior court of record. Cases are tried before a judge to decide *matters of law* and before a lay jury for *matters of fact*. The Crown Court has unlimited *jurisdiction* over all *criminal* cases. It sits in any centre in England or Wales as designated by the Lord Chancellor. Any High Court Judge, Circuit judge or Recorder, depending on the gravity of the offence, exercises its jurisdiction. The Crown Court (without a jury) may hear appeals from **Magistrates' Courts** and may sentence people committed for sentencing by those courts. Appeal from a Crown Court is to the Court of Appeal.

CSR see *Confined Spaces Regulations*.

cyclohexanone is a liquid with a peppermint or acetone-like odour. Its uses include cleaning leather or textiles, as a solvent in crude rubber, insecticides, epoxy resins and a sludge solvent in lubricating oils. It is hazardous to the respiratory system, eyes, skin and central nervous system. It is toxic by inhalation, absorption, ingestion and through contact. Symptoms include eye and mucous membrane irritation, narcosis, coma and dermatitis.

D

damages is a sum of money awarded by a court as compensation for a *tort* or a *breach of contract*. Damages are frequently (but not always) awarded as a lump sum. The purpose of damages in tort is to put the *plaintiff* in the position they would have been if the tort had not been committed, but the sum awarded may be reduced through *contributory negligence*.

The plaintiff must take 'reasonable steps' to reduce his/her 'losses' (including injuries) and undergo medical treatment for his/her injuries and/or seek alternative *employment*, if unable to follow his/her previous *employment*. Details of damages for *breach of contract* are outside the terms of reference of this work.

danger is generally considered to be an exposure to risk of death, injury or disease.

See also *hazard, risk* and *safety*.

dangerous article is any *article* used at work that manufacturers, designers, importers or suppliers have *not* (repeat **NOT**), so far as is reasonably practicable, designed and constructed so that it will be safe and without risks to health at all times when it is being set, used, cleaned and maintained by a person at work.

See also *Consumer Protection Act 1987* and the **HSWA** (especially s.6).

dangerous goods include:

(a) explosives;
(b) radioactive materials;
(c) goods named in the *Approved Carriage List* (ACL);
(d) any other goods having one or more hazardous properties;
(e) environmentally hazardous substances listed in the **HSWA** (*Application to Environmentally Hazardous Substances*) **Regulations** 1996.

dangerous occurrence is defined in the **RIDDOR**. Briefly it means 'an occurrence which arises out of, or in connection with, work and is a class as specified in' Schedule 2 of **RIDDOR**. Examples from the very long and wide ranging list include: an electrical short circuit accompanied by fire or explosion causing stoppage of the plant for over 24 hours; any accident or incident which resulted *or could have resulted* in the release or escape of a biological agent *likely* to cause severe human infection or illness; and the release of specified quantities of LPG.

dangerous substances is a term difficult to define because there is a large number of substances in commercial use, some of which are *dangerous to health* if used in a certain process, mixed with other substances (preparation) or treated in a certain way but otherwise (in simple terms) 'safe':

> **Approved Supply List reference** is necessary to comply with the requirements of the **CHIP**. The ASL only lists 'known' or dangerous substances already in use and is regularly updated and/or amended.

> **Codes of Practice** covering dangerous and *hazardous substances* are associated with various *Regulations* and contribute towards ensuring controls match the hazard of substance with its use.

> **Non-chemical** *dangerous substances* include *asbestos*, heavy metals, silica dust, mineral oils and compressed air.

> **New substances** are reportable under the *Notification of New Substances Regulations 1993*.

Dangerous Substances (Notification and Marking of Sites) Regulations 1990 require those in control of sites where there are 25 tonnes or more of dangerous substances present to carry out the following actions, including:

Cessation or reduction in the *dangerous substances* already notified or if there is a change in the list of any classifications of dangerous substances, requires a further notification to the local fire authority and **HSE**.

Mark such sites with the appropriate safety signs.

Marking signs must comply with BS 5378 1980/1982 standards and must be (i) displayed to give adequate warning to firemen *before* they enter a site in an emergency and (ii) additionally located on site where an inspector directs.

Notify the local fire authority *and* the **HSE** of:

> (a) the name and address of the person notifying;
> (b) the full postal address of the site;
> (c) a general description of the nature of the business;
> (d) a list of the *classifications* of dangerous substances held on the site;

(e) the date when it is anticipated that a total quantity of 25 tonnes (or more) of dangerous substances will be present.

Exceptions to the requirements include radioactive substances, Class 1 explosives, substances in aerosol dispensers, substances buried or deposited in the ground as waste.

dB or dB(A) see *decibel.*

decibel, in very simple terms, is a logarithmic measurement of loudness of, and pressure from, sound. Technically speaking, a decibel is a logarithmic measure, **one-tenth** of a bel, used to compare the sound level of interest with a reference level – sound power of 1000 Hz is the lowest that can be heard by someone with normal hearing.

Decibels are shown as dB, often with the letter (A), i.e. dB(A). The (A) means that the dB measurement corresponds to the frequency response of the human ear and thereby correlates with the human perception (or reception) of loudness.

There is a *time weighted average* of industrial exposure, beyond which workers must not be exposed. It must be noted that because it is a logarithmic scale every 3dB(A) increase actually **doubles** the dose. Therefore the following exposure scale demonstrates each measurement is the same dose and an exposure scale is as follows:

90 dB(A) or 8 hours
93 dB(A) for 4 hours
96 dB(A) for 2 hours
99 dB(A) for 1 hour

Examples based on averages are: jet engine at take-off, 140 dB(A); disco 110 dB(A); rock music from radios and personal stereos commonly played at 90 – 130 dB(A); diesel-engined lorry at 80 km/h, 90 dB(A); light traffic, 30 metres distant, 50 dB(A); living room, 40 dB(A).

decisions with regard to UK health and safety and the law, are basically of two types, UK judicial and those following EU Community legislation.

(a) **Judicial decision** *includes* listening to arguments put forward by counsel and providing a *finding* on disputed facts and an application of the law of the land, ruling on disputed questions of law. In simple terms, in the UK a judge or several judges (see **House of Lords**) issues a decision after considering the arguments heard in court and the law. Such a decision may or may not become a *precedent*.

(b) **Following EU Community legislation and *Directives*,** the Council and Commission of the EU/EEC may take *decisions* that are binding in their entirety upon those to whom they are addressed.

English courts 'must follow the same principles as the European Court' and 'look to the purpose and intent' of Community legislation when applying 'the meaning and effect of a Community instrument' with 'the Treaty of Rome ... the supreme law of the country, taking precedent over Acts of Parliament' (see *case law H.P.Bulmer Ltd v J. Bollinger SA [1974] Ch 401; Macarthy Ltd v Smith [1981] 1 All ER 111; Garland v BREngineering Ltd [1982] 2 All ER 402; per* Hoffman J. in*Stoke on Trent CC v B & Q [1990] 3CMLR867.*

Declaration of Conformity see *Supply of Machinery (Safety) Regulations.*

Declaration of Incorporation see *Supply of Machinery (Safety) Regulations.*

Declaration of Industrial Accident is obtained from an Insurance Officer through a 'victim' of *accident* (not necessarily a claimant or one including an injury or disease) completing a **BI 95** *each time* this occurs and forwarding the completed BI 95 to the **Benefits Agency.** If the application is successful, the 'victim' receives confirmation that the reported *accident* has been recorded on his/her **Benefits Agency** personal file and elsewhere as an *industrial accident.* The obtaining of this declaration of *industrial accident* **(whether or not an injury is known to have occurred)** is crucially important, particularly with regard to possible later claims.

define *(examination term)* requires a precise, concise, unambiguous explanation of something, which may be a term, expression, process, equipment, task or article.

definitions with regard to health, safety and environmental legislation terms are ultimately determined through judge's interpretation. Nevertheless, definitions are provided within legislation, sometimes with a whole section devoted to definitions. For example, see *articles, for use at work* **(HSWA** s.53(1))**.**

demography is the study of (statistics on) human population, such as growth rates, age, sex ratios, distribution, movement and density and their effects on socio-economic and *environmental conditions.*

demolition

demolition in health and safety terms, refers to the pulling or knocking down of, e.g. a building or structure. Much of health and safety legislation in the UK applies to demolition work, including that concerned with construction.

The steps that should be taken prior to or during demolition work are covered by legislation or general good practice. They include:

(i)   A survey must be carried out of the demolition building or structure, the site and its surrounds.

(ii)   Locate all services and ensure they are safe or made safe, referring to plans and the necessary authorities.

(iii)   Check on materials used in the **construction**, for example has **asbestos** or horsehair (possibility of **anthrax**) been used?

(iv)   Wherever possible, demolition should be carried out in the opposite order to **construction**.

(v)   **Risk assessments** should be carried out as legislatively demanded, monitored and, where or when necessary, reviewed.

(vi)   **Employees** should be provided with necessary **personal protective equipment**, e.g. safety boots with steel insoles.

(vii)   Debris and refuse removed on a regular basis.

(viii)   Trunking should be used where appropriate.

(ix)   Braces props or supports should be used wherever necessary.

(x)   Site illumination should be of good quality.

(xi)   Where demolition balls, explosives, pulling equipment or pusher arms are used, **employees** (and others) should maintain a safe distance.

(xii)   Catching platforms should be installed not more than six m below the working level wherever there is danger to the public.

(xiii)   Trespass to the whole or part of the site (especially with regard to children) should be prevented, so far as is reasonably practicable. For example, a secure fence should surround the entire site.

(xiv)   All machinery should be 'made safe' at all times and especially at the end of the working day or if the site is left unattended.

(xv)   Equipment, excavations and means of **access** (e.g. ladders and scaffolding) should be made and left safe, especially at the end of the working day or if the site is left unattended or without security presence.

(xvi)   An action plan and procedure to identify real and potential dangers should be drawn up and implemented, including inspections of the whole demolition site on a regular basis.

Department for Education and Employment (DEE) *Public Enquiries,* Century Buildings, Great Smith Street, London SW1E 6DE. Tel: 0845 609 9960.

Department of the Environment, Transport and the Regions (DETR) Public Enquiries, Ashdown House, 123 Victoria Street, London SW1E 6DE. Tel: 020 7890 3000.

Department of Health (DoH), Public Enquiries, Richmond House, 79 Whitehall, London SW1A 2NS. Tel: 020 7210 4850.

Department of Social Security (DSS) as Department of Health.

Department of Trade and Industry (DTI), Public Enquiries, 10-18 Victoria Street, London SW111 0HN. Tel: 020 7215 5000.

depression (in the workplace): each year, three out of every ten employees suffer depression in the workplace (note, not necessarily depression from the work or from the workplace environment). Employers have a duty to ensure a safe and healthy place and system of work, therefore where an employee suffers from depression an employer should investigate to establish if the depression is sourced from the work or the workplace. A useful aid for employers is a leaflet Depression in the workplace published by the Royal College of Psychiatrists, 17 Belgrave Square, Tel: 020 7235 2351 or www.rcpsych.ac.uk.

derelict land (acquiring, reclamation or improvement) is within the province of the local authority under section 89 of the National Parks and Access to the Countryside Act 1949. Planning authorities can obtain grants for land reclamation from the Exchequer under section 9 of the Local Authority Act 1966.

dermatitis is an inflammation of the skin. If it occurs as a consequence of work it is called occupational or industrial dermatitis. The condition may be **chronic** or **acute** and treatment is specific to the cause. The mnemonic **ERICPD** should be applied for the control and prevention of dermatitis. It is of two major types, contact dermatitis and allergic dermatitis:

(i) Contact dermatitis is caused by repeated contact with certain agents, resulting in the removal of natural skin oils, which cause drying, and cracking of the skin – usually but not invariably the hand (it can spread in severe cases). This process can leave the skin vulnerable to attack from other substances and biological infections. It may be prevented through avoidance or a reduction in exposure or substitution of the substance.

(ii) Allergic dermatitis is a reaction to specific trigger substances and requires complete avoidance of the trigger substance to prevent reoccurrence. Once sensitisation to a particular substance has developed, an adverse reaction to that particular substance will be found each time the substance is encountered. Preventive methods includes a complete avoidance of the substance causing the reaction **and** (not merely *or*) maintaining high standards of personal hygiene, requiring good washing facilities and the use of a barrier.

It is essential that *employers* ensure suitable containers are adequately labelled (a separate duty of the supplier). All relevant *employees* must be informed of the hazards and the control methods in place. Safety data sheet information must be made available to, and drawn to the attention of, all staff who come into contact with *hazardous substances*. It may be necessary for the *employer* to provide *health surveillance*.

In some individuals the work environment and **not** substances, e.g. warm air-conditioned offices, can induce dermatitis, although air-borne fibres from carpets should not be discounted. Some PPE (e.g. gloves) contain sensitising agents, which may induce dermatitis in wearers.

derogation is the annulment or restriction of an obligation or right by some subsequent act, frequently used in connection with property ('a landlord has an implied obligation not to derogate from his grant' *Ward v Kirkland [1967] Ch 194*), less so with health and safety. However, the *Working Time Regulations 1998* utilise the concept of derogation extensively, e.g. concerning hours of work and rest periods.

describe (*examination term*) demands a fairly detailed word picture of whatever is asked.

diffusion badge is a small clip-on unit worn to test for gas or vapour in the air of a work environment, depending on the tendency for gas or vapour to disperse according to its density in comparison with air.

dilution ventilation is a system which induces large volumes of flowing air to dilute a contaminant. In short, air in a specific area is in constant motion and *completely* changed within a specific time period. Sometimes fans are used, outlet and occasionally inlet, or sometimes it occurs simply through natural ventilation (e.g. open doors or windows). Dilution ventilation can **only** be used if *toxicity is low*, with a *small quantity of contaminant, steady rate of contaminant release*, the type of *contaminant is suitable*, and *heat loss or gain is* **not** *a problem*.

dioxan is a colourless liquid or, below 42°C, a solid with a mild odour. It is used in industry as a solvent for fats, oils and natural and synthetic resins, as a wetting agent for textile processing and in the manufacture of detergents etc. It is hazardous to the liver, kidneys, skin and eyes; it is toxic by inhalation, absorption, ingestion and contact. Symptoms of exposure include drowsiness, headache, nausea, vomiting, liver and/or kidney failure, irritation of the skin, eyes, nose and throat. It is carcinogenic.

See also *dioxins*.

dioxins is the commonly used (but incorrect) name of a family of chlorinated organic compounds, of which 2,3,7,8-tetrachlorodibenzo-p-dioxin is one important member – there are some 210 others, including *furans*. Dioxin can be the by-product of inefficient burning or industrial processes or residual in certain insecticides.

In summary, ingestion of dioxins can cause severe ill health and even death. Thus there are strict emission limits on dioxins, enforced by Her Majesty's Inspectorate of Pollution. Dioxin in the form of 2,4,5 T is banned from unrestricted use.

direct monitoring uses electronic devices. It is quick, simple and accurate, provided the user is suitably trained and the equipment well maintained.

directors' duty of care towards the company and its *employees* includes the duty to take care of its financial affairs as a whole (fiduciary duty) but, in financial terms, not liability for 'mere' errors of judgement (*Balstome v Headline Filters [1990] FSR 385*). In health and safety terms, the situation concerning the activities and duty of care of directors and more particularly Boards of Directors is less clear, with **ss. 37 and 40** of the **HSWA** outlining their duties but not clarifying **liability**. This situation is under review and it is advisable to check the current position.

Disability Discrimination Act 1995 (DDA) presents measures intended to end the discrimination which many disabled people face. It requires amongst other things, schools, colleges and universities to provide suitable information and facilities for disabled people. If 15 or more are employed, the **DDA** applies generally. However, while complying with the **DDA, *employers*** should not breach health and safety legislation. *Enforcement* of the **DDA** is through *employment tribunals*. Achieving compliance with health and safety duties may influence DDA decisions.

All things otherwise being equal, a disabled person should be considered for *employment* on equal terms with the non-disabled. Failure to employ a disabled applicant may lead to a successful discrimination claim at an industrial tribunal. *Case law* has yet to be established concerning this Act (see free booklet *Disability Discrimination Act 1995 What Employers Need to Know*).

Disability Discrimination (Employment Relations) Regulations

Some *employers'* groups consider the **DDA** places undue requirements on *employers*; on the other hand, some pressure groups for disabled persons declare that the **DDA** is inadequate.

Disability Discrimination (Employment Relations) Regulations 1996 are concerned to identify physical features of premises that **must** form part of an *employer's* duties regarding the disabled, including cover of any:

(a) feature arising from the design or construction;
(b) approach to, exit from or access to the building;
(c) fixture, fittings, furniture or materials in or on the premises;
(d) other physical element or quality of land included in the premises.

disabled employee is defined under the **DDA** as a person who has a physical or mental impairment (including incontinence or memory) which causes substantial long-term effects on abilities. The *employer* owes a disabled *employee* a higher *duty of care* than that for the *non*-disabled. *Paris v Stepney Borough Council [1951] AER 42* involved an *employee* with one eye who lost the sight of his good eye while at work and established that where there is a greater 'risk of injury to him than to a normal (sic.) *employee'* then the *employer* is under a *duty of care* to take *special* precautions.

See also *Disability Discrimination Act 1995*.

discharges into controlled waters are largely covered by the **WRA 1991** s. 85 which states '*it is an offence . . . to 'cause' or 'knowingly permit' any poisonous, noxious or polluting matter or any solid waste matter to enter any* **controlled waters'** *unless* a *discharge consent* (or other permit) has been obtained from the **EA**.

discharges into sewers are regulated by the *Water Industry Act 1991*. It is an offence to discharge prescribed substances or trade effluent from certain prescribed processes (see *Trade Effluent (Prescribed Processes and Substances) Regulations 1989* amended). The sewage system *does not* include septic tanks. The *Urban Waste Water Treatment (England and Wales) Regulations* provide minimum standards for the treatment of urban waste waters.

discovery in legal terms is properly termed 'discovery and inspection of docu-ments' in *civil* litigation, e.g. claims for *industrial injury* compensation. As an example, when a writ has been issued, the term automatically applies to documents that *must* be disclosed and made available for inspection, without the need for a request, to legal representatives (or concerned parties). They must not be withheld (see *Chipcase v Rosemund [1965] 1 WLR 153*).

See also *accident book* and *privilege*.

discrimination includes that which is favourable or unfavourable, direct or indirect, due to sex, race, religion, or disability. However, age discrimination is not yet covered by legislation in the UK.

Regarding health and safety, *employers* have the prime duty of care and therefore may appear to face a dilemma in the case of disablement. *Employers* must do everything, *so far as is reasonably practicable*, not to discriminate against the disabled yet at the same time *employers* must not expose such *employees* to any risks to their health and safety. The situation is at least partially covered by discrimination legislation but *case law* will further clarify the position. Equal treatment within the legislation is the objective (see *P v Sand Cornwall County Council [1996] IRLR 347* where the **ECJ** held that a transsexual who was dismissed for reasons associated with gender realignment could pursue a claim under the (EU) Equal Treatment Directive).

discuss (*examination term*) requires the debate, investigation and examination of different points of view concerning a task, process, statement etc., identified in a question and is more detailed than *explain* or *describe*.

discussion documents see *consultative documents*.

dismissal concerning health and safety (or most other) matters can be *fair*, *unfair* or *constructive*. In fact, only an industrial tribunal can determine if a dismissal is fair, unfair or constructive (appeals may progress in the normal way 'up' the legal system).

The general two years' service requirement for *employees* before being able to enter dismissal claims 'against' their *employer* does **not** apply to matters of health and safety. On the other hand, flagrant and/or gross breaches of legislation or failure to comply with health and safety requirements detailed in an *employee's* contract of *employment*, can lead to instant dismissal, with little chance of redress by the *employee* concerned (see **HSWA** ss.7 and 8).

For less serious breaches of company or (health and safety) legislative requirements, the established formal disciplinary procedure of the company should be carefully followed. It is possible that suspension (with or without pay) of the *employee* over the period during the running of the procedure may be considered fair. However, for unsuccessful appeals, the date of dismissal is the original date (*Bachelor v BRB [1987] IRLR 136*). The different types of dismissal include:

(i) **Constructive dismissal** – the termination of a contract of *employment* by an *employee*, usually through resignation, where the *employee* considers the *employer* does not intend to comply with some essential part of the contract and/or of statutory requirements. If the claim to an industrial tribunal is on a health and safety matter, the two-year exclusion clause does not apply. *Employees* may apply to an industrial tribunal as though an *employee* of the company concerned.

(ii) **Fair dismissal** – when a tribunal decides that an *employer* has acted reasonably in the circumstances and that the reasons (or grounds) on which the dismissal was based were sufficient and substantial.

(iii) **Unfair dismissal** – when an industrial tribunal finds that an *employer* acted unfairly in dismissing an *employee*. If an *employer* dismisses an *employee* who makes a complaint about some aspect of health and safety and the tribunal finds the complaint justified then, irrespective of the length of service, such dismissal would be found to be unfair.

Employees with two or more years' service who request a written statement giving the reasons for dismissal must be supplied with such a statement within two weeks of the request. However pregnant persons, regardless of length of service, must be provided with the written reasons for dismissal *without* having to ask for it. Those persons who work in areas of danger, e.g. where toxic fumes or substances are present, and who could become pregnant, should have reference to the possibility or probability of dismissal following pregnancy **or** what other arrangements have been made (e.g. alternative *employment*). However, *contracts of employment* cannot take away or change legal rights or legislation. The *employee* **must** inform the *employer* of her pregnancy as soon as it is known (see **MHSWR**).

display screen equipment (within the *Health and Safety (Display Screen Equipment) Regulations 1992*) means 'any alphanumeric or graphic display screen ... ' which ranges from most computers to microfiche.

Display Screen Equipment Regulations see *Health and Safety (Display Screen Equipment) Regulations 1992*.

disposal of hazardous waste requirements are in a state of continual change, with numerous discussion documents still under consideration. Basically there are EU Directives, such as the *Directive on Hazardous Waste (91/689/EEC)* and the *Landfill Directive (199/31/EC)* which provide the stimulus for UK legislation. However, the EU Directives are continuously changed, requiring legislators in the UK, in effect, to run to keep up with the changes, made more difficult (from a legislator's point of view) by the UK legal requirement to allow for discussion. See **EPA** and **Pollution Prevention and Control Act 1999**.

Divisional Court is one consisting of not less than two judges of one of the Divisions of the High Court. There are three Divisions, **Chancery, Family** and **Queen's Bench**. The function of the Divisional Court is to hear appeals in matters prescribed by statute and exercise *jurisdiction* of the high court over 'inferior courts'.

domino theory was originated by Heinrich (1959). His model identifies events, presented as five dominoes standing on end which Heinrich considered illustrated the sequence of events leading to an *accident* (hence *Heinrich's domino theory*). The events were identified by Heinrich as (a) ancestry and social environment, leading to (b) fault of person, the direct cause of (c) an unsafe act and/or mechanical hazard, which results in (d) the *accident*, which leads to (e) the injury. Unless action is taken to prevent the falling of one domino, then collapse of the 'series' will follow and an injury, death, damage or loss will be inevitable. Heinrich declared that if nothing is done, when the first domino falls, it automatically knocks down its neighbour and so on, the inevitable result being an injury, damage or loss. However, if any the first four 'dominoes' are removed (i.e.,action taken) the sequence is broken and there will be no injury, damage or loss. Heinrich considered that the most effective form of *accident* prevention would be to remove the middle domino – the unsafe act and/or mechanical hazard – thereby preventing the *accident*.

An attraction or advantage and disadvantage of the domino theory is its very simplicity. It is somewhat static, through not effectively identifying the inter-action between human beings and their environment, possibly underestimating or overlooking human processing perception and behaviour. This latter point is identified in the **Hale and Hale (1970) model of accident causation** and the later *Hale and Glendon (1989)* model which emphasises the dynamic element of human processing, perception and behaviour into the processes involved. Heinrich's theory has been much adapted and updated, e.g. by Bird and Loftus (1976), whose adaptation takes account of the important role of management in relation to *accident* prevention. The Bird and Loftus model is one of the cornerstones of loss control.

dose, in radiation, is the general term used to identify the quantity of radiation or energy absorbed; in chemical terms it is the quantity of a chemical absorbed.

double-barrelled action in simple terms, is when a claimant takes action in the *courts* against an offender for *negligence* and/or *breach of duty*. In effect, this combines *civil* and *criminal* actions. For example, a claimant sues a defendant for damages (*civil action*) for an injury (claimed to be) due to breach of a relevant statutory duty in health and safety (can be *criminal action*) see *Groves v Lord Wimborne [1898] 2 QB 402* and particularly *Kilgollan v William*

double insulation

Cooke and Co. Ltd [1956] 2 AER 294). The term is little used now, but may still be found in older texts.

double insulation is insulation comprising both basic and supplementary insulation.

drinking water of an adequate *wholesome* supply, readily accessible at conspicuously marked places (unless non-drinking supplies are clearly marked), **must** be provided for all persons at work *in the workplace*. Unless water is supplied via a fountain jet, the *employer* must also supply a sufficient number of suitable drinking vessels (see **CHSWR** and **WHSWR**).

If wholesome drinking water cannot be supplied direct from the mains, then suitable enclosed refillable containers of drinking water must be provided and refilled *at least* daily. Drinking water taps, so far as is reasonably practicable, must **not** be installed in sanitary accommodation or in places of possible high contamination.

DSER see *Health and Safety (Display Screen Equipment) Regulations 1992.*

due diligence is one of the statutory defences available to an accused, i.e. they 'took all reasonable steps and exercised due diligence to avoid committing the offence'. (Consumer Protection Act 1987 s.39)

dust sampling is usually carried out through the use of some method of filtration, whereby samples are collected 'on' a membrane through which contaminated air flows (see also *air sampling*).

dusts are fine grain solid particles suspended in air before eventually settling, unless disturbed or extracted by moving air. Dust particles range in size up to ten microns. However, in the US particles up to 25 microns are considered to be 'dust', which should be borne in mind when reading US occupational hygiene texts or considering US-manufactured engineering controls.

The solid particles (which become dust) are generated by handling, crushing, grinding, rapid impact and detonation of organic or inorganic materials such as rocks, ore, metal, coal, wood and grain. Dusts do not tend to stay in suspension except under electro-static forces, they do not diffuse in still air but tend to settle under the influence of gravity.

Dusts are frequently divided into the *organic* and **non-organic**. The *organic* (produced from animals or plants) can lead to, e.g. *asthma,* farmer's lung; the *in-organic* (not having the characteristics of living organisms) can lead to, e.g. *pneumoconiosis, asbestosis.*

Hazards arising from concentrations of dust include fire, explosion (flour dust is highly explosive) and various respiratory diseases, such as *pneumoconiosis, asbestosis, silicosis*, emphysema, byssinosis, bronchitis, farmer's lung.

duties of employers, in health and safety, are largely derived from *common law*, that is *employers* must take reasonable care to protect their *employees* and their immediate family from risk of foreseeable injury, disease or death at work. If the *employer* fails to take reasonable care regarding risks or hazards which *should have been known* and an *employee* is injured or killed at work, or suffers from a work-related disease, then the *employer* can be held liable.

The *employers'* duties at common law were established by the House of Lords in *Wilsons and Clyde Coal Co. Ltd v English [1937] 3 AER 628*. It is *common law as well as health and safety legislation* that requires all *employers* to provide *and* maintain:

(i)   a safe place of work;
(ii)   a safe system of work; and
(iii)   safe plant and appliances.

duty holder, basically, is a person identified, required by and defined in various legislation to carry out particular *occupational health and safety* or other duties. Experience, qualifications or *training* required may or may not be specified. A *duty holder* must be competent. As an example, a *planning supervisor* is a duty holder required by the **Construction (Design and Management) Regulations**.

duty of care requires everyone to avoid acts or *omissions* which one can *reasonably foresee* would be likely to injure one's neighbour, that is, persons so closely and directly affected by one's acts that they must be borne in mind when considering the acts or omissions called into question (summary of Lord Atkin in *Donoghue v Stevenson [1932] AC 562*) (see also **neighbour principle**).

The *employer* has the **prime** *duty of care, so far as is reasonably practicable*, towards his/her *employees* and *others who may be affected by their work activities*. Nevertheless, in health and safety, **everyone** has a *duty of care*, e.g. everyone must take care not to injure or damage one's neighbour *oneself*.

E

ear is the part of the body which translates sound waves into electrical energy, which is transmitted to the brain. The ear is extremely sensitive, reacting to *pitch* and *amplitude*.

Sound enters the *auditory canal*, which is about 2.5 centimetres long, and on to the *eardrum*. On the body side of the eardrum is the *middle ear*, completely enclosed in bone. Sound is transmitted across the middle ear by three linked bones, the *ossicles* to the *oval window* of the **cochlea**, a spirally wound tube (looking somewhat like a snail) which contains liquid and forms part of the *inner ear*. In response to sound, the liquid in the cochlea vibrates in turn stimulating small hairs to rub on a plate above them, producing electrical energy which travels along the *auditory nerve* to the brain, at which point the individual recognises the sound, e.g. as pleasant or unpleasant, loud or soft.

The hair cells situated nearest the middle ear are stimulated by high frequency sounds, with those located at the tip of the cochlea stimulated by low frequency sound. Hair cells can be irreversibly damaged or 'killed' by excessive or certain types of sound and **Noise Induced Hearing Loss (NIHL)** occurs. The onset of **NIHL** is sometimes first noticed when sound seems as though heard through a muffler wrapped around the ears, occasionally there is a sudden complete deafness or loss of hearing. Excessive periods of **noise** can cause a temporary loss of hearing, particularly at low **noise** levels. This is termed **threshold shift** and should repeated exposure to excessive periods of sound occur, it could lead to a permanent loss of hearing. Incidentally, hearing deteriorates. as one gets older, perhaps recognised when visitors say, 'your TV is loud, please turn down the sound!' The natural deterioration of hearing in older people is termed *presbycusis*.

Damage to the ear can be due to **acute** (a) or **chronic** (c) exposure to **noise**. Examples include, (a) or (c) tinnitus (ringing in the ears) affecting the auditory nerves, can be permanent if there is long-term exposure to **noise**: (a) acoustic trauma, affecting ear drum and ossicles, caused by explosions or similar; (a) temporary threshold shift affecting the cochlea, caused by short-term exposure to excessive **noise**; (c) **permanent threshold shift**, affecting the cochlea, caused by long-term exposure to excessive **noise**; (a) or (c**) noise induced hearing loss**, again affecting the cochlea and caused by exposure to excessive **noise**.

Many of the above (e.g. *industrially induced deafness*) are *prescribed diseases*.

eco-audit schemes see *eco-management and audit schemes*.

eco-management and audit schemes are a voluntary registration scheme adopted by the EU in March 1993. The objective is to reinforce the concept of total quality management in the field of environmental management. It is authoritatively considered by business that the biggest benefit comes from recognition of the implementation of cost-effective and/or cost-minimisation programmes which allow a company to gain competitive advantage.

ecosystem, since 1935, is the term used to refer to the collectivity of interdependent organisations and the physical environment in which they are found. The relationships are dynamic and change without altering the ecosystem's basic characteristics. *Ecosystem management* attempts to preserve and protect natural ecosystems.

ecotoxic applies to substances and preparations that present, or may present, immediate or delayed risks for one or more sectors of the environment.

See *special Waste Regulations* Part II H14.

effluent is the term commonly used to identify the gaseous or liquid waste, which may enter the environment treated, partially treated or untreated from residential, agricultural or industrial sources, sometimes discharged accidentally.

egress, in simple terms, means 'exit'. A safe means of *egress* is a requirement of health and safety legislation.

See the **HSWA** s.2; see also *access* for fuller discussion.

EH40, (updated annually), refers to *banned* substances as listed in a Schedule e.g. to the **Control of Substances Hazardous to Health Regulations** and most importantly, identifies *Maximum Exposure Limits* and *Occupational Exposure Standards*.

elected safety representatives, in simple terms, are non-union *employees*, in a non-unionised workforce, who are elected by members of that workforce under the **Health and Safety (Consultation with Employees) Regulations 1996** essentially to fulfil the role and function of a *safety representative*. Elected representatives effectively have the same rights and duties as appointed *safety representatives*.

electrical equipment is any item used for generation, conversion, transmission, distribution or utilisation of electrical energy (e.g. accessories, appliances,

Electrical Equipment (Safety) Regulations 1994

mains or generator electrically powered tools, machines, *transformers* or wiring materials).

Electrical Equipment (Safety) Regulations 1994 applies to electrical equipment of 50-1000 volts AC and 76-1500 volts DC (see **HSE** leaflet **INDG236L).** The *Regulations* include requiring:

(i) **CE marking** to be obtained and details securely fixed to electrical equipment;
(ii) **hired electrical equipment** to be safe;
(iii) **secondhand equipment** to be safe;
(iv) **protection** against risks to health and safety to humans *or domestic animals* and property damage.

electrical installation is an assembly of associated electrical equipment, supplied from a common origin to fulfil a specific purpose and certain co-ordinated characteristics, such as the complete electrical wiring of premises, including lighting and sockets.

electrical installation inspection and testing is recommended by the *National Inspection Council for Electrical Installation Contracting (NICEIC)* for new installations and at regular intervals thereafter. According to the *IEE Inspection and Testing Guidance Notes 16* (No. 3) a selection of the recommended lengths of time between tests and inspections are:

General	years	Buildings open to the public	years
Domestic	5	Cinemas	1
Commercial	5	Churches under 5 years old	2
Educational		Churches over 5 years old	1
Establish's	5	Leisure complexes	1
Hospitals	3	Public entertainment places	1
Industrial	3	Restaurants and hotels	1

Special installations		External installations	
Emergency		Agricultural and horticulture	3
lighting	3	Caravans	3
Fire alarms	1	Caravan sites	1
Petrol stations	1	Highway power supplies	6
Temporary installations	3 months		

The above provide typical recommended periods, the actual period will depend on circumstances which may make it shorter or longer. Furthermore, recommended intervals may be detailed and become a mandatory duty if the premises are subject to local authority licence or the premises are covered by subsequent legislation.

electrical precautions on construction sites must be taken when:

  (i)   excavating near underground cables, include:
        Isolate power supply;
        Identify location of cables from plans;
        Check location on site with track locators;
        Prepare test holes;
        Hand dig only;
        Mark location;
        Cover exposed cables, using sand/sieved soil over which appropriate tiles are placed, before back filling.
  (ii) working in the vicinity of overhead power lines, require:
        Contacting responsible electricity company, ensure electricity supply isolated;
        Erecting barriers either side of lines;
        Preparing passageways under lines;
        Erection of 'goal posts';
        Marking with warning signs;
        Ensuring adequate clearance distances;
        Excluding all metal ladders.

See also *Portable Appliance Testing* and *portable electrical appliance*.

Electricity at Work Regulations 1989 or **EWR** require people in control of electrical systems to ensure they are safe to use and maintained in a safe condition. The **EWR** are directed at *users*, not manufacturers or *suppliers* of equipment, with requirements such as *all systems must be constructed and maintained to prevent danger, so far as is reasonably practicable*. The EWR are concerned with the principles of electrical safety and its cover and requirements include:

All electrical systems are covered by the EWR.

All places of work, including factories, schools, installations in shops, are covered by the EWR.

All voltages are included in the cover of the EWR.

Electricity at Work Regulations 1989 or EWR

Construction of all electrical systems, *so far as is reasonably practicable,* must prevent danger (Reg. 4(1)).

Different levels of duty are specified in the **Regulations**, ranging from an *absolute duty*, through *reasonably practicable* to *reasonableness* levels.

Due diligence, exceptionally can be used as a defence, provided all reasonable measures have been taken and/or *due diligence* observed.

Electrical equipment includes 'anything in use, intended to be used, or installed for use, to generate, provide, transmit, transform, rectify, convert, conduct, store, measure or use electrical energy'.

Electrical installation certificates and reports are **NOT** a specific requirement of the **EWR** but are a recommendation of the *National Inspection Council for Electrical Installation Contracting.*

Electrical systems are all electrical equipment which is connected to a common source of electric power and includes both the source and equipment.

Electrical work must be carried out (or *closely supervised*) by trained, knowledgeable and experienced *competent employees*, in full possession of adequate information concerning the nature of the work, inherent dangers and the system.

Employees have to co-operate with their *employer*, so far as is necessary for the *employer* to comply with the **Regulations** (Reg. 3).

Exceptionally, work on live electrical equipment is permitted, provided 'suitable precautions are taken'. The Memorandum does *not* specify written procedures, only requires adequate information being made available, subject to a safe system of work (i.e. **Permit to Work**) being in place and operated, together with full details of precautions to be taken and followed.

Inspection and testing on installation and at regular intervals thereafter (see *electrical inspection and testing*) is **NOT** a requirement of the **EWR** but is a recommendation of the **National Inspection Council for Electrical Installation Contracting** as a means of checking if an installation meets the requirements of **BS 7671** and any other relevant standards. All persons carrying out inspection and testing of electrical installations must comply with the **EWR**.

Liability is strict where injury, damage or death is concerned, since electricity is a product within the cover of the *Consumer Protection Act 1987* and *product safety* requirements.

Maintenance of all electrical systems at all times, *so far as is reasonably practicable,* must prevent danger (Reg. 4(1)).

Superior or dominant legislation can apply; for example, in respect of personal protective equipment the **PPER** apply.

electrolysis is the chemical decomposition of an *electrolyte* by passing an electric current through it (see *spark erosion*).

electrolyte a compound that is capable of conducting an electric current when dissolved in a solvent or melted by the addition of heat.

electromagnetic induction is the transfer of electric power from one circuit to another by use of varying magnetic flux. Faraday's Law of Induction states that a conductor carrying current emits a magnetic force, which can be induced into another conductor cutting that magnetic force. The induced electromagnetic force is proportional to the rate of change of magnetic flux in the inducing circuit.

Fleming's rules offer further explanation, providing details of the magnetic field, flow of current and motion in an electric generator (using right hand) or motor (using the left hand). The method is to place the fingers and thumb at right angles to each other, whereby the thumb represents the motion, forefinger the field and second finger the flow of current.

See also *autotransformer* and *transformer.*

elevated work platforms can be masts or towers supporting a platform or cage, a platform supporting persons with their equipment, or a chassis supporting the tower or mast. Forks on forklift trucks may be fitted with a **DTI** *approved* specially constructed platform or cage. 'Cherry-pickers' is a common name for elevated work platforms used in warehouses.

The safe working load should be clearly marked on the equipment; only trained *competent person*s should erect, operate or dismantle the equipment; firm level surfaces should be provided; the equipment should only be raised or lowered if adequate clearance is available; unauthorised entrance into the work area must be prevented by suitable barriers; repairs and maintenance should only be carried out by trained *competent person*s.

emergency procedures are a statutory requirement, with the various legislation detailing requirements in many cases specific to the task or area covered. The emergency procedures must be described in the *Safety Policy Document*, and monitored, regularly reviewed and updated. They must be clearly understood by *employees* who must be *adequately and suitably trained* in the procedure or method. The cover and requirements include visitors, contractors and temporary workers. In addition, details of the emergency procedures may have to be provided to those who live in the vicinity of hazardous industries or processes or storage of large quantities of dangerous substances or goods.

Frequently, such as in the case of possible fire emergency or rescue from a *confined space*, regular practice sessions must be conducted *and recorded*, with the emergency procedures detailed in a *permit to work* as well described in the company's *Safety Policy Document*.

emissions into the atmosphere are largely covered by the **EPA 1990**, particularly those due to *prescribed processes*.

employee is anyone who is engaged to work under a contract of *employment*. However, for the purpose of the **HSWA** and many Social Security provisions, trainees and those on work experience are considered to be '*at work*' even though they may not be under a formal *contract of employment*.

The term *employee* includes supervisors, managers at **all** levels and for many health and safety requirements can include the *self-employed*. Company directors can be employees, if they are engaged under a contract of *employment*. This is very important because *employees* who are supervisors and/or managers have a double responsibility of duty of care – the usual one to take care of themselves and others who may be affected by their own work activity (**HSWA** s.7) and the duty of care as an *agent of their employer* (i.e. acting on behalf of the *employer*).

employee checks and records relating to health and safety will be carried out and held by the prudent *employer* on recruiting staff. These include checking *literacy* levels, what health and safety *training* their potential *employee* has received from previous *employers*, when that *training* was completed (i.e., is it up-to-date?), the level of such *training* (e.g. certificated by an approved body). While all general and trade *training* must include a component of health and safety, if the applicant has just completed a college or higher level course (e.g. plumbing or gas fitting) and particularly if the work environment or task is high-risk, it is useful to invoke the legislative requirement for *employers* and institutions of learning to provide a written statement of what health and safety *training* was provided to the *employee* or student, to be kept with the *employee's* records.

employer, in strict legal terms, is *'the master of a servant,'* that is, anyone 'corporate or incorporate' who employs, directs and controls the services of others in return for a wage or salary. Special arrangements cover those on work experience.

employer and employee relationship is governed by the terms and conditions of a *contract of employment*. The express and implied terms of a contract of *employment* cannot exclude statutory rights, for example, those concerned with redundancy and health and safety at work.

employer's and trade associations can be useful sources of health, safety and environmental information for their members. A *selection* of the larger associations, with the headquarters telephone number for their health and safety section, follows:

> **Confederation of British Industry (CBI)** Tel: 020 7379 7400
> **Association of British Insurers** Tel: 020 7600 3333
> **British Road Federation (BRF)** Tel: 020 7703 9769
> **Chemical Industries Association Ltd.** Tel: 020 7834 3399
> **Clothing Industries Association Ltd., British** Tel: 020 7636 7788
> **Construction Confederation,** Tel: 020 7608 5000
> **Master Builders, Federation of,** Tel: 020 7242 7583
> **National Farmers Union** Tel: 020 7331 7200
> **Passenger Transport UK, Confederation of,** Tel: 020 7240 3131
> **Retail Consortium, British,** Tel: 020 7647 1500
> **Road Haulage Association Ltd.** Tel: 01932 841555
> **UK Offshore Operators Association Ltd.** Tel: 020 7802 2400
> **UK Petroleum Industry Association Ltd.** Tel: 020 7240 0289

employers' defences when sued for breach of *common law* or *statutory duty* include the claiming of *contributory negligence* on the part of the *plaintiff*(s) and/or assumption of risk by the *plaintiff*(s) (*volenti non fit injuria*) or that an *employer* exercised *due diligence* and, in effect, should not be held either wholly or partially responsible.

*Employers' Liability (Compulsory Insurance) Act 1969 as amen-**ded*** includes the compulsory requirement for *employers* to insure for their liability against claims for personal injury, death, disease or illness sustained in the course of *employment* by the insured, in connection with the trade or business of the insured and occurring within the territorial limits.

employment

From January 1995 the Association of British Insurers, because of a huge increase in the number of claims and sums awarded in damages, placed a limit of £10 million (in most cases), with a *legal* minimum of cover at £5 million.

Employers must put their Liability Insurance Certificate (or a true copy of the Certificate) on prominent display at their place of business. The design and location of the Certificate must comply with current legislative requirements.

employment is the following of a vocation, profession or trade etc. under a *contract of employment*.

It is defined in the UK by the **Office of National Statistics** as 'anyone (aged 16 or over) who does at least one hour's paid work a week or has a job that they are temporarily away from (e.g. on holiday)'. Health and safety legislation *primarily* covers, protects and applies to those in *employment* (i.e. at work) and secondly covers those who may be affected by the activities of those at work. However, there are other definitions of *employment* within the UK, invariably for specific purposes, e.g. entitlement to certain benefits.

Employment Appeal Tribunal jurisdiction is set out by the *Employment Tribunals Act 1996* and consists of judges of the High Court and Court of Appeal, Court of Session and lay members, to hear appeals *on questions of law* relating to decisions of tribunals on, e.g. *Equal Pay Act 1970* and *Employment Protection (Consultation) Act 1978*. However, appeals on a *point of law* lie to the Court of Appeal, following leave of the court.

See also *employment tribunal*.

employment of young persons is covered by the *Health and Safety (Young Persons) Regulations 1997*, implementing the *EU Directive 94/33/EC* since 3 March 1997.

Its principle requirements include that where a person under the age of 18 is employed by more than one *employer*, the hours are accumulated and those in full-time education must not work for more than 15 hours per week.

employment tribunals were formerly called *industrial tribunals*; despite the change of name, their functions remain the same. However, the name *industrial tribunal* is still in common use and will be found in otherwise perfectly authoritative texts and works. Claims to *employment tribunals* are **only** initiated through obtaining from *ACAS* a Form IT 1, completing it and returning it to ACAS. Cases are heard by the tribunal, comprising three or (with ageement of the claimant) two members, the chair has legal training and the other two or one member(s) drawn from *employers* and '*workers*'. The functions of an *employment tribunal* include:

Hearing initial appeals against prohibition and improvement notices. Hearing claims for unfair dismissal, e.g. if an *employee* is dismissed for drawing the attention of the *employer* to a matter of health and safety; hearing claims against *employers* who may refuse time off to an appointed *Safety Representative* or *Elected Representative* who are refused health and safety *training;* claims concerning failure of an *employer* to allow rights under certain *Regulations* within the *Working Time Regulations 1998.* Appeals against *employment tribunal* decisions, which must be on points of law, are heard in an *Employment Appeal Tribunal* and thereafter go to the *Court of Appeal.*

Legal aid is not available for claims brought before employment tribunals. They are supposed to be informal and usually do not award costs, except sometimes in the case of frivolous, trivial or unreasonable claims. Before a full hearing or a case, on its own initiative or at the request of either party, a tribunal may consider the written *originating application* (complaint) to the tribunal and the written *notice of appearance* (answer) in response in a *pre-hearing assessment.* If the tribunal considers that *either* party is unlikely to succeed, the tribunal will warn that party that costs may be awarded against them if they insist on a full hearing. However, unless a pre-hearing has been held together with a warning issued or either party is found to have acted frivolously, etc., then costs will *not* be awarded. An *employment tribunal* cannot enforce its own awards, which must be done by application to a civil court.

Employment Tribunals Act 1996 was formerly termed *Industrial Tribunals Act 1996.*

EN means that an associated standard (e.g. **British Standard** (BS) has been 'harmonised' (provides universality) with European Union standards and will be accepted as such throughout EU member states.

endoparasite is a parasite that lives in a host, such as a tapeworm, which may live in a human or other animal.

enforcement officers (commonly called Health and Safety Inspectors) inspect premises in connection with health and safety and enforce the appropriate legislation. They can be 'from' the Health and Safety Executive or the local authority. The *Health and Safety (Enforcing Authority) Regulations 1998* list those who enforce health and safety legislation, where they do it and what is covered by whom.

enforcing authorities

enforcing authorities are always identified with each 'piece' of legislation with the function of enforcing legislation and providing advice and help concerning their area of responsibility. A useful source of reference is the *Health and Safety (Enforcing Authority) Regulations 1998.* In very broad terms, the *Health and Safety Executive* covers industrial activity; local authorities cover local commercial activities; the *Environment Agency* can cover either *and* the environment.

Except for Crown premises, enforcement can be transferred from the **HSE** to a local authority. This requires prior agreement and those affected should be notified of the change. It unfortunately can be confusing on multi-site or multi-premises undertakings establishing exactly who is the enforcing authority. It is prudent if undertakings check periodically if the enforcement authority has changed. Even if the correct procedure has *not* been followed by the enforcing authority an *employer* who is unaware of the enforcing authority can be held responsible for this lack of knowledge (see *Hadley v Hancox (1987) 85 LGR 402*).

engineering construction work see *work of engineering construction.*

environment is a general term that covers everything surrounding an organism, including for example, climate. There is invariably an interaction between an organism and its surroundings. However, whilst an emphasis is frequently placed on negative interaction or consequences, in fact there can be positive interaction between an organism and its environment. In the science of health and safety an objective of principal concern – consequential to moral, societal or legal pressure – in industrial or commercial activity is *environmental management* and associated legislative requirements.

Environment Act 1995 or EA amended several statutes (e.g. *Water Resources Act 1991*) established the *Environment Agency* and requires it to assess existing **and** potential pollution levels and identify options for prevention and/ or minimisation (s. 5), including identifying the costs involved.

See *Environmental Protection Act.*

Environment Agency was created, together with Regional Offices, under the *Environment Act 1995.* The Agency is primarily (but not only) concerned with the many aspects of pollution prevention and control, e.g. assessments and identifying costs involved. The Agency unified the various functions of the National Rivers Authority, Her Majesty's Inspectorate of Pollution (HMIP), the waste regulation authorities, disposal authorities, the Chief Inspector of radioactive substances and the functions of the Secretary of State formerly held under various legislation, e.g. the *Water Industry Act 1991* and the *Radioactive Substances Act 1993*.

environmental audit must be produced by manufacturers concerning their products and their influence on the environment, for example energy and material use policies, waste output and effect on the environment. The objective is monitoring purchasing contributes towards ensuring environmentally sound goods.

Environmental Impact Appraisal in developing countries suffers from great difficulties, largely because of lack of valid or verifiable data. There cannot be one single universally applicable 'best practice' (or appraisal) and therefore the Environmental Impact Appraisal must be tailored to national needs and capabilities, remembering that expertise in **Environmental Management** is frequently lacking or, at best, minimal in developing countries.

Environmental Impact Assessment or EIA is a method used to take account of environmental considerations and frequently used to construct an *environmental impact statement*. An EIA essentially obtains the following information:

(i) a description of the proposed development, including details of site, its design and its scale;
(ii) an assessment of the main environmental effects of the development;
(iii) the likely significant effects (direct and indirect) of the development on the environment (see *environment*);
(iv) a description of any adverse effects identified, together with a description of proposed measures to avoid, reduce or remedy such adverse effects;
(v) where public participation is involved, a summary in non-technical language of the information identified above.

Environmental Impact Statement or EIS is often a legal requirement *before* a new project (which may have an impact on the environment) can proceed. The *Environmental Impact Assessment* will provide the necessary information for the Statement.

environmental law, as its name implies, is legislation, controls and all other measures (including various agencies) introduced to protect the *environment* and society from ill effects from, or due to, industrial or other activity. Its core elements include the control of *pollution* and protection of natural resources,

Environment Management Systems

including wildlife and land. It is one of the fastest changing and developing sectors of law in the UK.

Environment Management Systems require companies to establish and implement environmental policies, objectives and programmes, as part of effective environment management systems. The standard, which primarily applies, is the BS EN *ISO 14000* series.

Environmental Protection Act 1990 is primarily concerned with ' . . . provision for the improved control of pollution arising from certain industrial and other processes'. Its application is largely overseen by the **Environment Agency.**

Part 1 of the Act provides for *prior authorisation procedures* for *specified processes* listed in the *Environmental Protection (Prescribed Processes and Substances) Regulations 1991*; emission limits are legally binding and operators must use the *best practicable environmental option* (BPEO) to control pollution and use the *best available techniques not entailing excessive cost* (BATNEEC) for preventing the release of substances and rendering harmless any residual substances. The cost of techniques including technology, equipment, design, **construction**, layout and maintenance of buildings, as well as number, qualifications, **training** and supervision of persons employed, can be taken into account, e.g. if the technology which reduces pollution emission by 95% costs four times that which would reduce pollution emission by 90%, then (unless the emission is very dangerous) the latter may be adjudged, *so far as is reasonably practicable,* to satisfy the requirements.

Enforcement may be by Her Majesty's Inspectorate of Pollution (central control) or by Environmental Health Officers (local control), both enforcement officers having similar powers to the **HSE** Enforcement Officers, including the issuance of Improvement and Prohibition Notices, in the case of pollution notices, appeals are made to the Secretary of State.

In summary, included amongst the provisions of the **EPA** 1990 are those covering: discharge and emission functions and objectives; authorisations, general provisions, conditions, variations of authorisations appeals; fees and charges for authorisations; obtaining information from persons and authorities; public registers for information (except that affecting national security or certain confidential information; financial assistance for environmental purposes; power to give effect to (EU) Community *and other international obligations.*

Environmental Protection (Prescribed Processes and Substan-

ces) Regulations 1991 provide classification details of processes 'prescribed' for local authority air pollution control and list the prescribed processes and substances for *integrated pollution control* by the relevant national Inspectorates.

See also *enforcement officers* and *Environmental Protection Act 1990.*

Environmental Protection (Prescribed Processes and Substances) Regulations 1991 (amended) divide processes and substances into two categories; Part A (subject to integrated pollution control (**IPC**) and Part B (subject to air pollution control by the *local authority*).

Environmental Technology Best Practice Programme was established in 1994 to help businesses with their environmental performance, in ways that are low cost and/or produce savings. The programme publishes guides to 'good practice' and Environmental Helpline Officers provide advice via a free Helpline (0800 585794).

ergonomic hazards include those derived from *anatomical* mismatch, e.g. machine not fitted to the individual, badly designed workstations or poor method of work; the *physiological*, e.g. task layout and/or sequence, fatigue, *stress*; the *psychological*, e.g. ability to learn, emergency reactions, *perception (e.g. of risk),* and *stress.*

ergonomics is the study of the relationship between a worker and the work environment. The best time to apply ergonomics is prior to and particularly at the design stage. However, assessments **must** be made of all existing workplaces and tasks, to establish where ergonomic improvements can be made. In some cases, a *generic assessment* may be sufficient.

As an example, in connection with the largely ergonomic based assessment of display screen equipment, the following four broad areas require assessment; organisation (e.g. software; breaks, task rotation etc.); equipment or process (e.g. position and/or layout of screen, keyboard, seating, posture, equipment design etc.); individuals (e.g. mental and physical capability, health, eye problems, etc.); environment (e.g. lighting, glare, temperature, workspace, *noise,* humidity etc.). Where significant risks to the health and safety of the worker/operator/user are found, action must be taken by applying the assessment findings, e.g. fitting the machinery and work environment to the human being – that is, **not** attempt to make the human being fit the requirements of the machinery or work environment.

EU Court see *Court of Justice of the European Communities.*

EU Directives

EU Directives see *European Union Health and Safety Directives.*

European Court of Justice see *Court of Justice of the European Communities.*

European Environment Agency co-ordinates and acts as a forum for European environmental matters. Postal address: Kongens Nytorv 6, DK-1050 Copenhagen K, Denmark. Tel: Copenhagen 33 36 74 00, website http://www.eea.eu.int.

European Union Court (commonly called EU Court) see *Court of Justice of the European Communities.*

European Union Decisions are those made by the *Council of Europe* with regard to the extent of compliance on specified matters by European Union Member States.

European Union Health and Safety Directives (commonly called EU Directives) begin with a proposal from the European Commission in the form of a draft Directive. The proposal then goes to the *European Parliament*, where the MEPs give it a first reading, then on to the *Economic and Social Committee* (ESC), for further discussion and revision.

The revised version of the draft Directive, following comments and amendments made and accepted by the EU Parliament and ESC, can be presented to the *Council of Ministers*. When a *common position*, via a *qualified majority vote* (QMV) is achieved (in 1996, it was 54 out of 76 votes), the Council has agreed to the proposed Directive. The EU Parliament then has a second reading of the proposed Directive and can make amendments. The proposed Directive then returns to the Commission, who considers the EU Parliament's amendments and presents the final version to the Council of Ministers for adoption. Article 5 of the Treaty of Rome requires member states of the EU to comply with Directives. Those who fail to comply can be brought before the *Court of Justice of the European Communities* for its decision, which may include the withholding of EU funds.

See also *challenging of EU Directives and legislation.*

European Union Legislation comprises three categories, *Regulations,* **Directives** and **Decisions.**

Please refer to various *Regulations*, which identify those originated following an EU Directive.

See also *European Union Health and Safety Directives* and *European Union Decisions*.

evaluate (*examination term*) means briefly considering and discussing all the evidence then coming to a conclusion as to the validity or otherwise of something, in other words is 'it' valid or not?

examination question techniques, together with answering examination questions, vary according to the individual, discipline, type of examination and its format. Students of the multi-discipline health, safety and environment find a very wide scope and range of disciplines. The principal problems for many candidates are illustrated by reference to the comments reproduced (by kind permission) from the Examiners Report for the National General Certificate Examination of the National Examination Board in Occupational Safety and Health.

From the *Management of Safety and Health* paper:

Question 9

(a) *Explain the meaning of the term 'competent person'.* (4)
(b) *Outline* **FOUR** *checks that could be made you help assess a person's competence.* (4)

Most candidates, for part (a), appeared to have a good idea of what constitutes a **competent person** by explaining that it is someone who has the necessary knowledge and skills (often gained by a combination of **training** and experience), and is able to apply them appropriately to a given situation. Better candidates also noted the importance of **competent person**s being able to recognise their own limitations. Part (b) was answered less well, often because simple lists were given rather than an outline of four checks that could be made. This was a question in which a few practical examples could be used effectively to demonstrate a full understanding. Checks that can be made include: seeking evidence of qualifications, level of **training** and membership of professional/trade organisations; undertaking written or practical assessments; and seeking references or recommendations.

From the *Identification of Hazards* paper.

115

excessive cost

Question 4

Outline the factors associated with the physical working environment that may affect the risk of injury when undertaking manual handling activities. (8)

Candidates who answered this question well noted that it referred only to the *physical* environment, and that the other factors affecting the risk of injury when handling loads (the individual, the task and the load itself) were not part of the question. The important elements of the working environment are listed in Schedule 1 of the Manual Handling Operations *Regulations* 1992 as space constraints, floor conditions (slippery, uneven or varying in height), extremes of temperature or humidity, air movements and lighting. Better candidates also identified that the physical layout of the workplace may lead to excessive carrying distances and/or excessive lifting or lowering distances.

Highlighting two of the problems faced by candidates, the assessment of answers to Question 9 (b) identifies a major problem, that is, understanding the difference between *list* and *outline* (see entries in text). Candidates who answered Question 4 fell into the fairly common trap of attempting to answer questions that were not asked – thus wasting time which in the 'real world' could justifiably be considered to be a cash loss to the company.

Such problems are common to most examinations. Similarly a useful technique to resolve most problems starts from *carefully* reading and understanding the questions, highlighting or underlining the key elements within the question and most important of all, **answering the question and ONLY the question.**

excessive cost includes consideration of the extent of reduction and improvement between comparative systems to control releases of, or render harmless, all substances from a process or activity. It also involves *so far as is reasonably practicable*; a simple example is considering if the cost of a scrubber fitted at the top of a chimney would exceed the benefits.

See **BATNEEC**.

expectant mothers see *new and expectant mothers.*

explain (*examination term*) means to provide in relevant detail a reasonable interpretation and account of 'whatever the question asks'.

explosive 'substances and preparations (are those) which may explode under the effect of flame or which are more sensitive to shocks or friction than dinitrobenzine' (H1 Part II *Special Waste Regulations 1996*). Dinitrobenzine also can cause *acute toxic hepatitis*.

Explosives Acts 1875 and **1923** are still wholly or partially in effect (but see *Control of Explosives Regulations 1991*). For example, the 1875 and 1923 Acts apply to explosives for industrial and commercial use. Explosives may **only** be kept in:

(i)   a factory or magazine licensed by the **HSE**;
(ii)   a store licensed by a local authority;
(iii) premises registered with the local authority.

Licensing of premises for the acquisition, storage and use of gunpowder or other explosives is covered by diverse requirements. Enforcement Officers can be from a variety of authorities, e.g. the **HSE** Explosive Inspectorate, Local Authority Officers, even the police.

extinguishant is a substance used to extinguish fires.

Exxon Valdez was an oil tanker which ran aground on a reef in Prince William Sound, Alaska, in March 1989 spilling some 38,000 tonnes of crude oil, contaminating around 1,000 kms of coastline. The episode is recognised as one of the major human-made environmental disasters of all time. The required clean-up took five years to complete, during which time many new and more effective technologies and techniques were developed for decontamination of areas subject to oil spillage. Regular monitoring of the area is showing that it and its wildlife is slowly recovering.

F

Factories Act 1961 is rapidly being replaced through piecemeal revocations, repeals and replacements, especially by incoming *Regulations* (e.g. for *machine guarding* by the *Provision and Use of Work Equipment Regulations 1998*). This essentially means the *Factories Act 1961* concerning health, safety and welfare in factories is becoming like a ghost – less and less of it applies, although its influence remains. In this basic text it is not advisable (or possible) to attempt to detail the causes of constantly changing *Factories Act* cover. Nevertheless, sometimes reference is made to the FA in this work for a useful or convenient definition (e.g. *factory*). It is recommended readers contact the *HSE Information Centre* (0541 545500) or consult professional in-depth texts, such as Goodman and Watkins *Encyclopaedia of Health and Safety at Work: Law and Practice,* (four regularly updated loose-leaf volumes and separate index), ISBN 1 86089 083 0 London, Gee Publishing Ltd, if they are concerned.

factory is any premises where goods are made, repaired, altered, etc., through the use of manual labour. However, the term 'factory' also includes dry docks, abattoirs, etc. (see s.175 *Factories Act 1961*)

Fahrenheit scale is a temperature scale, developed by Gabriel Fahrenheit (1686-1736), little used now, particularly for scientific or industrial purposes (see *Kelvin* and *celsius*. The melting point of ice is 32°F and the boiling point of water under standard atmospheric pressure is 212°F.

fair dismissal see *dismissal.*

family (staffed undertakings): irrespective of size or number employed, undertakings wholly family staffed have exemption from certain legislative requirements. For example, the conduct of, or form of, risk assessments **may** vary from the norm; *Employers' Liability* insurance **may not** be a requirement. Because of the wide range of legislation involved and high penalties for non-compliance, it is essential that authoritative and/or professional advice be obtained concerning possible exemptions.

fault, in 'legal' health and safety terms, is usually taken to mean *negligence, breach of statutory duty* or other act or *omission* which could lead to a more serious result than otherwise, both in relation to the conduct causing an *accident* and the conduct which influenced the severity of any injury (e.g. see *Bux v Slough Metals Ltd (1974) 1 AER 262:* plaintiff suffered eye injury, was not wearing (supplied) goggles which would have reduced severity of injury, damages awarded reduced).

filtration is the process by which unwanted substances are removed from a medium, e.g. solids from a liquid or gas. A filter, made from a porous material – ranging from paper to sand – through which the medium is passed, retains the unwanted substances. Filtration is one of the most commonly used and effective means of controlling or reducing the emission of pollutants into the environment.

fire classification and suitable *extinguishants* are shown in the table below.

fire extinguisher contents (*extinguishants*) and their action include:

water (used in its pure form or with various additives) which cools a fire and, in large quantities, can smother a fire;

dry power, which smothers fires through forming a powder blanket which cools the fire and chemically interacts, excluding oxygen. Has the disadvantage that the powder residue can mark items, i.e. computer cards in CPU's;

foam filled extinguishers, which on use form a foam blanket, smothering and cooling fires and excluding oxygen;

carbon dioxide (CO_2) which smothers fires with an inert gas blanket, excluding oxygen; halon which smothers and has a chemical interaction with some sources of fire, excluding oxygen. Has the disadvantage that if used in a confined space, e.g. a small room with little or no ventilation, it can suffocate the operator and/or other persons in the room;

sand which smothers fires through excluding oxygen;

fire blanket (non-asbestos) which smother fires through excluding oxygen;

wet 'blanket' comprising of any material soaked in water, even (strictly for emergencies *and not to be left*) thoroughly water-soaked newspaper, thrown flat over small fires, e.g. chip pan type of fire.

Fire Precautions Act 1971 or FPA (as amended) requires a fire certificate for *designated premises*. The FPA applies to e.g. boarding houses, schools, colleges, universities, libraries, factories and swimming baths, with additions through the *Fire Safety and Safety of Places of Sport Act 1987* and the *Fire Precautions (Workplace) Regulations 1997* and *1999 amendment*. These combine to provide a complete cover regarding fire.

119

Fire Precautions (Workplace) (Amendment) Regulations 1999

In summary, the FPA applies virtually everywhere where people work, subject to the conditions below.

In particular, a fire certificate must be applied for, by the occupier of factories, offices or shops, except in the case of part occupancy and/or ownership, on a prescribed form (obtainable from the local Fire Authority) where:

- the building has multi-premises occupancy (see below);
- more than 20 persons are employed on the ground floor, or more than ten on any upper floor;
- in factory premises where explosives or highly flammable materials are stored or used, the fire authority may decide to issue a fire certificate.

A fire certificate specifies the:

- means of escape in case of fire, which must be safe to use at all *relevant* times;
- use of premises;
- number and type of fire extinguishers;
- warning alarms.

The certificate *may* also specify:

- maintenance requirements for the fire escape;
- limits on number of persons on the premises at any one time;
- training requirements for staff.

In addition, all occupied premises, irrespective as to whether or not they have been issued with a fire certificate, **MUST** be provided with an adequate means of fire escape *and* a suitable means of fighting fires.

Premises are rated as high (e.g. where easily ignitable materials are used or stored), normal (e.g. offices and shops where a fire would be localised), and low risk (e.g. where heavy machinery is used). **NB** Offices and shops are virtually never categorised low risk.

Fire Precautions (Workplace) (Amendment) Regulations 1999
amended the *Fire Precautions (Workplace) Regulations 1997,* replacing once again the requirement for *employers* to carry out a fire risk assessment for virtually all premises.

Fire Precautions (Workplace) Regulations 1997 amended the *Fire*

Precautions Act 1971, particularly regarding those premises not requiring a fire certificate. It implements the general fire safety provisions of the *European Framework and Workplace Directives* not specifically dealt with by other legislation. The FPWR provide for minimum fire safety standards in places where people work, however some workplaces are exempt and others may be made exempt. *Workplaces* to which the FPWR does not apply or are exempt include:

- workplaces used only by the *self-employed*;
- private dwellings; and
- workplaces covered by a current fire certificate in force under the *Fire Precautions Act 1971.*

In alphabetical order, the main requirements of the FPWR are:

Emergency routes must lead as directly as possible to a place of safety. The routes must be clearly signed and number, distribution *and dimensions* of these routes must be adequate, having regard to the use, equipment and dimensions of the workplace and the *maximum* number of persons that may be present at any one time. Emergency routes requiring illumination must be provided with *emergency lighting* of adequate intensity in the case of failure of their normal lighting (Reg. 5).

Exemption of low risk premises from requiring a fire certificate can be granted by the local fire authority.

Exits must be kept clear *at all times* and be clearly signed. Emergency doors must not be locked or fastened so that they cannot be easily and immediately opened by any person who may require them in an emergency (Reg. 6).

External emergency services must be contacted and informed, to enable arrangements be made for rescue work and fire fighting (Reg. 4).

Fire fighting equipment, detectors and alarms must equip all workplaces. Fire fighting equipment must be appropriate, easily accessible, simple to use and indicated by signs. Additionally the *employer* must take measures for fire fighting and nominate an adequate number of *employees* to carry them out (Reg. 4).

Fire risk assessments must be carried out. The FPWR has amended Reg. 3 of the *MHSWR* to include the need for a *fire risk assessment,* the purpose of which is to determine the measures required to comply with those of the FPWR. This assessment is part of the health and safety assistance (Reg. 6) and to be done especially with regard to fire requirements or as part of a general workplace assessment. Information must be provided for *employees* (**MHSWR** Reg. 8) and is part of the co-operation and co-ordination efforts required by the **MHSWR** Regs. 9 and 10 (FPWR Reg. 3).

Maintenance of fire fighting etc. equipment must be carried out where necessary to protect *employees* in the case of fire. The workplace and any equipment and devices provided under Regs. 4 and 5 have to be maintained in an efficient state, in efficient working order and in good repair (Reg. 6).

Training and equipment available to nominated *employees* must be *adequate and suitable* (Reg. 4).

Local fire authorities have a responsibility for the supervision and control of compliance with the FPWR. If the fire authority thinks that there is a serious risk in the event of fire, the authority can issue an *enforcement notice* or a *prohibition notice*. Appeals in writing must be made within 21 days against the notice to an *employment tribunal.*

Fire Safety and Safety of Places of Sport Act 1987 amended and, to an extent, deregulated, fire precautions legislation. For example, through amending the FPA waivers (exemptions) from the requirement for Certification (*not* exemption from achieving the individual requirements) may be granted by the local fire authority.

fire triangle is a diagram where 'Ignition', 'Air' and 'Fuel' form and are displayed as the three sides of a triangle. With the removal of any one 'side' a fire cannot start or continue to burn. Sometimes the term 'air' is used in place of 'oxygen' and 'ignition' in place of 'heat'.

first aid has the objective, in very simple terms, of prolonging active life (or PAL). A qualified **first aider** does **not** provide comprehensive or full medical treatment. First aid is the provision of minimum treatment necessary for survival (such as applying a bandage), effectively making a victim comfortable and likely to 'survive' until a professional medical person can take over. The provision of first aid forms part of the general duty of care required by Section 2(1) of the **HSWA**. **HSE** free leaflet INDG215(rev) (or current version) is very useful and obtainable from **HSE Books**.

first aider is a person who is appointed in compliance with the *Health and*

Safety (First Aid) Regulations 1981 and the accompanying **ACOP**. A first aider **must** receive *suitable and adequate training* from an **HSE** approved *training* centre, *with additional specific, in-depth training* if employed in workplaces with unusual or uncommon risks. A person cannot be appointed or recognised as a first aider unless or until completion of the approved course and certification. A further course must be taken every three years to renew and update the first aid training.

In summary, the number of first aiders which should be appointed in relatively low risk workplaces (e.g. shops, offices) where there are 50-100 *employees* is one, with one more for *every* additional 100 workers; medium risk workplaces (e.g. light engineering, food processing, warehousing) one first aider for every 50 *employees* for the first 100 *employees*, one additional first aider for each additional 100 *employees*; high risk workplaces (e.g. construction, slaughter houses, chemical manufacturing) require at least one first aider for each 50 *employees*, one of which should have been trained in specific emergency action for those hazards which may demand extra first aid skills.

flammable generally refers to the capacity of a substance to be set on fire or support combustion easily, e.g. *liquid* substances and preparations which have a *flash point* equal to or greater than 21oC and less than or equal to 55ºC.

See also *highly flammable*.

flashpoint is the minimum temperature at which a flammable substance (usually a liquid) gives off sufficient vapour to catch fire when ignited. The *higher* the flashpoint 'figure' the *less likely* that the vapour will ignite, e.g., paraffin vapour has a flashpoint of 38°C, octane vapours a flashpoint of 15°C. A flashpoint is determined through heating a liquid in a standard capacity cup under prescribed conditions.

flocculation is the process during which suspended fine particles form large masses (floccules).

fluorocarbons are a synthetic organic compound, one of a group called halocarbons, in which some or all of the hydrogen atoms have been replaced by fluorine atoms. They have been used as refrigerants, coating materials, solvents and propellants. Halocarbons have been found to attack and destroy the *ozone layer* and their manufacture and use is being phased out.

food poisoning has a variety of causes arguably the best known of which is *bacteria*, typified by *salmonella*.

Food Safety Act 1990 provides powers to deal with unfit food and unhygienic premises and requires food handlers to be formally trained. It covers food businesses, defined as places where the act of producing, storing, delivering, selling, importing or exporting food takes place.

The presumption is that any food sold from or found in food premises is intended for human consumption (Section 3). If food on food premises is *not* intended for human consumption, for example, dog bones or meat in a butcher's, then it must be 'securely set aside' from food for human consumption and clearly labelled.

If someone sells or offers for sale unfit food as intended for human consumption, they are committing an offence (Section 8). If the unfit food is part of a larger batch, then the whole batch is considered to be unfit for human consumption

An authorised inspecting officer cannot be prevented from carrying out an inspection during any reasonable hour or at any time if the officer believes there is breach of the Act (Section 9). Unfit food for human consumption can be seized and removed. A Magistrate will view the food as soon as circumstances demand, and may condemn the food and either order it to be destroyed or stored. All expenses incurred are the responsibility of the owner of the food.

Improvement and prohibition orders apply, particular to food, e.g. unhygienic or defective premises (Sections 10 and 11). Supplying food not of the nature or substance or quality demanded by the purchaser is an offence (Section 14). Food businesses must be registered with the local authority (Section 19).

Convicted offenders on indictment are subject to an unlimited fine or imprisonment for up to two years or both; on summary conviction for breach of Sections 7, 8 or 14 a maximum fine of £20,000 or up to two years imprisonment or both, for breach of other sections a maximum fine of £5,000 or up to six months imprisonment or both (Section 35).

Food Safety (General Food Hygiene) Regulations 1995 require that the proprietor of a food business shall ensure that food handlers engaged in any food business are supervised, instructed and/or trained in food hygiene matters **commensurate with their work activity.**

The purpose of the **Regulations** is to create, use and maintain hygienic premises, work practices and procedures to prevent the risk of illness caused by food-borne bacteria. To satisfy the **Regulations** requires far more than mere cleanliness, it involves the:

(i) protection of foodstuffs from the risk of contamination *of any kind*;

(ii) *prevention of the multiplication of organisms* that pose such a risk;

(iii) destruction of harmful bacteria by use of *thorough* and *correct procedures*.

See also **bacteria, spores,** and *Hazard Analysis and Critical Control Points.*

Food Safety Regulations see *Food Safety (General Food Hygiene) Regulations 1995.*

forklift trucks (FLT) are of various types, including: pedestrian-operated stackers, both manually- and power-operated; reach trucks (mast and pantograph types); counterbalance; narrow aisle; order pickers. The power may be petrol, diesel, electric (using batteries), LPG.

Drivers of FLT must be over 18, of good health and trained in an approved scheme.

When operating the FLT drivers should drive with care, not carry passengers, not permit unauthorised use and when leaving the truck put controls in neutral, ensure the brake is on and *remove the key or ignition plug.*

The truck should be checked daily, using a pre-determined system of inspection before use or changeover.

The maximum load capacity of the FLT should **never** be exceeded and the load suitably located on the forks.

The hazards associated with petrol, diesel, electric (using batteries) and LPG powered FLT include:

Petrol/diesel/LPG FLT engines produce dangerous fumes, which means that they can really only be used in the open air.

Electric (battery) FLT operation presents several hazards, many associated with their maintenance and recharging.

FLT become *hoists or lifts* if they have a platform or cage fitted, the direction or movement of which is restricted by a guide or guides. No platform or cage should be fitted or used unless DTI approved.

formaldehyde is a near colourless gas with a pungent odour, often used in a water (aqueous) solution. Uses include textile, board and plywood manufacture, tanning, sandpaper and grinding wheels, with probably its best-known use being as an embalming fluid. It is hazardous and toxic by inhalation, ingestion and contact. Those with poorly functioning immune systems – e.g. children and the elderly – can be particularly affected. Symptoms include burning nasal passages, coughing, bronchial spasms, pulmonary, eye, nose and throat irritation, dermatitis; it is also carcinogenic.

formic acid (sometimes called methanoic acid) is a near colourless liquid with a pungent odour, often used in a water solution. It is used in textile dyeing and finishing, as a shrink and wrinkle-proofing agent, in dyes, refrigerants, pharmaceuticals, solvents, rubber latex, as an antiseptic in beer making, etc. Formic acid is hazardous to the respiratory system, the skin, kidneys, liver and the eyes. It is toxic by inhalation, ingestion and contact. Symptoms include eye and throat irritation, nasal discharge, cough, nausea, skin burns and dermatitis.

fossil fuels, technically speaking, are the residues of organic material. The uncontrolled use of (largely non-renewable) fossil fuels can significantly contribute to environmental problems such as acid rain or global warming.

free radicals are any atom or molecule capable of very short-lived independent existence containing one or more unpaired electrons, often extremely reactive. Hydrocarbon radicals, such as ethyl radical, can contribute to the toxicity of photochemical smog. Free radicals are also considered to play a role in mutations *preceding* the development of cancer and in damaging the liver and/ or kidneys, diabetes mellitus and ageing. However, it is difficult to establish if free radicals are the cause of a disorder or the result of some other agent.

frequency rates are part of the process of *accident statistics* and calculate the number of *reported* injuries per number of hours worked.

$$\frac{\text{Number of injuries}}{\text{Total number of hours worked}} \times 100,000$$

NB The frequency rate in some countries, e.g. the USA, is usually quoted per one million hours worked.

fumes are solid particles, usually formed by condensation from the gaseous state or break-up of liquids in the air. Fumes are generally generated from the gaseous state after volatization from molten metals and are often accompanied by a chemical reaction, such as oxidation. Fumes stay in suspension (flocculate) and coalesce.

fuse basically is a device which breaks the circuit in which it has been inserted when the current exceeds a given value for sufficient time. In effect, the circuit remote from an electrical supply is isolated. The 'fuse break' may be due to the melting of a conductor, which would require replacement before restoring the circuit. A melting type fuse protects the equipment but does **not** necessarily protect the user. It is essential to check and find out what caused the fuse to 'blow'.

See *Residual Current Device.*

G

gamma rays are high-energy *electromagnetic radiation* with a wavelength of less than 10 μmm, capable of causing *ionisation*, similar to *X-rays* but with far greater penetrative power. They easily enter the human body, leading to major cell damage including the initiation of various types of *cancer*.

gas, technically speaking, is a substance in the form of a completely elastic fluid in which the atoms and molecules move freely in random patterns. They have no volume or shape, but can expand indefinitely. Gases can spread widely and thinly (diffuse). Gas is one of three phases of a substance (solid, liquid and gas), especially one that does not become a solid or a hazard at normal pressure or temperature. Gases can be changed to the liquid or solid state *only* by the combined effect of increased pressure and/or decreased temperature.

Gas Appliances (Safety) Regulations 1992 see Gas Safety (Installation and Use) Regulations 1998.

Gas Safety (Installation and Use) Regulations 1998 or GSIUR and its associated Regulations protect the gas-consuming public from gas-related *accident* and injuries from supply and most equipment, including that using LPG, is covered. Excluded are mobile LPG appliances **except** when the appliance is under the control of an *employer* or *self-employed* person at a place of work. The *ACOP L56* should be referred to in conjunction with the GSIUR. This entry selectively considers key points from all GSIU Regulations.

The GSIUR cover gas fittings and gas fitters. Gas fittings are gas pipes, regulators, meters and an appliance used for cooking, heating or lighting. Only *competent person*s who must be members of an *HSE* approved body, i.e. CORGI, are allowed to carry out gas fitting or service pipework, installation and connection. The Regulations specify the content and requirements of *competent persons'* approved training courses. The GSIUR identify safety precautions concerning meters; pipe installation and maintenance requirements for *employers* and landlords.

The majority of gas appliances are covered by the *Gas Appliances (Safety) Regulations 1992* and include the requirement that appliances should be CE marked, or to an appropriate European or British Standard. The GSIU Regulation 35A requires landlords to check specified gas appliances and their flues, keep records concerning such tests or checks, e.g. date, address, location of appliance checked, defects identified, remedial action taken, name and signature of person carrying out the check. *A copy of the record must be provided to tenants* at specified times.

Gas Safety (Management) Regulations 1996 are concerned with the establishment of gas networks and appointment of a *network emergency co-ordinator* to prepare a 'safety case' for submission to the HSE prior to conveying gas in a network.

general duties in health, safety and environmental legislation are 'goal setting', allowing *employers* to decide how they are going to control the risks they identify within legislative requirements, with an emphasis on the word 'general'.

general duty of care, in the widest and simplest health, safety and environmental terms, means that *no one* at work should do anything that would endanger themselves, co-employees, or those who *could* be affected by their work activities.

Under the **HSWA**, the **prime** general duty of an *employer* is to take care, *so far as is reasonably practicable*, to provide a *safe place of work*, safe plant, tools, equipment and to provide *adequate and suitable instruction, information* and *training*, etc. The *employee* has a duty to take reasonable care not to endanger self and others, co-operate with the *employer* with regard to health and safety, follow the *employer's* instructions, etc. Breach of the **HSWA** is a *criminal act* and attracts criminal sanctions against convicted offenders.

On the other hand, there is also a general duty of care under *common law* which places a duty on everyone, in all situations, to take 'reasonable care' to ensure no one is injured. If they are, then civil action can lead to the awarding of compensatory damages from the convicted offender for failing to carry out this *common law* duty of care.

General Product Safety Regulations 1994 (GPSR) implemented EU Directive 92/59/EEC (Product Safety) and in practice largely supplement and extend the *Consumer Protection Act 1987*.

The main purpose of the GPSR is to ensure that *no producer shall place a product on the market unless the product is a safe product* (Regulation 7). This means that, under normal use, the product sold should provide a reasonably foreseeable high level of health and safety protection during its use, taking account of particular matters, e.g. the health and safety of children. The term 'products' includes secondhand and reconditioned goods.

The very important presumption is made in the GPSR that where products conform to UK health and safety legislation then, unless the contrary is proved, the products are safe. A product is defective if its safety is not to the standard that

generic assessment

may be reasonably effective (*case law* is awaited). Distributors (e.g. wholesalers and carriers) in the supply chain who supply products to a consumer must ensure that the GPSR is complied with, or be subject to being charged with committing a criminal offence.

generic assessment is basically an assessment carried out on one task, activity or workplace, which can apply to many others. As an example, in a large office with many workstations where the desks, chairs (suitable to take account of slight variations in staff size), computers, telephones, software, lighting, ventilation, temperature, etc., *are the same*, an assessment of one workstation may cover many other workstations or at least, the majority of an assessment may satisfy a large proportion of the assessment requirements.

genetic engineering is the manipulation of the genetic make-up of an organism to produce an (usually desired) effect. However in practice, if not carefully researched, applied and controlled, the ultimate effect may be unknown, unexpected, undesired or even disastrous.

geothermal energy is the energy available in the molten or semi-molten rocks beneath the crust of the earth. Commonly, power is generated by using the heat energy of crustal rocks; alternatively water is heated and used for commercial or domestic use. There are geothermal fields operating in Iceland, Italy, New Zealand and the USA but high cost of development and production reduces their competitive value.

goal setting (or setting of objectives) is an effective method towards providing effective health and safety management and thereby a high quality health and safety culture throughout an organisation.

According to *Successful Health and Safety Management* (**HSE**, 1993:32) all organisations need to set *achievable* health and safety goals 'for each of the following stages:

    (i)   defining, developing and maintaining the health and safety policy;
    (ii) developing and maintaining organisational arrangements;
    (iii) developing and maintaining performance standards and systems of control'.

grab sampling is where, for example, *stain detectors* (chemicals in calibrated glass tubes) are used for measuring airborne concentrations of gases and vapours (e.g. similar to the tubes packed with chemicals used by the police for breathalysing). In industrial air sampling, stain tubes are *calibrated* glass tubes packed with a chemical. Immediately before use, the seals on the tube are broken off, the tube placed in a suitable container and contaminated air drawn over the chemical in the tube through the use of a simple air pump. The chemical(s) change(s) colour in the direction of the airflow and the calibration indicates the concentration of the contaminant.

The *advantages* of grab sampling include cheapness, immediate results and ease of use. The *disadvantages* of grab sampling include some inaccuracy (indication only of presence of contaminant, with an estimate of extent of contamination), inability to measure personal exposure, no provision of a time-weighted average and the single reading which may indicate a long-term concentration. The chemical(s) in the tube may have a relatively short shelf life.

greenhouse effect is the ability of the atmosphere of the earth to be selective in its response to different types of radiation. Commonly described through reference to the operation of a greenhouse – sunlight in, heat trapped inside. Continuing the analogy, increased heat inside 'greenhouse' equates to process of *global warming*.

gross negligence may seem a misleading term, since it can be argued *negligence* is negligence. However, in usage negligence is something shown through the consequences of behaviour worse than that expected from the average person, therefore in effect there can be *degrees* of negligence, some 'worse' than others, e.g. death through manslaughter if the offender understood what could happen, but carried on, being an example of gross negligence.

Groundwater Regulations 1998 *require* the EA to use its powers under the regulations and other water pollution legislation to prevent the discharge of certain specified substances (List 1) and control pollution resulting from the discharge of List 2 substances.

groups see *workgroups*.

Guidance Notes are issued by the 'relevant authorities' to help people understand and comply with the law, through providing technical advice, best commercial or industrial practice and, to an extent, an interpretation of the law, (i.e., safe working of cranes or on scaffolds). They have no binding authority at law but those following 'Guidance Notes' will *almost* certainly be complying with the appropriate legislation; the courts will decide on compliance, if something 'goes wrong'.

See *Approved Code of Practice*.

H

HACCP see *Hazard Analysis and Critical Control Points.*

Hale and Hale model of *accident causation* introduces the dynamic element of human processing, behaviour and interaction into the processes involved and is in contrast to the somewhat static *domino theory.* Its dynamic nature means the Hale and Hale (1970) systems model of general human behaviour can be used to analyse *accidents.* It shows how failure of the 'processes described do not cope with controlling danger in the environment' (Hale and Glendon, 1985). Finally, it provides a key to understanding the process of *accident* causation – and, most importantly suggest several ways of preventing *accidents.*

See also *accident causation.*

half-life usually refers to that of radioactive materials, but not exclusively so (it can refer to the time taken for pollutants to be expelled from a biological system). For example, it describes the time taken for a *radionuclide* to lose one half of its radioactivity.

As an example, a *nuclide* with a half-life of ten years will lose 50 per cent of its original radioactivity after ten years, 50 per cent of the remaining radioactivity after a further ten years, and so on. After 30 years (frequently after passing through development into various other elements), such a substance will still contain 12.5 per cent of its original radioactivity. With some substances the time scale involved – from maximum radioactivity to nil – is immense. For example, uranium decays *over billions of years* into lead, passing through periods as *thorium* and *polonium.*

halons are synthetic organic compounds containing bromine, formerly widely used in fire extinguishers. They were found to be *extremely* destructive to the *ozone layer* (significantly more so than CFCs) and their use is now banned.

harm includes physiological (*physical injury, ill health*) and *psychological factors (i.e. stress)*, loss and damage.

harmful substances and preparations are those which, if inhaled, ingested or penetrating the skin, may involve health risks (*SWR Part II*).

hazard is something (technically, 'a condition') that has the *potential to cause harm*, e.g. tools, *machinery, work equipment, (hazardous) substance, work-station, system of work*, etc.

For example, a physical hazard with the potential to cause harm could be a flex connecting a photocopier to a power point and which lies on the floor where a tutor stands or moves. The tutor could trip over the flex, with outcomes ranging from a trip to breaking a limb (it should be noted that probably the tutor would be highly experienced in working under such conditions and is unlikely to trip, whereas students are less likely to be aware of the danger). Furthermore, because of the location of the flex (away from all main traffic/pedestrian routes) the probability of causing harm would be low – 'only' one experienced person is directly affected.

The following are widely recognised as the four major types of hazards:

(i) *Physical* e.g. *noise, vibration, temperature, radiation, fire* and *mechanical*;

(ii) *Biological*, including;
- *bacteria* e.g. *salmonella, listeria.*
- *viruses*, e.g. *hepatitis, flu*, *leptospirosis* or *Weills disease*, HIV;
- *moulds and/or fungi*, e.g. *hay*, cheese;

(iii) *Ergonomic* including:
- *anatomical* e.g. fit of machine, workstation or work method to person;
- *physiological* e.g. task lay out and/or sequence, fatigue and (sometimes) *stress*;
- *psychological* e.g. ability to learn, reactions in an emergency, *perception (of risk and/or danger)*, *stress*;

(iv) *Chemicals* including:
- *dust*, subdivided into:
  - (a) *organic* (produced from animals or plants) leading to e.g. asthma, farmers lung;
  - (b) *inorganic* (not having the characteristics of living organisms) leading to e.g. pneumoconiosis, asbestosis;
- *fumes*
- *gases*
- *vapours*
- *mists*
- *liquids*
- *solids*
- *fibres*

Hazard Analysis and Critical Control Points or HACCP is a system set out in Regulation 4(3) of the *Food Safety (General Food Hygiene) Regulations 1995* to ensure, *so far as is reasonably practicable*, that when handling, preparing and storing food, foodstuffs are *not* injurious to health. In simple terms, this means that an organisation has to have in place a *system to identify the hazards* **and** *put in place measures* to *control such hazards*.

The requirement is for the proprietor of a food business to identify any step in its activities which is *critical* to ensure food safety **and** ensure that adequate safety procedures are identified, maintained and reviewed on the following principles:

(i) analysis of potential food hazards in the food business operation;

(ii) identification of the points in those operations where food hazards may occur;

(iii) deciding which of the points identified are *critical* to ensuring food safety;

(iv) identification and implementation of effective *control* and *monitoring* procedures at those *critical points*;

(v) review of the analysis of food hazards, the critical control points and the control and monitoring procedures periodically and whenever the food business's operations change.

Hazard and Operability Study (or HAZOP) is the application of a formal, systematic, critical and extensive examination by a multi-disciplinary *team* (i.e. safety adviser, chemical engineer, mechanical engineer, production manager, works manager, etc.) of the process **and** engineering intentions of new facilities. The success of a HAZOP Study depends very much on the quality of the leader and the positive interaction, contribution and constructive attitude of the team members.

The team considers each logical unit of the plant, e.g. a pressure system with all its outlets or inlets, any electronic controls, the ergonomics of indicators, etc. The team leader questions every aspect, using e.g. 'What if . . . ?' 'What happens when . . . ?'

Usually HAZOP Studies are conducted early in the design stage, but it can be applied to existing premises, processes, plant and equipment. It has been found that a well conducted HAZOP Study eliminates 80-85 per cent of the major hazards (found) at that stage, thereby significantly reducing the level of risk in a plant *at maximum effect and at minimum cost*. A follow-up HAZOP, conducted when the detailed design is near finalisation, invariably reduces the level of risk even further.

hazard data sheet see *safety data sheets*.

hazardous properties or substances see *CHIP2, COSHH, dangerous arti-*

cle, *dangerous substances* and specific properties, for example, *carcinogenic, corrosive, harmful, highly flammable, infectious substances, mutagen* and *teratogenic.*

hazardous waste, in simple terms, is *waste* that is produced during industrial processes by human beings (e.g. *sewage*) or society generally, in such quantities that existing disposal systems cannot cope with it. **Hazardous waste** is extremely toxic (or *radioactive*) so that it threatens society or the *ecosystem*, or of such a long life that the waste can only be disposed of very slowly, or possibly not at all.

hazards, mechanical and **non-mechanical** see *mechanical hazards* and *non-mechanical hazards.*

haze are fine aerosols less than $1^{\mu m}$m in diameter produced by natural or human activities, held in suspension in the atmosphere. Individually the constituents of haze are invisible, collectively they can reduce visibility.

HAZOP Study See *Hazard and Operability Study.*

health and safety see *occupational health and safety.*

Health and Safety at Work etc. Act 1974: if any 'piece' of UK health and safety legislation can be described as being key legislation, the **HSWA** is 'it'. The **HSWA** applies to everyone at work **and** those who may be affected by the activities of those at work. Breaches of Sections 2-6 attract the highest **penalties.**

The following is a selective summary of Part 1 of the **HSWA**. Many words or phrases in the section summary have supplementary legislation offering updated and more detailed cover. A word of warning, very simply there have been many amendments and revisions or repeals to the original **HSWA** as enacted which are *not* shown in the current publication of the **Act**, e.g. s5 and s6 (briefly, due to Parliamentary practice). Contemporary texts such as *Encyclopaedia of Health and Safety at Work: Law and Practice* (Gee Publications, London) or Beatson C. (Exec. Ed.) *Health and Safety Competent Person's Handbook* (Gee Publications, London) both loose-leaf and regularly updated, should be consulted for in-depth review of the current situation and up-to-date legislation.

DUTIES OF EMPLOYERS *so far as is reasonably practicable.*

s.2   Duty of *employer to employees*

General *duty of care, so far as is reasonably practicable.* Ensure health, safety

Health and Safety at Work etc. Act 1974

and welfare at work (e.g., safe *plant, systems of work, articles* and *substances, access, egress* (exit), *information, training, supervision, work environment, safety policy, consult* with *safety representatives*).

s.3   Duty of *employer* to non-*employees* (*so far as is reasonably practicable*)

Ensure safety of work activities.

s.9   No charge to *employees* for requirements provided under statute

No charge should be 'levied' by *employers* for anything required *under relevant statutory provisions* (*Associated Dairies v Harley 1979*).

DUTIES OF OCCUPIERS *so far as is reasonably practicable*

s.4   Duty of occupiers to non-*employees*

Ensure safety of premises, *access, egress*, plant and substances to all non-*employees* (including visitors).

DUTIES OF PERSONS IN CONTROL OF PREMISES

s.5   Control of noxious or offensive substances

Persons in control of premises must prevent, by 'best practicable means', noxious or harmful substances emitted into air and render harmless and inoffensive such substances emitted.

The whole of **HSWA** s.5 was repealed by Sch.16 of the **EPA 1990** but its intentions and requirements are still covered, often far more stringently, by other updated legislation, e.g. see **Environment Act 1995** and various other emission **Regulations**).

DUTIES OF MANUFACTURERS etc. *so far as is reasonably practicable*

s.6   Duty of manufacturers and suppliers to users of articles and substances

Design/construct/install/supply (and provide information) to ensure health and safety prior to purchase, when used and when maintained.

Section 6 was amended (and actually completely replaced) to comply with EU requirements in 1987. See **Consumer Protection Act 1987, hire, producer,** *product liability, supply, Supply of Machinery (Safety) Regulations 1992* and amendments.

DUTIES OF EMPLOYEES *so far as is reasonably practicable*

s.7(a)   Take reasonable care of self and others.

s.7(b)   Co-operate with *employers* and others.

s.8   Not to misuse anything provided for safety.

DUTIES OF INDIVIDUALS (EMPLOYEES, MANAGERS, SUPERVI-SORS AND BOARDS OF DIRECTORS) *so far as is reasonably practicable*

s.36   Any persons who through their act or default causes an offence to be committed by another person, commits an offence themselves (Iindividual or *body corporate*).

s.37   The board of directors, individual functional managers, and senior managers may be individually liable for breaches of law and can be prosecuted if offence is found to be committed with consent or connivance of, or attributable by neglect to, any of these individuals.

s.40   Prosecutor has to prove only (i) breach of *Regulations* took place (ii) accused was responsible for the breach. Defences: the defendant has to satisfy the court that what he/she did was practicable, *so far as is reasonably practicable*, or to do what was required was not practicable or, not *reasonably practicable*, or the best practicable means was used to discharge duty.

DUTIES OF SELF-EMPLOYED *so far as is reasonably practicable*

s.3   Ensure safety of self and others affected by work activities **PLUS all other appropriate sections.**

See also *enforcing authorities, penalties* and the various *Regulations.*

Health and Safety at Work etc. Act 1974 (Application to Environmentally Hazardous Substances) Regulations 1996, in summary, lists certain *environmentally* hazardous substances, including those rated as *dangerous goods.*

Health and Safety Books is the (correct) name for what is part of the *Health*

Health and Safety Commission or HSC

and Safety Publications. They are the source of all **HSE** free leaflets and consultative documents, aside from other publications, at PO Box 1999, Sudbury, Suffolk CO19 6FS. Tel: 01787 881165.

Health and Safety Commission or HSC is a tripartite body corporate, established by section 10 of the **HSWA**. It is a *quasi-independent* body, comprising of a Chairperson and six to nine other members.

The functions of the HSC include:

- assisting and encouraging persons concerned with matters within Part 1 of the **HSWA**;
- making appropriate arrangements for research, publication of the results of the research and provision of **training** and information in connection with these purposes, including research and **training** by others;
- keeping advised and informed as it considers appropriate, government departments, **employers** and **employees**, on matters relating to these purposes;
- submitting proposals for **Regulations** to the appropriate authority;
- replacing and updating existing law and **Regulations** and preparing approved codes of practice.

The *Health and Safety Executive* **(HSE)** is the Executive arm of the HSC, some of whose functions are delegated to the **HSE**, including that of conducting many of the public inquiries into 'disasters' at work or those associated with work.

Health and Safety (Consultation with Employees) Regulations 1996 or HSCER

covers those workplaces where trade unions are not recognised (i.e. non-union workplaces). They broadly follow and offer somewhat similar protection to non-union members who are *elected representatives* as the *Safety Representatives and Safety Representatives Regulations 1977 (as amended)* offer to trade union appointed *Safety Representatives.*

Employers have the choice between consulting on a regular basis *directly* with their *employees* or through *elected representatives* (chosen and elected by *employees* and *not* by an *employer*) on matters which may substantially affect their health and safety. *Employees* **must** be involved in the planning, organisation and provision of health and safety *training*, be provided with *adequate and suitable information* on the health and safety consequences of the existing, and introduction of new, technologies. *Employers* must keep and provide to *employees* records of *injury causing* **accidents**, dangerous occurrences and specified diseases.

Health and Safety (Display Screen Equipment) Regulations

If *employers* choose to have Elected Representatives (ER), the ER must be nominated from the workforce in the workplace where the representative will serve, and effectively the ER has the same rights and privileges as the SR possesses under the **SRSCR**, e.g. time off with pay for health and safety *training*, rights of consultation with enforcement officers (i.e. **HSE** Inspectors), making representations to *employers* on potential hazards and general health and safety matters on behalf of *employees*.

The *Health and Safety (Consultation with Employees) Regulations 1996* amended Regulation 3 of the SRSCR, 'so that recognised trade unions can now appoint safety representatives to represent *employees* working at coal mines' (Reg. 3 – Guidance note 5). This amendment does *not* affect the *Mines and Quarries Act 1954* provision for the appointment of workers' inspectors; the authorities presume that agreement will be achieved between the parties concerned.

Health and Safety (Display Screen Equipment) Regulations 1992

or **HSDSER** cover most types of display screen equipment, except e.g. equipment in drivers' cabs; window typewriters; equipment intended mainly for public use. Important definitions within the HSDSER include:

Display screen equipment is any alphanumeric or graphic display screen regardless of the display process involved, but excludes screens for which the main use is to show television or film pictures.

Operators are self-employed persons, *including* contractors and self-employed temps.

Use means use for or in connection with work.

Users are those persons employed by the *employer*, including agency employed temps, who 'habitually use display screen equipment as a significant part of (their) normal work'. **NB** There is no case law decision established as to how long is a 'significant part', therefore it is open to interpretation and negotiation. **NB** *Employees* defined as 'users' are protected by the Regulations, whether they are 'required to work at their own *employer's* workstation, at a workstation at home, or another *employer's* workstation'.

Workstation, according to DSE Reg. 2(e) is an assembly comprising:

(i)   display screen equipment (whether provided with software determining the interface between the equipment and its operator or user, a keyboard or any other input device;

(ii) any optional accessories to the display screen equipment;

(iii) any disk drive, telephone, modem, printer, document holder, work chair, work desk, work surface or any other item peripheral to the display screen equipment; and

(iv) the immediate work environment around the display screen equipment.

A selective summarised review of the DSER principal requirements follows:

Assessment/analysis of workstations to assess and reduce risks (Reg. 2). Every *employer* must carry out 'suitable and sufficient analysis of workstations' to assess risks to which *employees* are exposed. The assessment is largely (but not solely) ergonomically biased and includes consideration of the VDU, seating, lighting, ventilation, software and identifying if there are, or are likely to be, physical (musculoskeletal), fatigue or stress problems. If a significant change in a workstation has occurred or the assessment is suspected to be no longer valid, then a review assessment is required. 'Significant change' includes major change in software, hardware, furniture, increase in time spent at DSE, relocation of workstation, modification in lighting and any *increase in task requirement*.

Daily work routine for users (Reg. 4) must be planned by an *employer* to ensure breaks or changes of activity be included in normal working time, and taken away from the screen. Ten-minute breaks every hour is considered healthier than 20 minutes every 2 hours.

Eyes and eyesight (Reg. 5). *Employers* **must** provide, at *employer's* expense, eyesight tests to 'users' or potential users *who request it*. If the test finds that due to their occupation, users require special corrective appliances, then the *employer* shall pay for and arrange for the provision of appliances at a cost suitable to correct the deficiency and prevent deterioration of sight. The tests should be repeated at regular intervals. This regulation does *not* apply to non-*employees*.

Home use of computers on company business/work. If a person, who is a user, is supplied by the *employer* with a computer, other than a lap-top (unless in prolonged use), for work at home for the *employer*, then strictly speaking the home workstation is within the *employer's* legislative duties under the DSER and, opinion states, other relevant legislation.

Provision of information (Reg. 7). Everyone who operates or uses DSE in a workstation must be provided with adequate health and safety information relating to such workstations. For example, those who use the equipment and workstation must be involved in the analysis and informed of the results.

Requirements for workstations (Reg. 3). Among those items specifically mentioned in the DSER are software, which is *also* covered by BS 7179 and other standards.

Training (Reg. 6). *Employers* have a duty to provide adequate health and safety training to users and to those who are about to become users. In short, all users must receive adequate health and safety training, with additional training following any substantial modification to the work or workplace.

Review analysis. The whole analysis (assessment) or part of the analysis must be reviewed should any change take place within the workstation.

Risks to the health and safety of *employees* must be reduced to the lowest reasonably practical level.

The basic legal requirements for a DSER assessment are listed in a schedule to the regulations. They form a useful checklist not only for assessing workstations but, slightly adapted, they provide a useful pro-forma for assessments generally and are therefore displayed in the *risk assessment* entry.

Health and Safety (Enforcing Authority) Regulations 1998 came into effect 1 April 1998. They revoke and re-enact (with amendments) the 1989 Regulations. An objective of the 1998 Regulations is to reduce dual inspection in small businesses.

Local authorities are identified as the enforcing authority (Reg. 3) for the activities listed in Schedule 1 of the Regulations, including:

- arts, entertainment, games, sports, games or cultural or recreational activities, their practice or presentation;
- catering services;
- childcare, playgroup or nursery facilities and their provision;
- consumer services that are shop-based (excepting dry-cleaning or radio and TV equipment *repairs*);
- garden centres (*not* agricultural activities);
- pre-school childcare (except when in *domestic premises*);
- retail or wholesale storage premises *which are part of a transport undertaking*;
- residential accommodation *provision*.

The *Health and Safety Executive* is identified as the enforcing authority (Reg. 3) for activities listed in Schedule 2 of the Regulations, including:

Health and Safety Executive (or HSE)

- agricultural (*not* horticultural activities in garden centres);
- electrical installations;
- fairgrounds;
- gas installations;
- mines or quarries.

Health and Safety Executive (or HSE): the Executive consists of three full-time members who are appointed by the HSC, with the approval of the Secretary of State (HSC 1992). It is the Health and Safety Executive and its staff who carry out the functions of the HSC, including inspection and enforcement of statutory provisions such as health and safety legislation. However, the HSE is only one of the authorities with the responsibility of enforcing the 'relevant statutory provisions' with, generally speaking, *all* inspecting and enforcing Inspectors having the same powers.

Inspectors operate in an administrative sectionalised or compartmental manner, with inspectors tending to specialise in different industries or sectors, e.g. education, factories etc. Local authority (LA) inspectors also carry out inspections in a wide range of undertakings or parts of undertakings, including Residential Care and Nursing Homes.

An important function of the HSE is to arrange and carry out enforcement. The appropriate *Secretary of State* may, by regulation, transfer enforcement responsibilities from the HSE to other enforcement authorities or vice versa (HSWA Section 18). HSE general functions include:

- appoint HSE inspectors and indemnify inspectors for honest mistakes.
- enforce duties provided under the **HSWA** and other health and safety legislation;
- carry out certain functions or duties on behalf of the **HSC**, aside from inspection and enforcement, such as health and safety research, education of persons, publicity concerning health and safety at work;
- publish guidance notes and advisory literature.

Health and Safety Executive Books (Tel: 01787 881165) see HSE Publications.

Health and Safety Executive Information Centre (Tel: 0541 881165) see *HSE Information Centre and Public Enquiry Point.*

Health and Safety (First Aid) Regulations 1981 (or First Aid Regs)

with 1997 ACOP lay down three general requirements:

Firstly, *employers* **must** carry out an assessment, conducted by an internal occupational health service (or occupational health advisor) to establish first-aid needs, taking account of the special factors related to the organisation (Para. 4 **ACOP**). The first-aid assessment is **in addition** to the duty to carry out the risk assessments demanded by·the *Management of Health and Safety at Work Regulations 1999* (*as amended*) Reg. 3).

Secondly, *employers* **must** provide, or make sure that it is provided, such equipment or facilities as necessary to ensure first aid is rendered to *employees* who are injured at work *or become ill* **at work.**

Thirdly, *employers* shall provide or ensure such number of suitable persons (i.e. having undergone HSE approved training, which must be updated/ renewed regularly) as is 'adequate and appropriate' in the circumstances for rendering first aid to persons who have become injured *or ill* **at work.** During absences of the *first aider*, e.g. holidays, another person must be appointed as cover. The explanation of key terms is found in the ACOP.

An important point about the First Aid Regulations is that they are very flexible, allowing the *employer* to take account of the degree of risk in the workplace/organisation and the *employer* to decide what provision to make, subject to the usual penalties if an enforcement officer or court decides otherwise. The 'equipment' and 'facilities' required are also dependent on risk. For example, a foundry (high risk) may require a 1 – 10 ratio of 'suitable persons' to *employees*; a relatively low risk library may require a ratio of 1 – 50. 'Suitable persons' can be HSE approved trained and certificated *first aiders* or '*appointed persons*' who have undergone suitable training, which need not be at as high a level as *first aiders*.

An appointed person must be provided by *employers* to take charge of emergencies (i.e. telephone for an ambulance) in the event of a strictly temporary short-term absence of the *first aider*. The appointed person is **not** an *alternative* to a *first aider*. A *first aider* should be provided **at all times** when *employees* are at work, with very few exceptions, such as in low hazard situations or if there are a very low number of *employees* when exceptionally an appointed person may be considered 'adequate or appropriate'. *Employees* **must** be informed of the names of the *first aiders*, appointed person and location and details of first aid equipment. Such information must also be included in the **Health and Safety Policy Document** organisation and arrangements (**HSWA** 2(3)).

Health and Safety Information for Employees Regulations

An *employer* is responsible for providing 'adequate and suitable' first aid cover for their *employees* working away from base. Where *employees* from two different companies are working on the same site, then a mutual agreement **in writing** can be drawn up concerning first aid provision, with each *employer* keeping a copy. There is a duty to ensure that provision meets the statutory requirements.

Where 400 or more persons are employed, or special hazards are present, or on construction sites with 250 or more employed, or when access to hospital-based casualty or emergency centres is difficult (through distance or other factors), then the *employer generally* should provide a suitably equipped and staffed first aid room. Furthermore, on construction sites where 250 or more persons are employed (including self-employed and subcontractors) a vehicle capable of carrying stretchers should be made available during working hours.

Access to the first aid room should be available whenever persons are at work, with the room suitably and adequately equipped and cleaned each working day. The room should be suitably signed and identified, together with a list, location and times of availability of first aiders and appointed persons affixed on the entrance door. The required contents of first aid rooms are listed in the ACOP and include such items as a sink with running water, drinking water, a list of dressings and bandages, couch, pillows and blankets (regularly cleaned), etc.

The **HSE** *free* publications INDG 214 *First aid at work: Your questions answered* and INDG 215 *Basic advice on first aid at work* are very useful and obtainable from **HSE Books**.

Health and Safety Information for Employees Regulations 1989
(as amended) require *employers* to display *approved* posters or *approved* leaflets providing essential health, safety *and welfare* information. For further mandatory requirements, especially that for health and safety information to be comprehensible to **all** *employees*, see the *Management of Health and Safety at Work Regulations 1999*.

Health and Safety Information for Employees (Modification and Appeals) Regulations 1995
repealed the requirement for abstracts of the *Factories Act 1961*, copies of exemption certificates (s. 46(9) *Office Shops and Railway Premises Act 1963*) and conditions of licence (*Petroleum (Consolidation) Act 1928*) to be displayed.

health and safety law in the UK **must not** be considered in isolation, but as part of the wider UK legal system, within a European Union legal structure. For example and as examples only, legislation 'from' Social Security covers much of the *accident reporting* procedures, and product liability, insurance and contract law is also involved in, or concerned with, health and safety. Internal to the UK, there are differences in the application of health and safety law (and the courts) between England and Wales, Scotland, the Isle of Man and Northern Ireland. More particularly, differences between legal systems of different countries sometimes lead to a total lack of understanding regarding transnational health, safety and environmental law and application. This dictionary concentrates on health and safety in England and Wales in the context of the European Union decisions and Directives, unless specifically identified.

health and safety management see *safety management*.

health and safety policy document is required, in writing, by all companies where five or more persons are employed. Where four or fewer persons are employed, a verbal health and safety policy statement may be required (e.g., where a single self-employed contractor tenders for work from a local authority).

The policy document consists of three parts:

(i)   general policy statement or *Statement of Intent*;
(ii)   *organisation* (in force for carrying out the policy);
(iii) *arrangements* (in force for carrying out the policy).

Aside from identifying those responsible for various aspects of health and safety within the company (e.g. organisation or who is 'in charge' of first aid) the document also details the arrangements for emergencies (e.g. for first aid).

The policy must involve all staff (*employees*) in establishing a positive health and safety *culture*, *management leading* with all *employees encouraged to co-operate* and in *ensuring all relevant legal requirements are complied with*. *Monitoring, reviewing* and *auditing* the policy document (and its implementation) are carried out by the *employer*, in *consultation with staff*.

See also *planning*.

Health and Safety (Safety Signs and Signals) Regulations 1996
are concerned with the duties of employers regarding safety signs and signals; they identify types of signs, the interchanging and combining of signs and signals.

The mandatory risk assessment will indicate where, after installing appropriate control measures and following work redesign, safety signs or signals are necessary. The signs must comply with the statutory requirements and be coloured as detailed:

- red = prohibition, danger or fire equipment;
- green = emergency escape, first aid or 'no danger';
- blue = mandatory sign, e.g. **must** do or **must** wear;
- yellow = warning sign, e.g. 'take care' or 'beware'.

Safety signs can be *permanent* (usually those demanded by statute) or *occasional* (e.g. 'beware: slippery floor'). Signs are largely pictorial, with minimal essential writing added.

health and safety standards are set by various relevant legislation, frequently established, interpreted and/or clarified by case law. As Denning L.J. stated in *Qualcast Ltd v Haynes [1959] AER 38*, 'The standard goes up as men become wiser. It does not stand still as the law sometimes does.'

Health and Safety (Training for Employment) Regulations 1990

extend the cover of the HSWA to trainees, such as those on work experience. This excludes those undergoing training in an institution of education or training under a contract of employment. In the latter case the trainee is essentially an *employee* and covered by general health and safety legislation.

hearing see *human hearing*.

hearing loss see *noise induced hearing loss* and *presbycusis*.

heat is a physical hazard, which can lead to impaired performance, an increased risk of accidents and/or heat induced illness. For example, the central nervous system may shut down the ability to sweat leading to loss of evaporative cooling and, if preventative action is not taken, death through heat stroke rapidly occurs. Preventative measures to reduce heat and its effects include *ventilation,* appropriate clothing, *suitable and adequate training*, provision of cooled rest areas and air dehumidifying.

Heinrich, H.W., was one of the 'founding fathers' of the scientific approach to health and safety. In 1931 he published his seminal work in the USA, *Industrial Accident Prevention*, which became the blueprint for modern safety programmes, suggesting the primary causes of accidents were *unsafe acts* (NOT just due to carelessness, but possibly lack of knowledge or training) and *unsafe conditions*, which could include those due to unexpected natural disasters (e.g. typhoon) or preventative human deficiencies (e.g. poor design). Heinrich was also responsible for developing the *domino theory*, an important model still used in accident prevention.

hepatitis is of various types, often *acute*, in which the liver becomes inflamed, often due to viruses. Examples include *acute toxic hepatitis* (e.g. affecting solvent workers); *acute cholestatic hepatitis* (e.g. affecting epoxy resin workers) and *acute viral hepatitis type B* (e.g. affecting some health care workers). Viral hepatitis is a *prescribed disease* and reportable under RIDDOR.

hertz is commonly referred to as *Hz* and is a measurement associated with *sound*. In simple terms, sound is detected by a human being following the reception of electrical pulses in the brain, created by variations in air pressure caused by vibration. The repeating pressure variations provide the *frequency*, given in units of cycles per second (called the *Hertz*).

hierarchy of control measures depend on what is being controlled. For *hazardous substances* the hierarchy of control measures would be covered by *ERICPD*. *Machinery* would require the following hierarchy:

(i)   fixed guards;
(ii)   other guards or protective devices, e.g. mechanical, trip, pressure mats, etc.;
(iii)   protection appliances, e.g. jigs, push-sticks;
(iv)   provision of *information, instruction, training* and *supervision.*

High Court of Justice is part of the *Supreme Court of England and Wales*, created by the *Judicature Acts 1873–1875*. It has unlimited civil jurisdiction, with appellate jurisdiction in both civil and criminal matters. It is divided into three Divisions, the *Queen's Bench, Chancery* and the *Family*. Usually High Court work utilises one *Judge*, sitting alone either at the Royal Courts of Justice in London or at 26 first tier *Crown Court* centres outside London.

highly flammable, according to the *Special Waste Regulations 1996,* means:

(a)   liquid substances and preparations having a *flashpoint* below 21°C; or
(b)   substances and preparations which may become hot and finally catch fire in contact with air at ambient temperature *without* any application of energy; or
(c)   solid substances and preparations which may readily catch fire after brief contact with a source of ignition and which continue to burn or to be consumed after removal of the source of ignition; or
(d)   gaseous substances and preparations which are flammable in air at normal pressure; or
(e)   substances and preparations which, in contact with water or damp air, evolve highly flammable gases in dangerous quantities.

Highly Flammable Liquids and Liquefied Petroleum Gases

Highly Flammable Liquids and Liquefied Petroleum Gases Regulations 1972 or HFLLPGR cover those liquids, liquid solution, emulsion or suspension classified as a highly flammable liquid (with its flashpoint determined by a method approved by the HSE), supporting combustion in accordance with Schedule 2 of the HFLLPGR Regulations 2(2A). It is recommended that, wherever possible or reasonably practicable, a totally enclosed piped system should be used, failing which suitable closed non-spill containers may be used (Reg. 8).

The HFLLPGR also covers any substance which would be a liquefied flammable gas at 20oC temperature and a pressure of 760 millimetres, but which is in liquid form as a result of an application of pressure or refrigeration or both (Reg. 2(2)). The cover of the HFLLPGR includes that for highly flammable liquids (HFL); liquefied petroleum gas includes commercial butane and commercial propane, or any mixture of them (Reg. 2(2)).

Build up of deposits of any HFL must be prevented, so far as is reasonably practicable, and if such deposits occur then 'effective steps' must be taken to remove the deposits immediately (Reg. 13(1).

Employees must comply with the Regulations and co-operate with their employers in carrying them out. In particular, employees must report any defect **immediately** to a responsible person (Reg.18).

Liquefied petroleum gas storage requirements are broadly similar to those for HFL, covering suitable underground reservoirs or tanks, movable storage tanks or vessels, pipelines and pumps part of an enclosed system, suitable cylinders kept in safe positions in the open air where this is *reasonably practicable*, or if not in a fire-resisting structure with the *sole purpose* of the storage of LPG and/or acetylene gas (Reg. 7(1)). LPG containers must be kept in suitable storage until required for use and empties immediately returned to storage. LPG containers *safely* connected *for* use may be kept in the workplace, even though not *in* use.

Marking of storerooms and all types of containers must be clear and bold, with signs stating *Highly Flammable* or *Flashpoint below 32°C* or *Flashpoint in the range of 22°C* (Reg. 6(1)). LPG should be boldly marked *Highly Flammable (LPG* (Reg. 7(4)).

Spills and leaks of HFL should be prevented so far as is reasonably practicable or immediately put into a suitable container, removed to a safe place, or rendered harmless (Reg. 8).

Storage must be in safe positions, e.g. suitable fixed tanks (with bund walls capable of containing 110% of the stored HFL, to allow for expansion) or closed vessels, protected against sunlight, with closed vessels held in safe positions or flame-resisting structure or, where up to 50 litres is stored, in suitable closed vessels in a suitably placed storage fire resistant cupboard or bin.

The HSE provide a range of HFL and LPG guidance; the information contained should be provided to involved *employees*, with appropriate free leaflets distributed to *employees* using HFL or LPG.

highly toxic relates to a chemical, preparation, substance, mist, fume, dust or concentration, which is lethal within prescribed limits.

highly volatile refers to a liquid that quickly forms a gas or vapour at room temperature. e.g. petroleum spirit.

homeworking: relevant health and safety legislation and policy are difficult to identify and discuss because homeworker is a general term, covering a variety of different work activities. In some cases an *employee* may be working at home without the knowledge of the *employer,* some work at home as outworkers, on a contract of employment, others are *self-employed*, finally there are many that work in what is termed the black economy. Furthermore homeworkers are often isolated, with certain activities (e.g. textiles and packing) performed by workers predominantly female and from ethnic minorities, many with low *literacy* levels and/or poor command of English. Unfortunately legislative protection and cover are only effective if they are known, understood and applied.

In summary because of the wide variation in terms and types of employment and work activities it may be difficult to establish which health and safety legislation applies or indeed who is the enforcement authority. Despite the enforcement *Regulations* the enforcement authority, for the same work activity, may differ from area to area (Grayham 1997). It is also difficult for enforcement authorities because they must be aware of the homeworker's existence, type of activity and location. Furthermore, some homeworkers do not wish to draw attention to themselves. It is a situation unlikely to improve until resource limitations are overcome – possibly following the introduction of charges for inspections, which in itself creates further problems. In the meantime, the likelihood of extensive inspections of homeworkers' premises is very low (Grayham 1987, 1995, 1997).

HSDSER see *Health and Safety (Display Screen Equipment) Regulations.*

HSE Books, PO Box 1999, Sudbury, Suffolk COP10 6PS, Tel: 01787 881165 is a source for Discussion Documents (on proposed legislation) and other publications. Staff are very helpful and courteous, as with *HSE* generally.

HSE Information Centre and Public Enquiry Point, Broad Lane, Sheffield S3 7HQ (Tel. 0541 545500 please note NOT 01541) is a most useful source of general health and safety information. The staff are exceptionally helpful and very patient, courteously steering callers to other sources when necessary.

HSE Publications see *HSE Books.*

HSWA is the acronym for the *Health and Safety at Work etc. Act 1974* (qv).

human endoparasites are parasites living inside their human host.

human factors, in specific health and safety terms, are defined in *HSE* HS(G)48 as:

> 'a range of issues including the perceptual, physical and mental capabilities of people and the interactions of individuals with their jobs and working environments, the influence of equipment and system design on human performance and, above all, the organisational characteristics which influence health and safety behaviour at work'.

However, beware of confusion. For example, if consulting health, safety and environmental literature and texts originated from or in the USA, the term human factors engineering (or human engineering) is widely found. These are not the same as (UK) human factors, but the US term for *ergonomics.* In addition, those who refer to authoritative UK psychology texts to learn more about human factors may find that little reference is made to what is often considered to be merely a 'sub-discipline' of industrial or organisational psychology.

human hearing can receive *sound* around the range of 20 to 20,000 Hz.

Human Rights Act 1998, or HRA, was not implemented until October 2000. It arguably presents UK legislation and its legal structure with its biggest challenge, even upheaval, since the introduction of common law. In summary terms, it provides the UK with a written constitution for human rights. It was deferred until the Home Secretary announced that its date of implementation was fixed for early October 2000. It will take many years for its full effects to permeate through the system, with possibly case law and health, safety and environmental law (particularly its application) likely to be affected.

human speech (or conversation) is about 300 to 3,000 *Hz*.

humidity monitoring is carried out through use of a *hygrometer* to measure the amount of humidity in the atmosphere of the workplace.

hydrogen bromide a colourless gas with an irritating odour. It is used (often in a water solution) in the manufacture of organic bromides used in photography, etching and lithographs, pharmaceuticals, textile finishing, fire retardant etc.; in the manufacture of brominated fluorocarbons for refrigeration, fire extinguishing and aerosols, etc. It is hazardous to the respiratory system, eyes and skin and toxic through inhalation, ingestion and contact. Symptoms include burns to eye and skin, irritation to the eyes, nose and throat.

hydrogen chloride (also Hydrochloric Acid), Hydrogen Cyanide, Hydrogen Fluoride, Hydrogen Peroxide, Hydrogen Selenide and Hydrogen Sulphide, are used in a wide variety of industries, processes and industrial products. They are highly toxic, hazardous through inhalation, ingestion and contact, with similar symptoms: respiratory problems, irritation to the eyes, nasal passages, skin and larynx.

hygiène et sécurité is the French term comparable with the English term *health and safety*.

Hz see *hertz*.

I

identify (*examination term*) is to select and name relevant items or parts in response to a question.

IEE Wiring Regulations, or more properly **Institute of Electrical Engineers Wiring Regulations**, currently Number 16, detail electrical precautions and wiring procedures; also termed **BS 7671**.

ignition, in technical terms, is the initiation of the process of combustion. In simpler terms, ignition includes the process of setting something alight or causing an explosion. The sources of ignition include: naked flame; chemical reaction, e.g. spontaneous combustion; electrical, e.g. arcing, overheating; hot surfaces, e.g. heating appliances; friction, unlubricated or worn machinery; static electricity, e.g. lighting, overalls, floor covering; hot work, e.g. welding, cutting, grinding.

ignition temperature is the lowest temperature at which a substance will spontaneously ignite through the heat contained in it. A *flashpoint* always has a lower value than an *ignition temperature*.

ill-health liability can apply in the case of non-*employees*. For example a person washing the clothes of another who may be employed in asbestos or lead processes, who contracts chronic ill-health associated with such processes, may succeed in a claim against the other person's *employer*, *provided* it can be proved that such ill-health could be foreseeable with a link between process and ill-health (legally termed *causa causans*).

illustrate (*examination term*) is to show what something is like, through the use of examples, perhaps supported by accurate tables, diagrams or graphs.

immediate cause (of an *accident*) is e.g. where an *employee* trips over a pallet on the floor of the workplace, the immediate cause is 'tripping over a pallet' but equally, if not more importantly, is the *root cause* (effectively, 'why was the pallet left on the floor as an obstruction?').

improvement notice is issued by enforcement officers when they consider someone or some business is not complying with relevant statutory provisions and some action should be taken. The enforcement officer, *before* issuing an improvement notice must discuss with the *duty holder what* is wrong, *why* it is wrong and by *when* the required remedial action should be completed (a minimum of 21 days). The improvement notice presents, in writing, the same points. Failure to take the necessary action could result in the offender being taken to the *magistrates' court* or exceptionally the offender prosecuted on *indictment* before the *Crown Court*.

Appeals against an improvement notice, which must be made before the specified time for action expires, are made to an *employment tribunal*. The requirements of the improvement notice are suspended until the appeal is heard. The grounds for appeal (followed by probability of success rating) may include: an inspector misinterpreted the law (low); solution proposed not practicable (success probability depends on whether *absolute liability* or *so far as is reasonably practicable* applies); degree of significance of breach (depends on circumstances).

incident rate forms part of the process of *accident statistics* and calculates the number of *reported* injuries per 100 *employees*:

$$\frac{\text{Number of injuries}}{\text{Average number employed during the period.}} \times 100$$

incidents are a sequence of events which **may** or **may not** result in an *injury, loss* or *damage*.

independent trade unions in broad terms, are those on the register of trade unions and are identified as not operating under the aegis of an *employer* or company (the latter are often termed 'sweetheart unions').

individual differences, in broad terms, identify the differences between individuals and are dealt with under three main headings: physique, intelligence and personality. Physique covers the attributes of the body, size, shape, speed, movement, the efficiency or otherwise of its senses; intelligence is the sum of the functions of understanding, learning, observing, problem solving and *perception*; personality can be defined as the total of all the various qualities that are shown in behaviour.

induction, electromagnetic see *electromagnetic induction*.

industrial health and safety see *occupational health and safety*.

industrial hygiene, in basic terms, is the science of recognising, evaluation and control of harmful substances, physical and biological agents in the work environment. In its fullest sense, it includes consideration of human and other factors which may lead to loss, damage, injury or disease, including stressors.

industrial hygienist is a qualified, trained professional who practices *industrial hygiene*.

industrial injuries are injuries that (a) have 'arisen out of and during the course of insured *employment'*, and (b) can be proven to have occurred during *employment* and in connection with an incident recorded as an *industrial accident*, irrespective as to whether or not sick absence is involved (see **BI 95** and **BI 76**). All *industrial injuries* and ill health must be entered in the *accident book* and may or may not be reportable under **RIDDOR**.

industrial injury benefits, paid to those who become disabled as a result of an *accident* at work or as the result of industrial disease, include *industrial injuries* disablement pension, attendance allowance and exceptionally severe disablement allowance, with in certain circumstances, disability working allowance. 'Disabled' has quite a wide meaning, e.g. it may include scars on the face or hands. *Even if the successful claimant returns to work, industrial injury benefit may still be paid.* It is paid on a percentage basis, i.e. in relation to the extent of the disablement compared with a person who is 100 per cent fit.

An industrially injured person may be entitled to additional benefits. The potential claimant must consider carefully *Benefits Agency* leaflets **NI 2**, NI 6, FB2 *Which Benefit*, obtainable from the local *Benefits Agency*, Post Offices, Job Centres and Citizen Advice Centres. Potential claimants are strongly recommended to obtain advice from an *industrial injury benefits specialist professional* (e.g. *Citizens Advice Bureaux or Local Law Centres*) BEFORE *completing and making any application* to the *Benefits Agency* (see **BI 95** and *Declaration of Industrial Accident*).

Industrial Tribunals since 1998 **no longer exist** under that name which was changed to *Employment Tribunals* (s.1 *Employment Rights (Disputes Resolution) Act 1998*) although the term Industrial Tribunal is still in common use.

Industrial Tribunals Act 1996 is changed to the *Employment Tribunals Act 1996* by s.1 *Employment Rights (Dispute Resolution) Act 1998.* The original Act established *Tribunals* and *Employment Appeal Tribunals* which still exist.

infectious substances contain viable micro-organisms or their toxins which are known, or reliably believed, to cause disease in humans or other living organisms.

information is knowledge (e.g. about risks to health, safety and the environment) and hence is a form of power, passed on to another person, with feedback received to ensure the information has been received and understood.

information sources, for health, safety and environmental matters, aside from personal networks, are built up by each individual over the years. The huge number available via the *internet* and the *world wide web* (*www*), include the following:

Official

- *Acts** and *Statutory Instruments* (e.g. *Regulations* and *Orders*)
- *Approved Code of Practice(s)*
- British Standards
- British Standards Institute publications
- Environment Agency
- Government bodies, e.g. Health and Safety Executive
- *Guidance Notes*
- Local authorities, e.g. Environmental Health;
- Office of National Statistics.

Authoritative sources (but see caveat below)

- Authoritative textbooks, e.g. GEE Publications
- Institutes of learning, e.g. Universities
- Professional bodies, e.g. *Institution of Occupational Health and Safety, Royal Society of the Prevention of Accidents (RoSPA), British Safety Council*
- Research institutions
- The Stationery Office publications.

Reliable sources

- Chambers of Trade and Commerce
- *Employers* associations, e.g. **Engineering** *Employers* **Federation, National Farmers Union**
- Industry Codes of Practice
- Industry Guidance Notes
- Manufacturers, e.g. data, *instruction* and information sheets;
- Reference libraries, e.g. local authority main libraries, university libraries, local law societies, public, hospitals
- Trade Associations
- Trades Union Congress
- Trades Union National and Regional Headquarters.

Informal sources

- Networks of professional colleagues and friends
- Non-professional magazine and newspaper reports.

ingestion

It will be noted that many of the information sources utilise reference to authoritative textbooks. Everyone involved with *health, safety and environmental management* should have an extensive reference library, if only to keep up-to-date. This raises the question of *understanding* and while there are many sources for health, safety and environmental information, obtaining unbiased, up-to-date, accurate, valid, reliable, *understandable* information can be difficult.

ingestion is the process of taking substances into the body by the mouth, which can lead to it being distributed throughout the body via the gastrointestinal tract and the blood, ultimately reaching vital target organs.

inhalable dust is that which can enter via the nose and mouth and is deposited in the respiratory tract (**COSHH** Reg. 2(1)).

inhalation is the process of breathing in a substance as a gas, vapour, fume, mist or dust, possibly causing lung disease. Toxins can pass through the lungs into the bloodstream ultimately reaching vital target organs.

inorganic: materials or substances (e.g. dusts) that are *mineral* and not *organic*. When inorganic dust is inhaled it can cause abnormal conditions of the lungs, e.g. anthrocosis, *asbestosis*, pneumoconiosis and silicosis.

insecticides are natural or synthetic chemicals used to kill insects. Natural insecticides, although relatively expensive to produce, *do not* persist in the environment, *do not* accumulate in organisms, *have low to moderate* toxicity for humans and other animals. Synthetic insecticides are frequently (but not always) relatively less expensive to produce but many have cumulative and sometimes long-lasting toxic effects (which may take some time to recognise).

As examples, organophosphates have a low persistence, do not accumulate in the environment but are highly toxic to humans and account for most of the deaths arising from insecticide poisoning; *carbamates* are stated to be the least dangerous of the synthetic insecticides, highly toxic to fish and deadly to honey bees.

inspectorate see *enforcement officers*.

Institution of Occupational Safety and Health (IOSH) is the largest of the associations in the UK for safety professionals with, at June 1997, some 20,000 members of all grades. IOSH can trace its ancestry back to 1916 under a variety of names or titles. The present title was adopted in 1980.

IOSH is highly influential in *occupational health and safety* and is particularly concerned in advancing levels of professional standards. Its address is: The Grange, Highfield Drive, Wigston, Leics. LE18 1NN (Tel: 0116 257 3100).

instruction is providing *information* in the form of an order or a direction, i.e. usually more specific and directed than with the provision of general information.

See also *adequate and suitable, information* and *training*.

Integrated Pollution Control (or *IPC*) was established by the *Environmental Protection Act 1990* s.4(2) to prevent or minimise pollution of the environment from potentially high polluting or technologically complex industrial Part A processes due to the release of such substances into the air, water or land. There are extensive changes being made and introduced piecemeal to IPC to comply with the Directive 96/61/EC *Integrated Pollution Prevention and Control*.

Integrated Pollution Prevention and Control EC Directive 96/61/EC (IPPC Directive) has the purpose of the integrated prevention and control of pollution from certain types of industrial installation, which will require a permit. The IPPC applies to manufacture, energy production, waste management and *some* forms of intensive animal farming. It will be fully implemented by the end of October 2007.

International Electrotechnical Commission, founded in 1906, is concerned with establishing international standards for electrical and electronic equipment. Its headquarters are at 389 Chiswick High Road, London W4 4AL.

International Labour Organisation, most frequently referred to as the **ILO,** is an international organisation, created in 1919 and now part of the United Nations, and is heavily involved with promoting an improvement in working (and living) conditions around the world. Britain is a signatory to the ILO convention, contributing economically and with personnel to ILO activity.

In real terms the ILO proves very effective, particularly with regard to providing initiatives in less developed countries. In addition, its publications on various labour topics, including health and safety, are useful texts providing achievable objectives for many countries.

International Organisation for Standardisation (ISO), as its name indicates, is a body which encourages worldwide standards. Founded in 1947, its headquarters are in Geneva, Switzerland. The **British Standards Institute** is a member of **ISO**.

International Register of Certified Auditors has a large number of certified auditors who specialise in environmental management.

internet provides a highway to many international sites and sources, e.g. for health, safety and environmental information, publications and legislation via the *world wide web*. Created in 1983, the internet connects computer systems world wide using a common addressing system. Where possible or available internet addresses are included in dictionary entries.

interpret (*examination term*) is to explain what something means using one's own judgement, supported by authoritative evidence.

ion is an atom or group of atoms that has become electrically charged through picking up (negative charge) or losing (positive charge) electrons.

ionising radiation can cause the material or body through which it passes to become ionised which can result in chemical changes and lead to alterations in living cells. The radiations that have this effect are either fast moving particles (for example electrons and protons) or electromagnetic rays, such as X-rays. The biological effects of radiation are not fully understood, although they are accepted to be broadly similar within living tissue. However, the *distribution of damage* throughout the body can vary significantly, depending on type, energy and penetrating power of the radiation involved. Control measures include shielding by enclosure; segregation by distance, e.g. remote handling; reduction of exposure time, e.g. rotation of workers; personal protective equipment, e.g. full suit/respirator; health surveillance; monitoring (and review); specific *training* and certification.

Ionising Radiations Regulations 1985 or **IRR 85** set out the basic safety standards for the health protection of the general public against the danger of ionising radiation arising from a work activity. In summary, according to **HSE** IND(G)96L(Rev) 8/94 the *Regulations* 'apply to all work activities with radioactive materials, including transport. The main provisions relevant to transport are those relating to driver *training* and the need under certain circumstances to prepare contingency plans for emergencies and enforced stoppages'. The Regulations incorporate three general principles of radiation protection:

(i)   exposure to ionising radiation must be justified by the advantages it produces;

(ii)   exposure must be kept as low as reasonably practicable;

(iii)   the sum dose received must not exceed certain specified limits.

The *Regulations*, which are in nine parts, contain 41 *Regulations* and ten schedules and are part of a three-tier regulatory framework including an *Approved Code of Practice (ACOP)* and *Guidance Notes*. The main requirements are:

Controlled or supervised areas must be set up where certain criteria, described in schedule 6, are met. If there is a likelihood of a person receiving a dose more than three-tenths of the annual dose limit the area must be designated a **controlled area**. If there is a likelihood of receiving a dose more than one-tenth of the annual limit the area must be designated a **supervised area**. Persons entering controlled areas must either be **classified persons** or have a **written system of work**.

Designate as classified persons any employee aged 18 or over likely to receive a dose of ionising radiation greater than 30 per cent of any relevant dose limit. Such persons must have an assessment of radiation received, preferably through use of personal dosimeters.

Dose limits are set for various categories of people, trainees, women of reproductive capacity, workers and members of the public. See schedule 1 of the *Regulations*.

Dosimetry services approved by the **HSE** are required for the regular assessment and recording of doses received by classified workers. Records of doses received must be made and kept for each person.

Health records must be kept of *classified persons* and *employees* who have been over-exposed to ionising radiation. Summary copies of records must be sent to the **HSE** within three months of the end of each calendar year (or agreed period), and originals kept for at least **50** years.

Manufacturers, designers, importers, suppliers, erectors and installers must ensure that equipment, devices and articles supplied for use provide optimum radiation protection and can be used in a way that keeps doses to as low as reasonably practicable.

Maximum dose limit from May 2000 is 100 mSv over a five-year period, with an average of 20 mSv per year, a maximum of 50 mSv in any one year in a five-year period. **NB** This may lead to a change in the Regulations.

Medical exposures have specialist considerations under the **Regulations**. Doses received by patients are excluded from the **Regulations**. However, doses received by patients due to other patient's exposure **are** included in the **Regulations**.

Medical surveillance must be given to classified workers by specially appointed doctors. Provision is made for a review of medical findings and for the **HSE** to require **employers** to make approved arrangements for the protection of any individual **employee**.

Monitoring radiation levels must be carried out in controlled and supervised areas. The equipment must also be tested and maintained.

Notification: with some exceptions, ionising radiation work and any significant changes in use must be notified to the **HSE**.

Personal protective equipment must comply with Regulatory requirements on dose limitation and an assessment made to determine suitability. **Only HSE** approved **respiratory protective equipment** may be used.

Radiation Protection Advisors and Supervisors, who are qualified, must be appointed where any **employees** are exposed to an instantaneous dose rate of more than 7.5 mSvh-1 (but see 'maximum dose'); they are appointed to provide expert advice and set up, apply and supervise safe working procedures.

Restrict the exposure of employees and other persons foreseeably affected, **so far as is reasonably practicable**, to ionising radiation. Engineering controls and good design features (e.g. shielding, ventilation) come before providing PPE.

Risk assessment is a requirement for all workplaces and work activities, a radiological-based assessment must also be carried out to identify the special hazards associated with the work and the **HSE** provided with a report of the assessment.

Sources of radiation must be controlled to keep doses as low as reasonably practicable. Sealed containers must be used for radioactive substances. Radioactive substances kept must be accounted for.

Training, information and instruction must be provided to workers and other persons affected by the work. This will include written systems of work or working procedures, emergency procedures, etc.

Washing and changing facilities must be provided and maintained in controlled areas.

irritants are substances and preparations which, through immediate, prolonged or repeated contact with the skin or a mucous membrane, can cause inflammation.

ISO 14000 is a series of standards concerned with the environment, ranging over the following areas:

ISO 14001 Environment management systems – Specification with guidance for use;

ISO 14004 Environmental management systems – General guidelines on principles, systems and supporting techniques;

ISO 14010 Guideline for environmental auditing – General principles;

ISO 14011 Guidelines for environmental auditing – Audit procedures: Auditing of environmental management systems;

ISO 14012 Guidelines for environmental auditing – Audit procedures: Qualification procedures for environmental auditors;

ISO 14040 Environmental management – Life cycle assessment: Principles and framework.

isolation is the separation of an area of 'infection' (e.g. hazardous substance, *noise* from machinery) from the individual(s) at work. The separation can be through the use of physical barriers or increased distance.

isophorone is a colourless or white liquid, smelling of peppermint. Its uses include: as a solvent in manufacturing vinyl resins, nitro-cellulose, herbicides; in organic synthesis in manufacturing lubricating oil additives. It is hazardous to the respiratory system and skin, being toxic by inhalation, ingestion and contact. Symptoms include narcosis, dermatitis and irritation of the eyes, nose and throat.

isopropylamine is a colourless liquid, smelling of ammonia. It becomes a gas in temperatures above 32.2C. It is used: in the synthesis of agriculture chemicals, insecticides; vulcanisation accelerators for sulphur-cured rubbers; in leather manufacture; in the purification of penicillin and streptomycin etc. It is hazardous to the respiratory system and the skin and is toxic by inhalation, absorption, ingestion and contact. Symptoms of exposure include pulmonary edema, skin and eye burns, dermatitis, irritation of the eyes, nose and throat.

itai-itai is a disease, first observed in Japan, caused by *cadmium* poisoning which is characterised by bone deterioration.

J

joule represents the work done when a force of one newton acts through one metre. In electrical energy terms it is the work done per second by a current of one ampere flowing through a resistance of one ohm.

judge in England is a state official, appointed by the Crown from experienced legal professionals (i.e. barristers and exceptionally, solicitors), with the power to adjudicate on disputes and other matters brought before the courts for decision. The Lord Chancellor provides advice concerning the appointment of English *circuit court* and **High Court** judges; the Prime Minister, regarding the appointment of judges in the **Court of Appeal** and the **Lords of Appeal in Ordinary**.

Once appointed, judges hold office during 'good behaviour' and, with the exception of the Lord Chancellor, not at the 'pleasure of the Crown'. Circuit judges can be removed by the Lord Chancellor for incapacity or misbehaviour, the remainder following a resolution from both Houses of Parliament and assented to by the ruling monarch. Judges have immunity from actions for personal damages *arising from the exercise of their judicial office.*

judicial precedent refers to the practice of judges not only giving their decisions, but also the reasons for their decisions. These become a *binding precedent* for decisions in lower courts and form a component of *common law.*

jurisdiction has several meanings which are related to context. Firstly, the power of a court to hear and decide a case or make a certain order; secondly, the territorial limits of the jurisdiction of a court, e.g. English courts have *jurisdiction* in England, Wales and Berwick on Tweed and claimed territorial waters; the area covered by the legislative competence of Parliament. Everywhere else is termed 'outside the jurisdiction'.

K

Kelvin is a SI unit of thermodynamic temperature, identical to the **Celsius** degree. However, the Kelvin scale is based on the *theoretically* lowest temperature possible (absolute zero). The range between the freezing and boiling points on the Kelvin scale is between 273 K and 373 K.

ketene is a colourless gas with a strong odour, used in the production of cellulose, vinyl acetate resins and plastics, acrylic resins, pharmaceuticals, etc. It is hazardous to the respiratory system, skin, and eyes and toxic by inhalation and contact. Symptoms include pulmonary edema, irritation of the eyes, nose, lungs and throat.

kier is a large fixed vessel used for boiling textile material, by use of boiling alkaline liquid circulated through use of steam or mechanically through a pipe, channel or duct (liquid is poured over material, seeping through it for scouring and bleaching).

There are two types of kier: one 'open', which operates at atmospheric pressure; the other 'closed', which may operate at 0.5 bar or more and is covered by the **Pressure Systems and Transportable Gas Containers Regulations 1989**. No one may work in a kier unless authorised to do so by a **competent person**, as required and described by the **Regulations** – with the use of a **permit to work** system.

kinetic energy is the energy an object possesses as a result of its motion. Kinetic energy is highly relevant for reducing the risk element in manual handling.

kinetic handling principles include using kinetic energy, e.g. balanced positioning of feet, arms and chin held in, load close to the body and, importantly, a straight back.

L

ladders, unless reasonable to do so, must **not** be used as a place of work but can be used as a means of *access* to or *egress* from a place of work. Ladders must be in a sound condition, of sufficient strength for the purpose, used in a 1-4 position (the distance of one rung out for every four rungs up), should be 'securely fixed' when over three metres in length, near to their highest resting place **or** where fixing is impracticable, footed **or** securely fixed at their base to prevent slipping. Ladders in excess of nine metres vertical length, where practicable, should be provided with sufficient safe landing or rest areas at suitable intervals. The surfaces on which ladders rest must be firm, level and stable, of sufficient strength to support the ladder and its load. Care must be taken to ensure there are no overhead dangers, with which the ladder could come into contact (e.g. power cables). The top of ladders used for *access* purposes to another level must extend sufficiently above the *access* level to provide a safe handhold, *unless* a suitable alternative is provided. (**Construction (Health, Safety and Welfare) Regulations 1996**)

A ladder is in sound condition if it has no visible flaws or breaks in its sides or 'steps'. Wooden ladders must *never* be painted, except for identification marks (painting could conceal splits or fractures). Metal ladders must not be visibly defective or used near overhead power. Ladders must be suitably maintained.

laser is the acronym for *light amplification by stimulated emission of radiation*. The radiation emitted by lasers is **non**-ionising. The laser beam is due to forcing atoms of a particular gas to emit an invisible stream of electromagnetic radiation of zero rest mass, travelling at the speed of light, the wavelengths depending on the source medium (photons or quantum). Lasers are used in surveying, welding, microsurgery, **communications** and for military purposes etc. Lasers present hazards directly or through *diffusion* to all 'parts' of the eye (i.e. retina, iris etc.) and the skin.

Preventive measures include isolation of the installation, the laser beam terminated by a non-reflective and fireproof material, special goggles (suitable for the wavelength of the laser being used), worker education and regular eye tests for users.

lead is a bluish-grey metal, with no smell. It is used in the manufacture of batteries, sheet lead (for use, e.g. in construction/roofing), paint, containers, etc. Lead pollution and exposure are found in the air, water, food or soil from domestic, industrial and commercial activity.

lead poisoning has long been recognised as a hazard, but its true extent is only recently becoming fully recognised. This under-recognition has been partly due to the fact that the symptoms of low-level lead poisoning are shared with many other ailments and the true extent of the problem remained undiagnosed. Lead poisoning includes the hazards from inhalation, ingestion or contact with lead including those to the respiratory system, reproductive system, blood, central nervous system, kidneys and the mental and physical development of children thus exposed. Symptoms include cerebrovascular disease, hypertension, weight loss, cancer, miscarriages, still births, colic, hepatic and renal effects, irritability, poor attention span, headaches, muscular spasms, memory loss, hallucinations, paralysis, coma and death. See the **Control of Lead at Work Regulations 1998**.

leader, in industrial terms and health, safety and environmental management, is derived from and based on psychological concepts and analysis. In simple terms, a leader is anyone who holds a position of authority, dominance or influence in *every* group. Importantly, a leader can be formally appointed (e.g. by an **employer**) or informally accepted as such – sometimes despite the presence of a formally appointed 'leader'. When applying health and safety in the **workplace** it is the informal leader who must be identified and taken account of, despite the fact that the term 'leader' in industry is commonly used synonymously with manager or supervisor.

leadership is an apparently simple term, relatively easy to define. Actually there are many definitions, subject to a tremendous amount of analysis, research and discussion. This is understandable when we recognise we are dealing with that most complex of creatures, the human being and entering the world of psychology (which includes **human factors**).

Nevertheless, when selecting and appointing a **manager** (leader), in all aspects of business, which includes (as part of the normal function of **management**) the design, application, implementation, monitoring and review of an effective health, safety and environmental programme, a knowledge and understanding of the many facets of **leaders** and leadership is essential.

In very basic terms, there are many 'types' and 'styles' of manager and **management**. Each 'type' or 'style' may prove effective in a particular work environment (situational models) or to carry out a particular task (functional models). They include the following:

(i) *authoritarian* leadership style is where the **leader** has absolute authority, does not consult with others, seldom if ever thanks subordinates for a job well done, in the worst examples, shouts rather than informs, frequently attempts to 'build empires', placing self interest above those of the company; often susceptible to heart attacks and severe stress. Examples are found throughout industry, but particularly (for perhaps acceptable reasons) in the military, where this style may be useful;

(ii) *bureaucratic* leadership style where the **leader's** authority comes from the official position held and may also have the attributes of any of the other types, singly or in combination;

(iii) *democratic* leadership style is one where authority comes from group consensus. The **leader** listens to and takes account of the views and opinions of all concerned, individually and collectively, a style of leadership which may lead to non-decision making and inaction;

(iv) *laissez-faire* leadership style allows **leaders** to distance themselves from their group, in effect providing a non-leadership style. The individual members of the group effectively make their own individual decisions, turning to the laissez-faire leader for advice or information. A weakness of this style is that it can lead to non-decisions and inactivity. An example where this leadership style may prove effective is in research teams.

Effective organisational occupational health and safety is dependent on a variety of factors, but it commences from the top and therefore leaders and leadership style constitute a crucial influence. A very simplified review of the salient features of leadership has been presented here. Aside from specialist books on the subject, all good management texts spend many pages on leaders and leadership.

legionella see *legionellosis.*

legionellosis is an acute bacterial disease found in two distinct forms: *Legionnaires Disease* and *Pontiac fever*. Incubation time is 2-10 days for Legionnaires disease and 5-66 hours for Pontiac fever. Persons under 20 are rarely affected and neither form is communicable from person to person. Both are caused by *legionella pneumophila*, a bacterial organism which frequently grows in the warm waters of building cooling towers. Outbreaks have also been associated with contaminated industrial water sprays, hospital showerheads, hot baths and possibly contaminated soil or air. Control measures include use of antibiotics, cleaning and disinfectant of cooling tower water and treatment of water supplies. (**Notification of Cooling Towers and Evaporative Condensers Regulations 1992**)

legionnaires disease see *legionellosis.*

Legislation (L) Series in effect are guides, sometimes at *Approved Code of*

Practice (**ACOP**) level, to various **Acts** and **Regulations**. For example, L1 is *A guide to the Health and Safety etc Act 1974*; L27 is an **ACOP**, *Control of Asbestos at Work*.

leptospirosis see *Weills disease*.

liability is an important legal term. For a person to be liable they must have (i) personally brought about a wrongful state of affairs and (ii) been in a state of mind in relation to the wrongful conduct that was reprehensible. The following are the 'types' of liability at law:

Civil liability is a legal duty, which may lead to action being taken by a person affected. Where safety **Regulations** do not specifically mention *civil liability* (i.e. are *silent*) an action may still be possible. Irrespective of any right of action at common law for negligence, there is also the possibility of civil action for damages for breach of statutory duty, commonly called the **double-barrelled action** against an **employer**, e.g. see *Kilgollan v William Cooke and Co Ltd [1956] AER 294* whereby an **employee** sued for damages *simultaneously* but *separately* on the grounds of *negligence* and *breach of a relevant statutory duty*.

Under s.47 of the **HSWA** there is an exclusion of civil liability for breach of *general* statutory duties, i.e. breach of s.2-8 of the **HSWA** and where **Regulations** made under the **HSWA** (e.g. **MHSWR**) specifically state otherwise. However, **opinion** declares that it is possible that in the event of a breach of s.2-8 of the **HSWA**, since these have been drawn from negligence rules at common law, it still may be possible to claim common law liability for negligence (see *Kilgollan v William Cooke and Co Ltd* above. See also the Woolf Report *Access to Justice* HMSO 1996).

Corporate liability is where liability for an offence is extended to companies and corporations. Lord Denning stated in the case of *Bolton Engineering Co. vs Graham & Sons (1957) 1 QB 159* 'In cases where the law requires a guilty mind as a condition of a criminal offence, the guilty mind of the directors **or managers** will render the company itself guilty.' (Emphasis added). This decision has been supported many times since.

Criminal liability is better subsumed for basic understanding in the term **criminal negligence** (qv).

Personal liability is where an offender, on conviction, is found to be *personably liable* for a criminal act or **tort**.

Product liability defines the liability of manufacturers and certain others for defective products. In short, a product is defective if its safety is not such as persons generally are entitled to expect. Liability under the CPA cannot be excluded by contract or notice. A possible defence is that the user contributed to his/her injury (or death) through failing to follow the instructions or misused the product (see *contributory negligence)*.

Strict liability is divided between the **criminal and civil law (tort)**. The term is sometimes loosely used in place of *absolute liability*. In outline, strict liability is when someone commits an act which is absolutely forbidden by law, then an offender is liable to punishment, whether or not that offender has good reason or the breach of law was intended or not (see *mens rea*). Strict liability applies in *tort*; as an example, where dangerous machinery is found on the premises without secure *guarding*, or, under certain circumstances, relating to *products liability*, the occupier can be considered to be 'strictly liable.'

Vicarious liability is that placed on one person for torts or crimes by the actions of another. For example, if a *tort* or crime (such as *a breach of statutory duty*) is committed by an *employee*, an independent contractor or an agent, during the course of **and** arising from that person's *employment*, then the liability applies, even if the person held vicariously liable (e.g., the *employer*) *is not at fault*. For example, if an employed truck driver commits a tort in the course of his/her *employment*, then the *employer* will be held vicariously liable if the driver be found guilty of the offence; whereas, should the driver physically assault the driver of another vehicle and be found guilty of the offence, then the offender is **personally liable**.

lifting equipment is defined under Reg. 2(1) Of the *Lifting Operations and Lifting Equipment Regulations 1998* as 'work equipment for lifting or lowering loads and includes its attachments used for anchoring, fixing or supporting it'.

Lifting Operations and Lifting Equipment Regulations 1998 (or LOLER) came into force December 1998, consolidating the law into ten 'goal setting' *Regulations* which (selectively) cover:

competent persons should inspect lifting equipment at suitable intervals *between* thorough examinations;

defects found during thorough examinations and inspections must be reported to *employers* and, if the defect is likely to lead or has led to a serious personal injury, reported to the enforcing authority (Reg. 10);

evidence of examinations to accompany lifting equipment used outside an undertaking (Reg. 9(4));

exception from regulation 9 (Reg. 5(1)) for winding apparatus at mines;

exposure to conditions causing deterioration of lifting equipment, which could result in dangerous situations, must be thoroughly examined: (a) for lifting persons, at least every six months; (b) accessories for lifting, every six months; (c) other lifting equipment, at least every 12 months. The examinations must be planned, and also carried out each time that exceptional circumstances have occurred, liable to jeopardise the safety of the lifting equipment;

lifting equipment, before being put into service for the *first time*, must be thoroughly examined unless the equipment has an EC *Declaration of Conformity,* which must be kept for as long as the lifting equipment is operated; or it is obtained from the undertaking of another person; and it is accompanied by physical evidence that the last thorough examination required has been carried out;

lifting person's equipment must be such as to prevent a person using it from being crushed, trapped, struck or falling from the carrier;

marking on lifting equipment and accessories must show its safe working load and special characteristics which affect its safety (Reg. 7);

organisation of lifting operations, properly planned by a *competent person,* appropriately supervised and carried out safely (Reg. 8);

positioning and installing of lifting equipment, *so far as is reasonably practicable*, to prevent the load drifting, falling freely or being released unintentionally (Reg. 6);

records to be kept of inspections and examinations (Reg. 10 and Sch. 1);

reports to be made of thorough examinations (Reg. 10 and Schedule 1);

strength and stability of lifting equipment must be suitable (Reg. 4);

safety of lifting equipment for lifting persons which depends on the installation conditions, must be thoroughly examined to ensure it has been installed correctly and is safe to operate: (a) after installation and before being put into service for the first time; (b) after assembly and before being put into service at a new location (Reg. 5).

Lifting Plant and Equipment

Lifting Plant and Equipment (Records of Test and Examination etc.) Regulations 1992 were revoked by LOLER.

lifting tackle is defined in Reg. 2(1) of the *Lifting Operations and Lifting Equipment Regulations 1998* as 'work equipment for attaching loads to machinery for lifting'. The main hazards with lifting tackle are as follows:

> **Chains:** breakage, either through manufacturing defects, caused through careless use (e.g. dragging) or unsuitable storage (e.g. not carefully hanging from suitable supports).

> **Hooks:** breakage or failure (hooks 'opening' and/or load falling off). Hooks must be fitted with safety catches.

> **Rings, shackles and swivels:** breakage or failure, through inadequate testing and/or poor maintenance.

> **Ropes:** breakage, through overloading, natural wear and tear (more likely if natural fibre, not suitably checked and/or tested), unsuitable storage (as 'chains' above). Natural fibre susceptible to attack from oils or chemicals.

light is a form of radiant energy coming from atoms violently disturbed by electricity or heat.

lighting is covered by various legislation, the *superior* taking precedent, e.g. although the *Workplace (Health Safety and Welfare) Regulations 1992* generally apply, the *Electricity at Work Regulations 1989* are *superior* for electrical equipment.

The recommended illuminance for various work activities is presented in the *HSE* Guidance Note HSG(G)38 *Lighting at Work*. In summary, light fittings must be regularly maintained, without glare, the light distributed evenly (without pools of darkness contrasting with adequately lit areas), preferably diffused to prevent uneven spread and without flicker.

liquid is an intermediate between a solid and a gas, maintaining a fixed volume but offering no resistance to a change of shape.

liquid propane gas (LPG) is a colourless, odourless gas, to which a pungent odour is frequently added, shipped as compressed liquefied gas. It is used in the manufacturer of petrochemicals, polymers and as a fuel for equipment and cars. It is hazardous to the respiratory system and central nervous system and is toxic by inhalation and contact. Symptoms include drowsiness and light-headedness.

list (examination term) is to enumerate a number of items, to place in a catalogue.

literacy of *employees* should be checked by *employers*, otherwise they (albeit without intent) may be in breach of the **MHSWR 1999** (Reg. 10; *ACOP L21* para 64)) requirement that health, safety and environmental *instruction*, information and *training* **must** be comprehensible to *employees*. Some *employers* (such as the Ford Motor Company) provide *literacy* courses, free of charge to *employees*.

A quick, useful, simple although admittedly unscientific indicator of staff *literacy* is through assessing 'reading age' (usually associated with level of education, formally **or** informally acquired) through observing which newspaper is read by an employee. The *Sun* requires a reading age of ten years old, *The Mail* 14 and *The Times* a reading age of 19 years old. Beware of those who cannot read but hide this fact by buying a newspaper, pretending to read it during breaks, but DO NOT embarrass such individuals. Many persons with poor literacy feel inadequate and respond well to and need help and assistance.

local authority is one of those terms which is commonly used but seldom defined or used correctly. In legal terms a *local authority* is a body of councillors elected by the inhabitants of a local government area. In common usage, a local authority is the name given to an administrative body, a form of government made up of several different sections and departments, run by local civil servants, ostensibly controlled by elected councillors – which is actually *local government*. In general application and usage, each reference to 'a' local authority is usually identified or located by context, e.g., in a discussion on fire the local authority may be presumed to be the Fire Service; education, the local authority is the Local Education Authority, and so on. The position is compounded by the fact that services in the same area may be controlled by local authorities (or local government) *not* located in that area, or the same occupation or task may be enforced by different agencies in different areas (e.g. *homeworkers).*

local government see *local authority.*

lone workers include those who work alone, as part of their contract, as well as those who work isolated from the remainder of a workforce. There is no general prohibition on working alone, but certain specified dangerous activities and/or environments have constraints. For example, young persons cannot work on dangerous woodworking machinery, except under supervision, until they have been fully instructed and trained; lone working is prohibited during activities using certain hazardous substances covered by **COSHH**. *Risk assessments* will identify any special risks faced by lone workers.

All workers **must** be provided with *adequate and suitable training*, which most likely will include specialised *training*, irrespective of which lone workers should be highly experienced in their work. What is considered *adequate and suitable* may ultimately be determined by a court of law. The lone worker is likely to be self-supervising, although an *employer* has the duty under the *HSWA* s.2(2)c to provide, *so far as is reasonably practicable, adequate and suitable* supervision.

Employers have the general duty to ensure a safe system of work (preferably especially designed) for lone workers; safe plant and equipment; lone workers must be fully aware of the risks and safety measures associated with their work environment and activity. The *Safety Policy Document* should provide full information, regularly reviewed and updated, on the health and safety organisation and arrangements for lone workers which must be brought to their attention.

long-term sampling involves the taking of air samples for several hours to obtain an average concentration measurement of the contaminant. Long-term sampling may be *personal* (via an attachment to the operator, e.g. *diffusion badges*) or through measurements taken at various places in the workplace (known as static or area sampling, e.g. via *stain tubes*).

Lord Advocate is the chief law officer of the Crown in Scotland, corresponding to the Attorney General in England. The Lord Advocate has ultimate responsibility for criminal prosecutions in Scotland, assisted by a Solicitor General, advocates depute and *procurators fiscal*. Almost invariably the Lord Advocate is a supporter of the ruling party and resigns from office on a change of government.

Lord Chancellor is the head of the judiciary, who is a government minister (normally of Cabinet rank and Speaker of the House of Lords. The Lord Chancellor is appointed by the Crown, on the advice of the Prime Minister, and combines judicial, executive and legislative functions.

Lord Chief Justice ranks second to the *Lord Chancellor* in the judicial hierarchy and is the chief judge of the Queen's Bench Division.

lumen is the flux per *unit* from a uniform source of light of one candle.

M

machine guarding, in summary, is required for all machinery or work equipment which has a part (or whole) which is dangerous, e.g. can cause injury to any person acting reasonably in normally expected circumstances (see *Walker v Bletchley-Flettons [1937] 1 AER*).

The principle legislation covering machinery guarding in workplaces, aside from the general duties in s.6 of the *Health and Safety at Work etc. Act 1974*, includes (for the supply and manufacture of machinery) the *Supply of Machinery (Safety) Regulations 1992* or SMSR, together with its 1994 amendment and (covering *employers* and users) the *Provision and Use of Work Equipment Regulations 1998* or PUWER. In summary, relevant legislation covers machinery design, manufacture, supply, maintenance and use, with specific duties also placed on *employers* and *employees*. The *Consumer Protection Act 1987* and the *General Product Safety Regulations 1994* are concerned with *product safety*, which includes guarding.

All guards should prevent persons being injured when the machine is in motion and have 'fail safe' operation, e.g. where operated through electric power, if the power supply is interrupted, the guard should remain or move to the safe position. The types of guards are identified in the mnemonic **FIAT** and are the following:

Automatic guards close automatically when the machine starts, preventing operator *access*, and will not open until the machine ceases operation. An example would be the guard on the blade of a hand-held portable circular saw, which automatically springs back to cover the cutting edge.

Fixed guards which must be secure, only openable using special tools, e.g. for maintenance purposes. The preferred option for moving transmissions.

Interlock guards should prevent moving parts becoming active and should stop parts from moving when the interlock guard is open. A simple press guard typifies application.

Trip guards operate through the operator 'tripping' a protective device, e.g. standing on pressure mats placed in front of a press; or electronic beams arrayed across a machine, which break the electric eye and the machine will not work.

machinery (or mechanical) hazards include abrasion/friction/contact, crushing, cutting, drawing in/running nips, ejection, entanglement, flying objects, high pressure fluid injection, impact, shear, stabbing and punctures.

See also *MNEMONICS (ENTICE)*.

magistrate is a justice of the peace sitting in a *magistrates' court.* Most magistrates aside from Chairpersons) are lay persons, have no formal legal qualifications and are unpaid, with the exception of *stipendary magistrates* who are paid and are appointed in major cities.

Magistrates' Courts were created by the Justices of the Peace Act in 1361 following the appointment of 'one Lord and with three or four of the most worthy in the Country –at the time, England and Wales)' to keep the peace in each locality. They are restricted to England and Wales. Scotland has the Sheriff Court, which is equal in status to the County Court. Magistrates' courts can sit any day of the year, exceptionally including Christmas or Good Friday.

A Magistrates' Court is now presided over by two to seven *magistrates* (with approximately 25,000 magistrates in England and Wales) or a single *stipendiary magistrate* (of which there are approximately 60, mainly in inner London), with the principal function of providing a forum within which all criminal prosecutions are initiated (and holding limited *jurisdiction* in civil matters, e.g. debt or matrimonial proceedings). The *magistrates' court* can sit as *examining justices* to consider whether or not there is sufficient evidence to commit defendants to the **Crown Court** with regard to an **indictable offence,** e.g. the offence of murder, rape or robbery.

Magistrates' Courts also deal with offences **triable either way** that is, those which are listed in Schedule 1 of the Magistrates' Court Act (1980), such as malicious wounding or burglary, or those for which the penalty is specified by the Act creating the offence. A defendant in a case **triable either way** may elect for a *summary trial.* Magistrates' Courts deal with around 98% of all criminal cases summarily and commit the others for trial or sentence to the **Crown Court.** In summary cases the Magistrates' Court acts as a *court of summary jurisdiction* (i.e. a **criminal court** of trial, without a jury but assisted by the **clerk to the justices**). Most cases brought under the Health and Safety at Work etc. Act 1974 are **triable either way,** that is they may be summarily tried by the magistrates or on indictment at the Crown Court. At Magistrates' Court level in England and Wales the prosecutor may be an enforcement officer (in the **Sheriff Courts** in Scotland an enforcement officer acts as an advisor to the prosecutor, the **Procurator Fiscal**).

major accident see *Control of Major Accident Hazards Regulations 1999.*

Management and Administration of Safety and Health at Mines Regulations 1993 (with ACOP) or MASHMR: Schedule 3, Regulation 41(1) and (2) of MASHMR repeals the whole of Sections 2-18, 20, 60, 91, 147-149, 158 and 168 of the *Mines and Quarries Act 1954*, with repeals or modifications to several other sections.

The MASHMR were made under the **HSWA 1974** to 'take account of modern working practices in mines and . . . the need to ensure that all mines have an effective administrative management structure staffed by individuals who are aware of their duties for the safe operation of . . . (all mines) . . . and who are competent to carry out those duties' (Para. 1 Introduction MASHMR).

Included in the MASHMR provisions are: duties for owners; structure of health and safety management, supervision and inspection of mines; qualifications; *training* requirements; surveyors and plans; records and information; exemptions; repeals, modifications, revocations and savings. In all cases, the MASHMR apply to *self-employed* persons as if the *self-employed* person were an *employer* and an *employee.*

management of change is a prime component of health, safety and environmental matters and a key activity of the *safety professional.* Unfortunately a full analysis and discussion of the techniques and application of change is clearly beyond the scope of this work, the following is provided as a useful outline and guide.

Inevitably, successful safety management means the successful management of change, since at all levels – organisational, legislative, role and in respect of hazards – change is inevitable. The most successful management 'style' or 'technique' depends on what and where the change is required, the choice and application of the most appropriate technique, the people involved (influenced by their personality, life experience, education, company selection process and *training*) and the organisation culture. The majority of textbook discussion on change in organisations tends to concentrate on motivation and financial matters, with little focus on health, safety and environment *per se*, where the cost benefits are less obvious and, in all honesty, difficult to measure effectively.

As an example, Pettigrew (1989) provides considerable useful discussion on the theory and practice of change but the discussion is (a) intentionally academic, (b) business oriented, and (c) requires adaptation before it could be used for health and safety (see A.M. Pettigrew (1989) 'Longitudinal methods to study change: Theory and Practice' in R. Mansfield (ed.) *Frontiers of Management*, London, Routledge). In essence, safety professionals and other managers want results from a technique and (unfortunately) do not have time to 'do the course'.

One effective approach is to consider an organisation or company as a 'society', with its own culture, structure and different individuals. The objective is to achieve long term and if possible permanent change in the individual groups and members of an organisation. To achieve success, certain steps should be taken including:

- finding out what is wanted by whom (known as *initiating circumstances of change*);
- measuring sick absence, efficiency, profitability and pay before, during and after the introduction of change (known as *manifest goals of change*).

Beware of the *latent goals of change*, exemplified by the spoken 'I believe in health and safety' hiding the thought 'so long as it does not interfere with production' or the divisional manager who overtly embraces change but covertly is looking for ways to protect and expand his/her 'empire'.

The actual change technique which 'works best' depends on many factors. These include the **organisation culture**, the person introducing the changes and influences, which can lead to the technique style chosen. The technique can be structural (e.g. **Taylorism** with its autocratic leadership, individuals and groups 'do what they are told to do'); human resource based (e.g. **Maslow** suggested providing opportunities for individuals to realise their potential at work, psychologically and developmental); or any current 'fashion', which often means combining aspects from the major approaches. However, whichever change technique is chosen, there is usually still some resistance to change.

There are ways which can minimise resistance to change. They include:

(a) involve all concerned in discussions during planning and organising the changes, as well as before the details of the changes concerning health and safety are finalised (a **legal** requirement);
(b) precisely define changes to be introduced;
(c) reduce to a minimum fears concerning job security;
(d) preserve, wherever possible or appropriate, existing work groups (split up those which are not successful);
(e) monitor and review the position during and after the change process.

The above (a)–(e) is a successful general procedure or technique for initiating the change process, whatever its purpose. However, in matters of health and safety, discussion and the provision of information and (re-)*training* are legal requirements.

If the changed behaviour is based on changes in *belief,* the change in behaviour is most probably permanent. Many effective permanent changes can be the result of the person leading or initiating the change agent having learnt from life experience. Nevertheless, theoretical knowledge, understanding and underpinning from a directed course of study are the best ways for effective professional understanding, application and monitoring of change techniques and achieving the resultant *desired* change, as with all management techniques.

Management of Health and Safety at Work Regulations 1999 or **MHSWR**, accompanied by **ACOP** and **Guidance L21**: the **MHSWR** is another key piece of health and safety legislation, derived from what is termed a *mother* **EU Directive**. The selective details provided draws from both the Regulations and their associated **Approved Code of Practice (ACOP)**.

The element of the **MHSWR**, *which has received most publicity and discussion,* has been the duty placed on employers to carry out risk assessments. This duty is considered immediately below, followed by a selective review of the **MHSWR** requirements. Incidentally, because of their general nature, the **MHSWR** overlap with other regulations, e.g. carrying out a **COSHH** assessment satisfies the **MHSWR** requirement for a risk assessment.

risk assessment to be carried out by *competent persons.* The purpose of a risk assessment is to determine the measures needed to comply with relevant statutory provisions – therefore the *employer* and/or the *competent person* must know, in outline at least, the statutory provisions relevant to the area where the risk assessment is carried out.

To satisfy the **MHSWR** risk assessment duty:

additionally, a 'suitable and sufficient assessment' of risks to *young persons*, pregnant workers and persons who have recently given birth **must** be carried out where applicable;

carrying out a 'suitable and sufficient assessment' of risks to workers and *others who may be affected* (e.g. *employees*, visitors and students);

record in writing all significant findings from risk assessments, if five or more persons employed (see below);

self-employed to assess **risks to self** and others affected.

Other **MHSWR** requirements include:

Accident prevention **measures** are required to be taken by *employers* under Schedule 1 Reg. 4 of the **MHSWR**.

Arrangements (for health and safety) **should be recorded** if five or more persons employed (*in addition* to other records).

Capabilities, training and refresher training (Reg. 11). Every *employer* shall ensure that *employees* are provided with adequate health and safety information, instructions and *training* at induction, on transfer to new work and following any changes in technology employed or in the system of working.

Co-operation and co-ordination – where two or more *employers* share a workplace or site (Reg. 9), even on a temporary basis, health and safety information should be exchanged to enable relevant provisions to be complied with and health and safety measures co-ordinated.

Criminal and/or civil proceedings, exceptionally, may follow breach of the **MHSWR**.

Employers **must consult** with all concerned on health, safety and environmental matters.

Health and safety arrangements to be made within the undertaking, part of which includes application of the normal management functions of *Planning, Organisation, Control, Monitoring and Review* (Reg. 5).

Health and safety assistance for *employers*, including general definition, appointment and utilisation of *competent persons* is covered in Regulation 6.

Health surveillance must be arranged for *employees*, where found necessary following the assessment (Reg. 6).

Host places of *employment* – comprehensible information *must* be provided to persons working (including e.g. work experience persons, students) in host *employers'* or *self-employed* persons' undertakings (Reg. 12) regarding the risks to health and safety, fire precautions and procedures. *Employers must* take all reasonable steps to ensure that persons working in their undertakings should be informed of the identity of persons nominated to implement evacuation procedures.

Information for employees (**Reg. 8**) *must* be provided by every **employer** which must be **comprehensible** (i.e., **employees** including students, speaking poor English, must be provided with information in a manner or language which they can understand) and particularly relevant information on risks and precautions. (See 'literate staff' immediately below).

Literate staff and knowing the standard of **literacy** of **employees** are necessary, because of the requirements of Reg. 10.

Procedures for serious and imminent danger (Reg. 8). *must* be established by employers to be followed in the event of serious or imminent danger (such as in the case of fire or explosion); with **competent persons** (defined as above) to implement the procedures; ensure no **employee** has **access** to areas of serious or imminent danger *unless* the **employee** has adequate health and safety **instruction** (these arrangements and organisation must be included in safety policy required under the **HSWA** s.2(3)).

Sufficient (paid or salaried) time must be provided by the **employer**, together with adequate resources to enable the risk assessment to be carried out effectively.

Temporary workers and those on fixed duration contracts (Reg. 15) – **employers** must advise **employment** agencies of any safety requirements (and special risks in the undertaking) prior to temporary workers being engaged. The **employment** agency in turn *must* ensure that the temporary worker is informed of such safety requirements. This requirement does *not* absolve the new **employer** from complying with any relevant statutory requirements, e.g. **employers** must provide an induction 'course' to all **employees** with a health and safety component.

Training *in health and safety* **must** be provided by an **employer** to **employees** following introduction of new work equipment or a change respecting equipment in use, new technology, a new or changed system of work. The training must be **adequate and suitable**, repeated periodically and must take place *during working hours* (Reg. 13).

Workers who become pregnant (Regs 16, 17 and 18):

(i) **MUST** inform their **employer** as soon as this fact is known; and
(ii) **employers** **MUST** then carry out a review assessment, taking account of the pregnancy.

(iii) An assessment is also necessary for workers who have recently given birth or are breastfeeding (see **HSE** Guidance Note *New and expectant mothers: a guide for employers*).

Employees also have duties under the **MHSWR**, which include:

(i) **full co-operation** with their *employer* to ensure safe working;

(ii) **machinery, equipment, or substance** etc., **must** be used in accordance with the instructions and *training* provided by their *employer* (Reg. 14);

(iii) **notifying** their *employer* or the appointed *competent person* of any perceived dangers, including unsafe systems of work and/or unsatisfactory (from a health and safety perspective) *training* programmes.

manager is one who controls, plans, organises and directs the activities of one or more persons (other than self), acting as an agent for the *employer*. Therefore the term manager *includes* supervisors, forepersons and chargehands. Such persons have in effect and actuality, 'double duties' under health and safety legislation – their duty as an *employee and* their duty as an agent (i.e. 'acting on behalf' of their *employer*).

mandatory duties are those which must be carried out, albeit sometimes at the *so far as is reasonably practicable* level.

manganese is a shiny brittle metal. It is used for such activities as the manufacture of wood preservatives, safety matches, glass, ceramics, signal flares and fireworks; it can be released during welding, etc., and is hazardous to the respiratory system, central nervous system, blood and kidneys. Symptoms include Parkinson's disease, mental confusion, insomnia, dry throat, cough, vomiting, general malaise and fatigue.

manual handling, according to Reg. 2(1) of the *Manual Handling Operations Regulations 1992*, means:

' . . . any task which involves transporting, carrying or supporting a load through the use of hand or bodily force. It includes lifting, putting down, pushing, pulling, carrying or moving . . . .'

Human effort, not mechanical, is required to move *or hold* the load, e.g. scanning goods at a check-out, packing products into boxes, lifting boxes or packets and pushing or pulling trucks; a hand operated pneumatic drill is *not* manual handling within the **MHOR**, it is covered by the **MHOR** when moving the drill to and from the actual place of use.

Manual Handling Operations Regulations 1992 or MHOR

Manual Handling Operations Regulations 1992 or MHOR came into force 1 January 1993. In outline the MHOR require *employers* to:

(a) avoid the need for workers to carry out any manual-handling task that may result in injury;

(b) if (a) cannot be achieved, arrange for a risk assessment, considering the 'risk factors' listed in the *Regulations*, to be carried out by a **competent person.**

TILE identifies the risk factor *areas* which must be considered in the MHOR assessment, a pro-forma of which is included in the *Regulations* (it may be freely photocopied for use). TILE comprises:

(a) **Tasks** – do they involve awkward bodily movement or posture, carrying loads long distances or sudden movement of loads?

(b) **Individual capacity** – does the task require unusual strength, height etc.?

(c) **Loads** – are they heavy, difficult to grasp or sharp?

(d) **Environment** – are there extremes of temperature or humidity, gusts of wind, space constraints preventing good posture?

The *Regulations* state *employers* must carry out the following:

Adequate and suitable training to be provided in manual handling, specific to the job which they do, for **all** *employees.*

Avoid manual handling wherever possible.

Eliminate or reduce manual handling risks *employees* face when away from their own workplace (e.g. delivery drivers), duties shared with the *employer in control of the premises*, who **must** co-operate in respect of specific risks (**HSWA** *and* **MHSWR**).

Heaviest side of load, with an off-centred centre of gravity, must be marked and information provided to *employees.*

Inform *employees* of the risks they face when carrying out the task and from the work environment.

Manual handling which cannot be avoided must be subject to a full *assessment* (i.e., **TILE**).

Monitoring and reviewing the manual handling procedures must be carried out and methods introduced to improve them, shared with the *employer in control of the premises*, who must co-operate.

Personal protective equipment provided for *employees* must comply with the PPE *Regulations* (the *superior legislation* for PPE).

Reassessment must be made of the risks associated with TILE in the event of an *accident* occurring during manual handling.

Risk to *employees* carrying out manual handling **must be reduced** to the lowest *reasonably practical* level.

Weight of each load, wherever possible, must be provided to *employees*.

Employees have their duties under the *Regulations*, these include:

reporting to their *employer* **any deficiencies** in the PPE supplied by their *employer* or the *employer's* representative (e.g. manager);

systems of work provided by the *employer* must be fully used and properly carried out by *employees*.

mass of a body is defined in terms of its inertia or resistance to a change of motion – i.e. a body with a large mass will be difficult to move and, once in motion, more difficult to stop than one with a small mass.

Maximum Exposure Limit (or MEL) for a *substance hazardous to health*, in technical terms, means 'the maximum exposure limit approved by the *Health and Safety Commission* for that substance in relation to the specified reference period when calculated by a method approved by the *Health and Safety Commission*'. (*COSHH* Reg. 2(1)) In simpler terms, an MEL is the maximum concentration of an airborne substance, hazardous to health, averaged over a reference period (e.g. eight-hour called 'long-term' or 15-minute 'short term') to which an *employee* may be exposed at work.

maximum permissible dose is the maximum amount of ionising radiation that an individual should not exceed absorbing over a given period of time. The maximum dose is almost invariably determined by law and, most importantly, is subject to change (increased or lessened) following current research findings.

measurement techniques include those suitable for *long term, continuous* and *spot* measurements. The technique used depends on several factors related to the *hazard*, which can produce **chronic** or **acute** reactions.

The measurement techniques for chronic hazards include: continuous personal dose measurements (e.g. using radiation 'badges'; continuous measurement of average background levels; spot readings of contaminant levels at selected positions and times). The techniques for measuring acute hazards include: continuous personal monitoring with rapid response; continuous background monitoring with rapid response; spot readings of background contaminant levels at selected positions and times. There are times when it is necessary to find out if an area is safe to enter, this requires the use of direct reading instruments which can provide qualitative and quantitative particle analysis.

See also *sampling techniques.*

mechanical hazards see *machinery (or mechanical) hazards.*

megavolt is a unit of electromotive force equal to one million electron *volts.*

megawatt is a unit of electrical power equal to 1,000 kilowatts or one million *watts.*

MEL see *Maximum Exposure Limit.*

melanoma is a malignant, often fatal form of skin *cancer*, caused by over-exposure to ultraviolet-B radiation.

mens rea (*Latin: guilty mind or wicked mind*) means that someone had the *intention* to carry out an act which broke the law (*Allard v Selfridges Ltd [1925] 1 KB 129*); this may include recklessness (*Sweet v Parsley [1970] AC 132*).

See also *liability.*

mercury is a silver heavy colourless liquid. It is used in the production of chlorine and caustic soda (from brine), the manufacture of inorganic and organic compounds such as pesticides, antiseptics, germicides and skin preparations; mildew-proof paints, felt etc. Hazardous to the respiratory system, skin, central nervous system, kidneys and eyes, its contact symptoms include cough, chest pain, bronchial pneumonitis, anorexia, irritation of the eyes and skin.

mesothelioma is a (rare) cancer of the membranes of the lungs, heart or stomach. The tumour may form thick sheets covering the internal organs. The recovery outlook is poor. Sometimes it is called *celothelioma*. It is linked to contact with *asbestos.*

metal is a malleable, ductile element, which has a high relative density (specific gravity) and is a good conductor of electricity. The negative effects on the environment during extraction, manufacture and final disposal temper its usefulness.

methanoic acid see *formic acid*.

method statements are a written, systematic, description of the way a particular task or work activity will be carried out, including reference to health and safety measures required and which will be put in place. Their major purpose is to ensure a *safe system of work*. Method statements are frequently requested by clients (or their agents) from contractors, even though method statements for the same task may differ from department to department, or company to company. A typical method statement will include such things as:

(a) current legislation and practice;
(b) the type of machinery and equipment used;
(c) the materials used;
(d) the method and sequence of operations;
(e) the provision of protective clothing and equipment;
(f) local conditions and weather;
(g) emergency procedures and first aid provision;
(h) *access* and *egress*; and
(i) provision of *information, instruction* and *training*.

MHOR is an acronym for *Manual Handling Operations Regulations 1992.* (qv)

MHSWR is the acronym for *Management of Health and Safety at Work Regulations 1992 (with amendments).* (qv)

micro-organism is an organism, such as bacteria, viruses and some algae and fungi that can only be seen through a microscope.

See **COSHH**.

Mineral extraction: Legislation arising from the EC Directive 92/104/EEC covering mines and other mineral-extracting sites. A short, selective resume follows.

New workplaces (those brought into use after the 1994 *Regulations* were implemented) must comply with the 1994 *Regulations* as specified.

Old workplaces (those working before the 1994 *Regulations* commenced) have to comply as soon as possible and, at the very least, nine years after 1994.

Common minimum or special health and safety requirements apply to:

(i) **surface and underground** mineral extracting industries;
(ii) **ancillary surface** installations;

which include (alphabetically):

- danger areas;
- electrical equipment;
- explosion risks;
- fire hazards;
- first aid;
- harmful atmospheres;
- lighting;
- mechanical equipment;
- mines and rescue;
- organisation;
- plant;
- sanitary installations;
- stability;
- supervision;
- traffic routes;
- transport;
- ventilation.

Minimum Acceptable Flow (MAF) requires (UK) local river authorities to work towards determining the flow that would allow the normal uses of a river to be maintained.

mists are suspended liquid droplets formed by condensation from gaseous or break-up of liquids in air.

mnemonics are the use of a word where (usually) each letter in that word represents a term or phrase, thus assisting recall of the whole. They are frequently used as an aid to memory on health and safety *training* courses and safety professionals use them to assist in remembering or explaining certain concepts or activities. In alphabetical order, the following are some of the best known and in common use:

AIDIM = (safety management) Assess, Identify the hazards, Develop a system (bring in **ERICPD**), Implement, Monitor.

mobile cranes

COILS = (test of reasonableness) Cost, Obviousness of risk, Inherent nature of the risk *versus* Likelihood of risk, Severity of risk.

ENTICE = (machine or *mechanical hazards*) Entanglement, Nips, Traps, Impact, Contact or Cutting, Ejection.

ERICPD = (to control hazards and risk, prevent *accidents*).Eliminate, Reduce, Isolate, Control, PPE, Discipline.

FIAT = (types of machine guards) Fixed, Interlock, Automatic and Trip.

NAFOF = Never Assume, Find Out First (general).

PEME = (safe systems of work) People, Equipment, Materials, Environment.

POCMAR = (safety management) Planning, Organisation, Control, Monitoring and Review.

PROBE = (*accident* investigation technique) Persist in questioning, Respect or Relax the situation, Open mind-no blame, Background, Explain the reasons and findings.

SPAME = (human factors) Skill, Personality, Attitude, Motivation, Experience.

TILE = (Manual Handling) Task, Individual, Load, Environment.

mobile cranes require special precautions in use, including: checking they are suitable for the task, e.g. adequate and identified Safe Working Load (SWL); outriggers used; the ground on which they are used is stable and in good condition, e.g. avoid excavations; ensure there are no overhead (or other) obstructions; good visibility; adequate *communication*; lifting tackle is suitable and pre-inspected; all test certificates are up-to-date; the driver and banksperson are competent; the area is clear of non-involved personnel; the area is adequately signed; the load is carried at appropriate height; and care taken when travelling on sloping ground. *Do not confuse mobile cranes with overhead travelling cranes.*

models are idealised and usually simplified, mathematical or physical representations of complex phenomena, e.g. models are used to describe and explain as well as forecast the effects of change.

(See also **Hale and Hale model of accident causation**).

molecule is the smallest part of an element or compound, which retains the composition and chemical properties of the element, or compound.

monitoring can be *pro-active* (before an event) or *re-active* (after an event).

Pro-active monitoring (sometimes called 'active monitoring') is:

- concerned with the *prevention* of *injury, ill-health* or *loss*;
- *action* taken *before injury, ill-health* or *loss*;
- a *system* that involves *routine, regular inspections*, re-assessments and/or *sampling*.

Reactive monitoring is:

- concerned mainly with *responding* to *incidents*;
- action taken after such *incidents*;
- a *system* that involves *inspections, investigations* and *audits*.

motivation is one of the key psychological concepts for use or application by the safety professional and managers generally. Unfortunately, it is a most difficult and complicated concept or behaviour to define and more pertinent, to apply effectively. Of course, we utilise and apply motivation techniques throughout our lives, often without realising *exactly* what we are doing. We are all amateur psychologists and demonstrate this through motivating our partner into thinking we are 'the best' out of the billions of potential partners, or children to do what we want them to do, reasonably happily, even if they did not originally want to do it. The difference is a professional psychologist is repeatedly successful and can select or adapt a technique from a wide range of techniques to suit all circumstances.

However, this entry is not intended – nor is it possible – to convert every reader into a professional psychologist, nor can this entry cover the subject of motivation in any great depth. It provides a basic understanding of the concept of motivation, identifies some of the different approaches, illustrates its usefulness with regard to health and safety, suggests different motivational techniques for the workplace.

Motivated safe behaviour at work is goal directed, purposeful and is what the safety professional ideally strives to achieve, along the way of changing externally motivated behaviour to internalised self-motivation. In short, change from the external encouragement or motivation of *employees* to 'work safely', possibly through the operation of a bonus scheme, to 'working safely' through internalised self-motivation, because *employees* can see the benefit of so doing. It is cheap to utilise and can be very effective. The different techniques of motivation can partly depend on the school or persuasion of the psychologist. As examples:

Behaviourists search for reinforcement schedules. In extremely simple terms this means positive behaviour is rewarded, negative behaviour punished. Skinner, a leading behaviourist, thinks it is unnecessary to consider motivation as a separate concept, since he thinks all behaviour derives from reinforcement. However, Hull, who is also a behaviourist, disagrees with Skinner.

Cognitive psychologists will relate behaviour to a persons thinking.

Humanist psychologists will relate behaviour to self-actualisation. A typical exponent is Maslow and his hierarchy of needs.

Neurobiological psychologists will look for processes in the nervous and endocrine systems, and other bodily systems and processes.

In summary, typical with social science generally and psychology in particular, there is **NO** one theory or concept of motivation that is 100 per cent 'right' – or 100 per cent 'wrong'. Each of the various approaches makes a contribution to understanding of motivation and becomes the preferred choice in a particular circumstance.

Maslow's theory is very idiographic, that is, recognises that every individual is unique. With development and adaptation, Maslow remains one of the leaders in the field. He considered that everyone is subject to two different sets of motivational forces. Those that ensure survival and satisfy needs, such as safety, love, belongingness and esteem. Next are those which promote a person's *self actualisation*, that is, realising ones full potential, becoming everything that one is capable of becoming.

mutagen is a substance capable of causing genetic change or mutation in an organism that may be passed on to succeeding generations. Mutagenic substances and preparations are those which, if they are inhaled, ingested or penetrate the skin, may induce hereditary or permanent genetic effects or increase their incidence. Many mutagens are also carcinogens.

N

National Examination Board in Occupational Safety and Health

(or NEBOSH) is an *independent* awarding body in *occupational health* and safety founded in 1979. One of the objectives of NEBOSH is to raise professional standards in *occupational health* and safety and offer recognised professional qualifications. NEBOSH does not run courses, but establishes standards, compiles course syllabi and examines.

The NEBOSH qualifications commence with the National General Certificate and the National **Construction** Certificate, with courses run at approved centres. At a higher level there are the Diploma 1, Diploma 2 and Environmental Diploma, with their courses run by accredited bodies. Success in the Diploma is recognised by the *Institution of Occupational Safety and Health* (Tel: 0116 288 8858) and other professional health and safety associations.

National Health Insurance is a compulsory weekly or monthly payment made by all *employees, employers* and the *self-employed.* With regard to health and safety, the principal role of National Health Insurance is to provide monies (*not* **compensation**) to a *claimant* who satisfies certain legislative conditions, following an *industrial accident* to that person.

National Inspection Council for Electrical Installation Contracting

is a non-profit making body, supported by all sectors of the electrical industry, consumer bodies and local and central government. Its purpose is to protect electricity users against unsafe and unsound electrical installations and it operates as the industry's independent regulatory body on electrical safety matters.

natural gas is a mixture of hydrocarbons in gaseous form, found in pockets beneath the earth's surface, usually in association with liquid petroleum. It is comprised of 85 per cent of methane, with other hydrocarbons.

natural hazards are an element or circumstance in the natural environment, having the potential to cause harm to persons or property. Natural hazards include those originating in the *atmosphere* (blizzards, droughts, floods), those which are *terrestrial* (earthquakes, landslides), *aquatic* (floods, storm surges), *biological* (infestations, viral diseases). Planning and forecasting, including the use of *models*, can help prevent or mitigate natural hazards.

NEBOSH see National Examination Board in Occupational Safety and Health.

negligence, in summary, is failing to do something the average reasonable person would do, e.g. a breach of duty that deserves blame (culpable). In basic terms, the key terms and conditions, which must apply to establish, for example, the tort of negligence, are:

(i)   duty (e.g. there must be a duty of care);
(ii) breach (there has been a breach of that duty of care);
(iii) injury, loss or damage occurred (i.e. as a direct result of that breach of duty of care, there has been an injury, damage or loss).

Should the above outline three conditions be satisfied, then the tort of negligence is applicable. For example if, as a consequence of a breach of statutory duty concerning health and safety, someone is injured or killed then the offender may be liable to criminal charges, *as well as* a civil action for damages. However, if it is unclear whether or not a statute confers the right of civil remedies, the courts decide the situation.

Negligence means more than heedless (or careless) conduct, whether in omission (*unknowingly* not doing something, which should have been done) or commission (*knowingly* not doing something), referring to the complex concept of *duty*, *breach* of that duty and *damage thereby suffered* by a person to whom the duty was owed – summary of part of a very important judgment made by Lord Wright in *Lochgelly Iron and Coal Co. Ltd. v M'Mullan [1934] AC 1*. Actions for negligence can be civil (compensatory) and, as Lord Diplock said, 'judgments of the courts say all'. Where negligence is 'self-evident' and the 'facts speak for themselves' (referred to in 'legal-speak' as *res ipsa loquitur*) the defendant has to show he/she 'took reasonable care'; if unable to do so, the defendant 'automatically' is adjudged negligent.

If negligence is the basis of **criminal liability**, it is not a defence to show that one has done something *so far as is reasonably practicable*. However, if someone is negligent through carelessness, then a civil liability may not apply, **unless** the offender has failed to conform to the standards of the reasonable person and there was a *breach of a duty of care* owed to the **plaintiff** and *that breach caused damage* to the plaintiff, the offender therefore being negligent.

See also **contributory negligence**.

negligence, criminal see *criminal negligence*.

neighbour principle is where 'persons who are so closely and directly affected by my act that I ought reasonably to have them in contemplation as being so affected when I am directing my mind to the *acts* or *omissions* which are called into question' (per Lord Aitkin in *Donoghue v Stevenson [1932] AC 562*). In somewhat simple terms, each worker and *employer* must work or take actions which will not knowingly adversely harm or affect those next to or around them (including non-*employees*).

neutron is an elementary or subatomic particle that carries no electrical charge. Neutrons are part of the nuclei of all atoms, except hydrogen. Their mass is slightly greater than protons, the other component of a nucleus.

new and expectant mothers are defined in the *MHSWR* as '*employees* who are pregnant, who have given birth or miscarried within the previous six months, or who are breastfeeding (which could continue for a longer period than six months)'.

NI 2 is a booklet issued by the *Benefits Agency* providing details of *industrial injuries* for which social security compensation is an automatic entitlement, **subject** to the claimant satisfying certain conditions and requirements.

night work by *employees* is generally defined as work that is carried out between midnight and 5 a.m., but there are specified exceptions. A principal point is that night workers must not exceed eight hours work over a 24-hour period (**WTR**). The legal requirements covering those on night work broadly include those described in the earlier entry, *lone workers.*

However, of particular importance is the way that the body clock must adapt to the new pattern of life demanded by working nights. The body clock pattern is termed *circadian rhythm*, the entry for which should be considered.

Generally there are no exceptions or exemptions concerning staff required to work nights, although new or expectant mothers may be suspended. This would be subject to them obtaining and producing a medical certificate stating that they may suffer ill health if they work nights.

NIHHSR see *Notification of Installations Handling Hazardous Substances Regulations 1982.*

NIHL see *noise induced hearing loss.*

nitrate, in chemical terms, is a salt or ester of *nitric acid.*

nitric acid is a colourless, yellow or red fuming liquid with an acrid, suffocating odour. It is used, for example, in the following processes; fertilisers, foams, insecticides, metallurgy, metal refining, nylon, ore recovery, photo-engraving. Symptoms of exposure include delayed pulmonary edema, pneumonitis, bronchitis, irritation of the eyes, mucous membrane and skin.

NNSR see *Notification of New Substances Regulations 1993.*

noise is *unwanted sound*. However, what one person considers unwanted sound

Noise Act 1996

(*noise*), may be welcomed by another (e.g. hard rock may be seen as *noise* and unwelcomed by one person but welcomed by someone else).

Noise Act 1996 includes placing a duty on officers of local authorities to investigate at night complaints about excessive noise. If the complaint is justified the officer must provide proof of identity, enter the premises and seize and remove the equipment or serve a warning notice; if the excessive noise continues an offender on summary conviction is liable to a fine not exceeding level three on the **standard scale**.

Noise and Statutory Nuisance Act 1993 includes, amongst its principle provisions that *noise* from machinery, equipment and vehicles (under specified conditions of use, i.e. **not** traffic) can be considered to be a **statutory nuisance**. The Regulations cover: operation of loudspeakers in streets or roads; audible intruder alarms.

Noise at Work Regulations 1989 or **NWR** cover *employers, employees,* trainees and the *self-employed* within Great Britain. The NWR places various duties on *employers, self-employed, employees, machine designers and suppliers* to reduce the risk of hearing damage to those at work to the lowest possible level. Exempted are those on board aircraft and shipping.

In particular, *employers* have a duty to purchase and install machinery with minimum *noise* levels reasonably practicable, and to install appropriate *noise* control measures. *Employees* have the duty to comply with their *employer's* instructions concerning the operation of control measures installed or, as a last resort, wear any PPE issued to reduce *noise* at work.

Certain duties in the **NWR** are **not** constrained by the term 'reasonably practicable' and are *absolute duties*, e.g.:

- *noise* assessments;
- provision of PPE to *employees* exposed to certain levels of *noise*, (see below);
- ensuring all relevant *noise* control equipment is fully and properly used.

Reg. 2 includes a definition of *three action levels*, establishing daily personal *noise* exposures at or beyond which the *employer* has to take certain actions and about which *employees* must be informed, instructed, trained *and their compliance ensured.*

The *action levels* are:

First **action level** 85 dB(A); between 85 dB(A) and 90 dB(A) *employees* can request ear protection. *Employers have no legal duty to ensure they are worn.*

Second **Action level** 90 dB(A); at or above this level, *employers* **MUST** *provide suitable ear protection and* **ENSURE IT IS WORN.** *Ear protection zones* must be allocated, signed and **all** *employees* **MUST** wear protectors in such zones.

Peak (or Third) **Action level** 200 **Pascal's** (140 dB(A)), the peak level for impact *noise*, the measurement of which requires a special sound level meter.

In summary, the **Regulations** require:

Adequate record *must be kept of the assessment* and kept by the **employer** until a new assessment is made **(Reg. 5).**

Ear protectors, only issued as a **last resort** requires that:

(a) they must be suitable for the purpose;
(b) compatible with other protective equipment;
(c) the equipment must be maintained.

Employers to reduce, so far as is reasonably practicable, in all cases, noise levels to the lowest level possible. Where *noise* levels are at 90 dB(A) or above, *employers must* take action to *lower noise levels* to the lowest level reasonably practicable **(Reg. 6)**, *without the use of ear protectors* **(Reg. 7).**

Employees likely to be exposed to *noise* levels 85 dB(A) or above must be:

(i) informed of their right to request hearing protection if exposed to *noise* between 85 dB(A) and 90 dB(A) and the **employer's** duty to provide it;
(ii) informed of the duty of the **employer** to supply *adequate and suitable* hearing protection if *employees* are exposed to *noise* levels of 90 dB(A) or above and of the **employees'** duty to wear it;
(iii) instructed and trained in its use and maintenance;
(iv) informed of the risks to the **employees'** health and safety and damage to the ears from exposure to the *noise* and of the steps the *employees* can take to minimise the risks.

Employees (and others who could be affected by the *noise*, e.g. visitors) have the duty to:

(i) wear PPE supplied by the **employer**;

(ii) report to their *employer* any defects in the hearing protection, e.g. wear, cracks etc., and exchange defective for effective equipment.

Noise assessment *must be carried out by a competent person.* The assessment findings and report will inform the *employer* what action and control measures are necessary to comply with their statutory duties (Reg. 4).

The principle objective for *employers* must be the use of effective control measures, which requires the accurate measurement and assessment of the *noise*, its source and the sound levels in *and* from the workplace.

noise control methods must be considered prior to purchase and commissioning of machinery or equipment (a requirement of the **Supply of Machinery (Safety) Regulations 1992** with 1994 amendment) or put in place following a *noise assessment*. Control methods include, in order of preference:

(i) reduction of *noise* at source – the preferred option for existing tasks, plant and equipment;
(ii) isolation, e.g. through enclosing of the source of *noise*;
(iii) the provision of *personal protective equipment*, the last resort, in the form of ear protection for workers exposed to *noise* in excess of the appropriate *action level*. PPE must be of good fit, compatible with other PPE used by the *employees*, who must be trained in its use and, where appropriate, its maintenance;
(iv) reduction of the exposure time for workers likely to be affected – which may include workers outside the immediate work area.

noise induced hearing loss (*NIHL*) can be caused by long duration exposure to *noise*, thereby damaging the hair cells of the inner ear, causing a reduction of hearing capability at particular frequencies and ultimately *permanent* threshold shift. If *noise* induced hearing loss occurs despite (**only** as a last resort) the wearing of suitable personal protective equipment, it may be because of one or more of the reasons given in *personal hearing protection, limitations of* (qv).

noise measurement is usually carried out by electronic equipment, such as hand held portable sound level instruments or personal dose meters.

There are three principle elements of *noise* (sound) measured and recorded, which are: (i) vibrations in the air from the *noise* source, recorded as cycles per second, known as **Hertz** (Hz); (ii) the sound intensity, measured in *decibels* (dB) usually expressed as dB(A) with the addition of an adjustment weighting biasing the measurement of sound *against* the low frequency end of the spectrum (since the high frequencies of sound are those with greater ear damage potential); and (iii) the magnitude of the sound measured as air pressure waves, known as *Pascals*(Pa).

non-mechanical hazards include those from biological sources, chemical emission, dust, electricity, ergonomics, explosion, fire, manual handling, *noise*, pressure, radiation, stress, temperature extremes, vibration.

Non-mechanical hazards can be quite complicated. For example, *dust* is subdivided into the *organic* (produced from animals or plants) leading to such conditions as asthma, farmers lung, and the *inorganic* (not having the characteristics of living organisms) leading to conditions such as pneumoconiosis, asbestosis.

See *machinery (or mechanical) hazards*.

notice boards can be an effective means of *communication* of a wide variety of health and safety instructions and information. However, to be effective they must be carefully located and highly visible. The notices concerning health and safety, as far as is practicable, must be written so that all the workforce can understand 'what they are about' (a legal duty, see **MHSWR** Reg. 10(1)). Cultural requirements must be recognised and taken into account, including customs or conventions regarded as characteristic of or essential to a community (*mores*). Old *communication*s should be removed from notice boards or regularly moved around, rather than the same pattern (boringly) displayed week after week.

notifiable refers to 'something' or some activity that must be notified to a named authority or agency. For example, some diseases must be notified to the appropriate authority, often (but not always) Environmental Health. Alternatively, demolition is a notifiable activity – the **HSE** must be informed prior to commencing demolition work if lasting more than 30 days or more than 500 person days.

Notification of Cooling Towers and Evaporative Condensers

Regulations 1992 cover 'notifiable devices' (i.e. a cooling tower or evaporative device), but **not** one in which the water is not *exposed to the air* or where the electricity or water supply is not connected. The principle requirement of the *Regulations* is for *employers* and/or occupiers of factories, hospitals, nursing homes, laboratories, schools and *construction* sites with water systems incorporating, as examples, a cooling tower or an evaporative condenser, hot/cold water services (*irrespective of size*) in particularly susceptible premises (e.g. health care premises), spa baths or pools where warm water is recirculated, **must identify and assess sources of risk.**

Notification of Installations Handling Hazardous Substances

The assessment should pay particular attention to: droplet formation; water temperature; risk to anyone inhaling water droplets; means of preventing and/or controlling risk. *Employers* must prepare schemes for preventing and controlling risk, implement the precautions, inform *employees* and keep records of implemented precautions.

Notification of Installations Handling Hazardous Substances Regulations 1982 require those who store, manufacture, process, use or transfer specified quantities of dangerous or hazardous substances on sites or in pipelines to inform the *HSE* at least three months before the storage or other activity commences (or within any lesser time as the *HSE* requires), following a specified format. Schedule 1 of the Regulations identifies the minimum quantities of named substances, which must be notified to the *HSE*.

Notification of New Substances Regulations 1993 require manufacturers to send to the appropriate authority full details of: an evaluation of *foreseeable* risks; the tests and their conduct; any unfavourable effects of the substance; and, in the case of hazardous (dangerous) substances, how they are going to comply with the supply requirements of the *Chemicals (Hazard Information and Packaging for Supply) Regulations 1994* and its amendments (or replacement).

noxious substances, in *occupational health* and safety terms, are harmful (= noxious) particular natural or artificial (including micro-organisms) kinds of matter, having more or less uniform properties. See *Environmental Protection (Prescribed Processes and Substances) Regulations 1991*, as amended, for a list of substances considered to be noxious and/or offensive.

nuclear energy is that released during nuclear fission. If uncontrolled it leads to an explosion; if controlled via a nuclear reactor it can be used to generate electricity. France produces around 73 per cent of its electricity through the use of nuclear reactors, the UK some 20 per cent.

Nuclear Installations Act 1965 is a relevant statutory provision under Schedule 1 of the *HSWA*, concerned with the right and terms to conduct a nuclear installation.

Nuclear Installations (Dangerous Occurrences) Regulations 1965 require the *licensees* of nuclear installations to report immediately to the *Health and Safety Executive*:

    (a) any release of radioactivity or toxic substances causing or likely to cause death or serious injury;

(b) any uncontrolled criticality excursion; any explosion or fire likely to effect safety;

(c) any occurrence during the transport of nuclear matter which is likely to cause death or injury from radioactivity; or

(d) the breaking open of a container of nuclear matter.

nuclear waste is the waste product produced by the nuclear industry and characterised by its radioactivity, which creates special problems in its disposal.

nucleus, in general terms, refers to the core of an object.

nuclide is the nucleus of an *atom* with a specific atomic and mass number. See *half-life* and *radionuclide*.

nuisance, in simple terms, is any unreasonable or unnecessary interference with the use or enjoyment of property or of a piece of land (including that caused by *noise* or air pollution, vibration or odours). It can be the cause of action in *common law*. The purpose of the action is for the *plaintiff* to obtain an *abatement* of the *nuisance* and obtain *compensation* for the *damages* caused.

Nursing Homes and Mental Nursing Homes are covered by the general health, safety and environmental legislation, as well as specialist legislation, e.g. the *Nursing Homes and Mental Nursing Homes Regulations*. Of particular concern for Nursing Homes are fire precautions and procedures to be taken in the event of fire. Regular fire practices should be held, recorded and checked for effectiveness. Accident prevention is of high priority, with staff trained in *first aid*. Nursing Homes are open to 'lawful' visitors and therefore occupier's liability is of prime importance. Nevertheless, general health, safety and environmental legislation provides the main cover for Nursing Homes.

O

Occupational Exposure Standard (or OES) for a *substance hazardous to health* 'means the standard approved by the **Health and Safety Commission (HSC)** for that substance in relation to the specified reference period when calculated by a method approved by the **HSC**' (**COSHH** Reg. 2(1)). One source of information regarding OES standards is the **EH40**. Substances that have allocated an OES should, *so far is reasonably practicable*, be kept below the OES and when exceeded, brought down to OES or below as soon as possible.

occupational health is concerned with the health of people in the workplace and, in its widest sense, concerned with the effects of work and the work environment on the health of workers and those in the vicinity.

occupational health and safety is a very wide ranging term, covering a multiple of disciplines, which cannot easily be defined, largely because of the wide variety of occupations, locations, and vast *individual* and role *differences*.

A working definition can be assembled from the components of the term: (a)*occupations*, defined by the Oxford Dictionary as '. . . one's *employment*'; (b)*health* as 'the state of being well in body or mind, a person's mental or physical condition'; (c) *safety* as 'being safe, freedom from risk or danger'. Hence:

> applied *occupational health and safety* enables a person to carry out his/her *employment*, well in body and mind, safe and free from risk and danger.

Occupational health and safety is not a static term or discipline. For example, it has (unfairly) been said in the UK that *occupational health* seems to be considered at the Cinderella end of the medical profession. However, in France *occupational health* is pre-eminent in health and safety; in Germany engineers predominate, together with insurance, etc.

These national differences are highly relevant when comparing the multi-discipline health and safety between countries, the dominant discipline influencing the perspective of health and safety, sometimes identifying or reflecting the 'group in control'.

As with many multi-discipline professions which are gaining in importance (and the opportunity to make money), various groups attempt to establish pre-eminence (e.g. the medical profession, chemical engineers). This manoeuvring is inevitable, not necessarily dysfunctional, but the situation has not yet been resolved in the UK. However, professionals and other persons concerned with health and safety should be aware that if a company is large or more particularly foreign owned or controlled, there may be a misunderstanding or even breakdown in *communication* regarding aspects of applied occupational health and safety.

occupational health and safety management see *BS 8800, risk management, safety management, total loss control and total quality management.*

occupational health and safety professionals see *safety professionals.*

Occupational Health Nurse (OHN) or Physician are persons who have received general professional medical *training* and during their *training*, or some time after qualification, carried out a specialist course of study and qualified in *occupational health.*

In industry some organisations employ *occupational health* nurses, perhaps with a suitably equipped *occupational health* section or department. *Occupational health* physicians may be employed on a full- or part-time consultant basis. The *Employment Medical Advisory Service* is virtually the *occupational health* section of the *Health and Safety Executive.*

The RCN definition of an OHN includes stating that they provide immediate care to ill or injured workers and when they return to work; educate and promote good health; devise *accident* prevention programmes; monitor the workplace regarding all aspects of *occupational health* and have a health and safety function. However, for an OHN effectively to carry out health *and* safety functions it is essential to ensure that, additional to health professional *training* and qualifications, the OHN has professional safety *training* (regularly updated) **and** relevant qualifications.

occupational hygiene see *industrial hygiene.*

occupational medicine has a concern with persons at work and the effects of work on health. It also ensures that health and safety in the workplace are of high standard, **provided** practitioners have received adequate and relevant professional health and safety *training* and qualifications (including covering legislative requirements).

occupier is someone who has control over premises, *even if that control is exercised* *through a manager.* Interestingly enough, 'occupation' and 'occupier' are NOT specifically defined in the **Occupiers' Liability Act 1957** or **OLA 1984**. Instead the definition is obtained by reference to the duty of care under common law and recognition that an occupier is someone who has sufficient control over a premises to exercise reasonable care on behalf of visitors.

In summary a *case law* definition of occupier is , 'Wherever a person has sufficient degree of control over premises to realise that any failure on (their) part to use care may result in injury to a person coming lawfully there, then (they are) an "occupier" (*Wheat v Lacon & Co. [1966] AC 552*).' The **OLA 1984** extended this to include, subject to certain conditions, trespassers.

occupier's liability extends both to invited visitors ('invitee' – e.g. shop customer) and non-invited visitors to the premises (i.e. 'trespassers' – e.g. entering land or taking away goods without consent) if the occupier is aware of any danger due to the state of the premises or has reasonable grounds to believe that the danger exists. Trespass is a *tort*. Incidentally, under the **Unfair Contract Terms Act 1977** an occupier cannot exclude or restrict liability in contract for death or serious injury, *except* regarding trespassers.

Occupiers' Liability Act 1957 deals primarily with *civil liability* and the duties of *occupiers* to lawful visitors to those premises. It is based on negligence. Managerial control can constitute an 'occupation,' sometimes determined to be a 'joint control'. (See *Wheat v Lacon & Co. [1966] AC 552* where a public house customer suffered an injury and the manager *and the brewery* were adjudged to be 'in control'.)

Protection under the Act is afforded to lawful visitors who enter for the occupier's benefit, e.g. clients or customers, or for their own benefit, e.g. policemen or **HSE** Inspectors. Occupiers have to erect warning signs near dangerous places; in one such instance when a surveyor fell into a deep pit where there was no lighting and injured himself, the court held that the occupier should have erected a warning (*Rae (Geoffrey) v Mars (UK) [1990] 3 EG 80*, but the occupier does not have to provide lighting at night when no use is made of the premises under normal circumstances (*Capitono v Leeds Eastern Health Authority [1989]*.

However, occupiers owe a greater duty of care towards children than adults and have to take account of the possibility of children entering the premises, with children likely to be treated as an 'implied licensee'. In any event, the OLA '57 declares 'an occupier must be prepared for children to be less careful than adults'. The **Occupiers' Liability Act 1984** more specifically considers unlawful visitors.

Occupiers' Liability Act 1984 is concerned with *civil liability* and the duties of *occupiers* to visitors, whether they have lawful authority or not to be in the vicinity, who may be at risk of injury in the occupier's premises, always providing the occupier:

(i)   is aware of the danger or has reasonable grounds to believe that it existed;

(ii) knows or has reasonable grounds to believe that a trespasser is in the vicinity of the danger concerned or that he may come into the vicinity of the danger; and

(iii) is aware the risk is one against which, in all the circumstances of the case, he may be reasonably expected to offer some protection.

Case law has established that occupiers hold some liability towards certain classes of non-*employees*, such as fire fighters and window cleaners. Fire fighters should be warned of 'traps' that the occupiers know to exist (under the **neighbour principle** (*Hartley v British Railways Board [1981] SJ 125*) and a similar situation applies for **employers** of window cleaners working on premises other than their own **unless** the cause of an *accident* was due to a structural defect (*General Cleaning Contractors Ltd v Christmas [1952] 2 AER 1110*).

See also *Workplace (Health, Safety and Welfare) Regulations.*

offensive substances see *noxious substances, hazardous properties, substance.*

office health and safety can be considered in two ways: firstly, by reference to legislative requirements, such as the *Workplace (Health, Safety and Welfare) Regulations 1992*; and, secondly, as a means to increasing profitability and/or productivity, by e.g. reducing sick absences from a variety of sources such as *accidents* at work, fumes from photocopiers or arising from poor ergonomic design.

There is a mandatory **duty** placed on all *employers* for a *risk assessment* of all *workplaces* to be carried out by a *competent person*. The risk assessments will identify the hazards, their risk to the health and safety of *employees* and suggest what action should be taken. As examples, the assessment would include the office design, its workstations (not restricted to Display Screen Equipment workstations), *noise*, ventilation, copiers, phones – with equipment complying with CE marking requirements. Also included in the assessment should be office consumables, such as toners, carbonless paper (which may contain formaldehyde), despite the fact that suppliers **must** provide *safety data sheets* with such products.

Office of National Statistics

The *hazards* associated with office work are frequently overlooked or ill-considered; frequently only the effects are recorded without identifying cause, consequence or preventive measures required. Slipping and tripping hazards from slippery floors, trailing wires and cables, swinging doors, filing cabinet drawer obstructions etc., are the more obvious hazards. However, while the possibility of back problems arising from lifting may be recognised, the possibility of back problems due to poor ergonomic design of chairs may not be identified.

The structure of the building and its services may also be the source of *hazards*. These hazards include: (a) possibility of asbestos in the structure, particularly relevant in the case of buildings built between 1930-1976; (b) radon can accumulate from granite, brick or cement used in *construction*; (c) allergies and respiratory infections can develop and persist from micro-organisms located in air (possibly from air-conditioning, humidifying systems, evaporative condensers, water storage or cooling towers, for which see *legionnaires disease*.

Office of National Statistics, commonly known as ONS, according to its introductory literature, provides demographic data for the UK, based on two sites at Newport (Tel: 01633 812973, email: library@ons.gov.uk) and Pimlico, London (Tel: 0207 533 6262, email info@ons.gov.uk). They provide data on e.g. the population, production, prices, *employment*, socio-economics, and 'working with Eurostat, data of every aspect of life in the European Union'. The Government Statistical Service (GSS) internet home page address is www.statistics.gov.uk the ONS home page is www.ons.gov.uk accessed through StatBase, accessed through the GSS Home Page, which includes StatSearch, the search engine (based on a keyword facility) for information, publications, censuses, statistical data bases and other information sources. Part of StatBase is StatStore, which allows viewing and downloading of data online. StatBase also provides *access* to Navidata 2, allowing exploration, manipulation, charting and mapping time series data and a programme called Beyond 22/20™ enabling cross sectional analysis.

Office of Population Statistics or OPS see *Office of National Statistics.*

Offices, Shops and Railway Premises Act 1963 or OSRPA is virtually dead, following piecemeal revocations, repeals and replacements by various *Regulations*. It has reached the point where providing details of the **OSRPA** may prove misleading, even though reference to **OSRPA** requirements may be found in older health and safety publications and otherwise authoritative works. However, always check the up-to-date position regarding **OSRPA** provisions by contacting the **HSE Information Point** (Tel: 0541 545500).

omission: where there is a known duty to act, such as the general duty of care placed on *employers* by the *Health and Safety at Work etc Act 1974*, and there is a *deliberate* failure to comply with that known duty, then a crime is likely to have been committed. As an example, following inaction from which a death results, that death can then be considered to be the consequence of murder.

open cast mining (commonly called *open pit mining* in the USA) is a form of mining used to extract minerals close to the earth's surface, whereby overlying soil and/or rock is removed to expose the ore. Open cast mining is cheaper than underground mining but currently usually causes greater environmental damage.

operator definitions can vary according to a Regulation. In **COMAH** an operator is the person (or company) who is, or proposes to be, in control of an operation or installation and can include *employees, self-employed persons, contractors* or (*self-employed*) temps. If the person who will be in control is not known, then the operator is the person who commissioned the design or construction.

opinion, strictly speaking, is a term restricted to judgements delivered by the *Law Lords* in the *House of Lords*. However, in popular common usage the term opinion is used: (i) to identify one based on *professional* knowledge and understanding gained through education, *training* and experience; or (ii) meaning a legal opinion, from one or more solicitors or barristers. The term can be carelessly used and misleading, care should be taken when making reference to 'opinion'. Most importantly, the term must not be confused with *decisions* or *precedent*.

organic means materials or substances (e.g. dust) that are of plant or animal origin, containing carbon in their structure. Ill health can be caused, e.g. when inhaled organic dust causes breathing problems (*asthma*, byssinosis, hay fever).

organisational culture derives from the internalised beliefs, ideologies, behaviour and norms (individual and group) that develop within a particular undertaking or plant and expresses itself as the 'culture' of an organisation. To establish and maintain an effective health and safety programme requires an understanding of the culture and how to change or utilise it to achieve the desired effect.

Organisational culture within a large company, with several different geographic locations, can be at two levels, local (in each individual plant of the whole) and national (or international) throughout the company. Contributing factors include the extent, type and way in which *training* is used or applied throughout the organisation and the response to the influence of local area culture. As extreme examples, in some parts of the UK *employees* are known to be relatively compliant, even with trade union affiliation – they consider the *employer* 'knows best', working conditions are accepted virtually without question; however, in other parts of the UK a less compliant workforce may question working conditions (from a health and safety standpoint), continuously seeking *training*, information and improvement. Influencing variables include employment opportunity, *leadership*, *group norms*, training, information, education, literacy level, religion, race and gender.

Even within one company the variation in culture can be so great that visitors or staff travelling from one company location to another may see what appears to be completely different companies, e.g. within the Post Office. This difference can exhibit itself at all levels, from differences in the way customers are treated or dealt with (despite training and systems), to different methods in carrying out the same task. Departments or sections within the same premises can each develop individual own cultures. Finally, the stronger the *group* or organisational culture the greater the resistance to change.

outline (*examination term*) means giving the main features, principles or factors of something, without entering into excessive detail.

overhead crane is a crane that travels on tracks on the ground, usually with a high gantry and cabin from which it is operated. 'Effective measures' **must** be taken to ensure the safety of *employees* and others working on or near the wheeltracks (not merely at the base) of overhead cranes – warning signs alone are insufficient to comply with this *absolute duty*. Do not confuse with *mobile crane*.

overhead travelling crane is one where it is not possible to lift the load higher than the lifting mechanism of the crane; the crane therefore usually travels on overhead tracks, either inside or outside buildings. Do not confuse with *mobile crane*.

oxidising substances and preparations are those which exhibit highly exothermic reactions (characterised or formed with evolution of heat) when in contact with other substances, particularly flammable substances.

ozone is a blue gas with a very strong odour. It is developed during welding processes; operations involving high-voltage electrical equipment and high intensity ultra-violet light; during certain food preparations. It is hazardous to eyes and the respiratory system and toxic by inhalation.

See also *arsine*.

ozone layer is a diffuse layer of ozone, located at 20-50 km in the atmosphere above the earth's surface. It protects the earth's surface from the ill effects of *ultra-violet radiation*. The actual amount of ozone is very small – if brought to sea level it would form a band around three mm thick – nevertheless, it is very effective in its ability to absorb the *ultra-violet radiation*. It has been found that the growth in the use of ozone-destroying chemicals has led to greater levels of *ultra-violet radiation* reaching the surface of the earth, thereby (it is claimed by many scientists) increasing the possibility of skin cancer, genetic mutations, etc.

P

Packaging of Explosives for Carriage Regulations 1991 place certain requirements on those who *package* explosives for transporting, especially such packages being safe to handle and secure. For *labelling* of tankers and vehicles, see *Carriage of Explosives by Road Regulations 1996*.

paraquat is a yellow solid or a methyl sulphate, used as a herbicide, defoliation agent, desiccant, etc. Hazardous to eyes, respiratory system, heart, liver, gastrointestinal tract and the kidneys, symptoms include *dermatitis*, damage to the fingernails, the heart, liver and kidneys, *acute* pulmonary inflammation, irritation of the gastrointestinal tract, eyes, nose and epistaxis.

parasite is an organism that lives in or on another organism and uses that relationship to obtain food energy. Parasites in humans can cause blindness, sickness and death and reduce the possibility of their achieving full development. They can enter the human body through a variety of ways, ranging from ingestion to eggs being laid in the *epidermis*.

Pascal is a *SI unit* of pressure, equal to the force of one Newton per square meter.

PAT see *Portable Appliance Testing*.

pathogen (or pathogene) is any organism that produces disease in a host and may alter the response of the host to other disease processes. *Pathogenic* is acting as a *pathogen*.

penalties are the punishment for a crime, which must be clearly stated before enforcement, and can be financial or imprisonment. Penalties 'awarded' by the courts for health and safety offences to convicted offenders range from the maximum of £20,000 plus the option of up to six months imprisonment on *summary conviction* for breach of the *HSWA* sections 2-6 (£5,000 generally) at *Magistrates' Courts* to the unlimited fine plus up to two years imprisonment for *each offence*, plus the possible award of costs against the convicted offender.

Position in the company is of little account. Imprisonment for managing directors convicted of manslaughter due to gross negligence does occur. The managing director (Mr Kyle) of OLL Limited, after conviction for manslaughter due *to gross negligence*, was sentenced in 1994 to three years imprisonment (OLL Ltd was fined £60,000). A ship's captain and owner (Mark Litchfield) in 1995 was held responsible for the deaths of three members of his crew through failing to comply with health and safety requirements and was sentenced to imprisonment.

Since such convictions are 'criminal' there are several important repercussions for the convicted offender, apart from any fine or imprisonment imposed and irrespective of size of fine. Firstly, the convicted offender will have a criminal record. Secondly, because of the criminal record, this must be declared as such when, for example, completing an entry visa for a foreign country, which can mean the refusal of a visa and entry to the country concerned (e.g. USA).

The **Court of Appeal** judgment in *R v Howe and Sons Engineering Ltd. (1998)* concluded that penalties: (a) must be large enough to drive home (to convicted offenders) the seriousness of failing to provide a safe environment for workers and the public; (b) generally fines should not create the risk of bankruptcy, although in serious offences perhaps the offender should not continue in business; (c) if the offence is very serious then magistrates should consider carefully the need to pass the case on to a higher court, for suitable higher penalties; (d) the standard and duty of care is the same for all companies, regardless of size. The judgment stated that particularly bad are offences where breach of legislation is due to profit motives, failure to carry out the general duties identified in the **HSWA** and/or failure to heed warnings. Mitigating factors noted by the judgment included: (a) prompt admission of responsibility; (b) prompt guilty plea; (c) a good safety record.

perception is the giving of significance to sensations through mental processing. For example what is seen, heard or felt is translated into knowledge and understanding through mental processing into felt pain, or pleasure, or any stage between. It is highly individualistic – each person's perception (i.e. of danger or people) is different.

A problem in health and safety is that an individual's perception of danger or what is dangerous is partly dependent on a mix of past experience, *information*, *training* and/or individual differences (e.g. hearing, colour blindness). These factors contribute to provide the necessary knowledge and understanding of danger. For example, an airborne *toxin* may be invisible but with a fairly strong recognisable odour, which the untrained or uninformed person may be unlikely to recognise (or perceive) as being dangerous. In situations where there is little or inaccurate knowledge and understanding, there can arise serious errors in perception of danger because the reference points are inaccurate or erroneous.

period of employment is defined in s. 176(1) of the *Factories Act 1961* as '. . . the period (**inclusive** of the time allowed for meals and rest) within which persons may be employed on any day' and is still valid.

periodic table

See also *Working Time Regulations*.

periodic table is the classification of elements in tabular form, based on the periodic law of Mendeleev, which declared that the properties of elements were related to their atomic weights. Modern versions of the periodic table arrange elements in order of their atomic numbers.

permanent threshold shift is irreversible damage to hearing from exposure to *noise*, frequently (but **not** invariably) over a long period.

Permits to Work are a written, formalised, systematic statement of work to be done, safety precautions to be taken, confirmation that associated dangers and hazards have been identified, countersigned before entry and after completion of the task. In itself, a Permit to Work is NOT a safe system of work but confirms that precautions have been taken. Typically, a Permit to Work would be drawn up and issued for working in areas with high voltages (above 1,000 *volts*) in *confined spaces*.

Permits to work should be in triplicate, self-carbonated and serial-numbered. The person carrying out the work should retain the original; the first copy given to the person in charge of the area where the work is going to be carried out; the second copy retained by the originator. In detail, a Permit to Work comprises or identifies the following:

(a) who is to do the work;

(b) the time for which it is valid;

(c) the work to be done;

(d) the precautions necessary;

(e) the fact that the Permit to Work cancels all other instructions;

(f) during the application of the Permit to Work, no one must work on tasks not recognised as safe by the permit;

(g) if work is not covered by the permit, no one can carry out such work;

(h) any change in work or workpersons must mean the Permit to Work is amended or cancelled *by the originator of the permit*;

(i) in an emergency situation, another person formally takes over and assumes full responsibility, returning the Permit to Work to the originator;

(j) there must be liaison between the Permit to Work area and other areas which may affected by the work activities;

(k) where appropriate, the limits of the Permit to Work area must be clearly defined and suitably marked;

(l) contractors on site must be briefed prior to commencement of the work;

(m) compliance with all health and safety legislation and procedures, including Permits to Work, must form part of all contracts.

When the work covered by the Permit to Work is completed, the Permit to Work is cancelled *and returned to the originator*. The originator signs the Permit to Work in confirmation that all personnel, plant, equipment and waste has been removed from the area covered. The person responsible for the plant etc. must check that all has been returned, that the Permit to Work has been correctly cancelled and accept final responsibility for the plant etc.

personal hearing protection, limitations of, include (with method of resolution in brackets): incorrect wearing (*training*); fitted incorrectly (improve selection, *training*); incompatible with other PPE (improve selection); interference with normal *communication* (improve selection); easily damaged (improve selection, *training*, assess work environment); unhygienic (improve selection, *training*). *Consultation* with employees, a legal duty, can eliminate or minimise many of the problems.

personal protective equipment generally means 'all equipment (including clothing affording protection against the weather) which is intended to be worn or held by a person at work and which protects (them) against one or more risks to (their) health or safety, and any addition or accessory designed to meet that objective'. **PPER**,Reg.2(1)).

PPER is the acronym for *Personal Protective Equipment Regulations* (see below).

Personal Protective Equipment Regulations 1992 and the *Personal Protective Equipment (Amendment) 1994* **(*PPER*)** requires that *employers* carry out an *assessment* and where necessary, provide **as a last resort**, after **all** other measures have been considered (i.e. **elimination, substitution or controls**), appropriate personal protective equipment (PPE).

The *employer* must ensure:

assessments are carried out (which will identify where and which control measures are necessary, with PPE the last resort;

charges are not made for any PPE supplied to *employees* (or visitors) as a requirement of health and safety legislation;

compatibility of PPE with other equipment;

consultations are carried out with the proposed user concerning the PPE, its selection, use and maintenance;

personal sampling

EC approved and marked PPE must be purchased;

employers must ensure PPE supplied as a consequence of legislative requirements is worn, maintained, stored correctly, etc.;

ergonomic factors must be taken account of;

footwear must be suitable for the purpose, i.e. non-slip, toe-protectors;

instruction and training must be provided to relevant *employees* (and lawful visitors) in the use **and** maintenance of the PPE supplied;

proper use of PPE must be made by wearers, supervised by *employers*;

storage accommodation must be provided, of adequate nature;

sufficient standard and quality of PPE supplied in accord with the Regulations and subsequent amendments;

suitability of PPE, e.g. must fit the intended wearer.

Employee's **legal duties** include:

maintaining the PPE, following instruction, information and training;

reporting any defects in the PPE;

storing the PPE in the *adequate and suitable* storage accommodation provided by the *employer*;

wearing of PPE that has been supplied by the *employer*.

It is a criminal act, under the **HSWA**, **PPER** and other regulations, if *employers* fail to provide suitable and adequate PPE. Equally, any *employee* who refuses or fails to wear or maintain supplied PPE, after suitable and adequate training, can be prosecuted and/or dismissed. PPE does **not** include uniforms, ordinary working clothes or protective clothes provided for food handlers for food hygiene purposes, unless such items also perform a health and safety function. However, the PPE Regulations cover wet weather wear.

personal sampling is where a measurement, for example of air or radiation, is taken and recorded via an attachment to an operator. The attachment may be a tube, drawing in air to a sampling device, which may be displayed, for example on a meter or a hazard/substance sensitive strip, which e.g. changes colour, displayed on a badge.

persons at work are defined in s.52 of the HSWA as *'employees* in the course of their *employment* and *self-employed* persons throughout the time they devote to work as *self-employed* persons'. It should be noted that persons not at work but who may be affected by the activities (in the widest sense of the term) of those at work can also be covered by the HSWA and much associated legislation.

pesticides are products, almost invariably chemical, used to kill or restrict the development of pests (those organisms considered undesirable by society). They include *fungicides, herbicides* and *insecticides*. However beneficial pesticides are, they may present environmental hazards and problems, and demand controls and great care in their manufacture, application and use.

phenol is a near colourless crystalline solid, with a sweet odour, used in manufacturing plywood, industrial coatings, the synthesis of synthetic resins, detergents, polyester, disinfectant agents etc. Hazardous to the liver, kidneys, skin and toxic by inhalation, absorption, ingestion and contact, symptoms include anorexia, weight loss, muscle aches, dark urine, liver and kidney damage, dermatitis, tremors and convulsions, etc.

photocopier hazards include the possibility of emissions of e.g. ultra-violet light and ozone which can cause sickness and severe headaches. Companies who routinely maintain photocopiers should provide a written statement that the machine, after maintenance, satisfies all relevant health and safety legislation; for example that toners comply with **COSHH** and *Safety Data Sheet* supplied.

photon is an invisible unit of electromagnetic energy emitted by radiation or light source having zero rest mass.

See also *laser*.

physical hazards include *noise, vibration, temperature, radiation, fire* and *mechanical hazards*.

See also *control limits, control measures* and *mnemonics* (ERICPD).

place of work, in the simplest possible terms, is virtually anywhere and everywhere in the UK or offshore in territorial waters where an employed or *self-employed* person works. As with all simple explanations or definitions, questions are raised such as 'are sales representatives covered by health and safety legislation while driving and travelling?', since the sales person's car interior could perhaps be defined as a specific 'place of work' but the law is unclear on this matter (although lorry cab interiors *are* recognised as places of work). **Case law** intervenes: the Court of Session decided that *a fork lift truck, operating inside and outside buildings, could not be described as a place of work*. However, this decision was disapproved of by the High Court during *Cox v HB Angus Ltd [1981] ICR 683* (cab of fire engine was determined to be a place of work).

Unfortunately with legislation answers can depend on many factors. The answer for the sales person can depend on factors *outside* the place or activity, including interpretation of fine legal points (e.g. was the sales person **in the course of (his/her) employment**), and ultimately on decisions of judges who are constrained by the recognition that, 'the law is not concerned with facts, it is concerned with the law'.

A prime objective of all health and safety law or legislation is to ensure the provision of a **safe place of work** by an **employer**. A place of work has extensive cover from health and safety legislation, particularly the principal legislation, such as the **HSWA**, the **WHSWR** and the **CHSWR**. According to the **HSWA** s.2(2)(d) the **employers'** duty towards their **employees** includes that of providing, **'so far as is reasonably practicable'**, the maintenance of any place of work under the **employers'** control, safe and without risks to health including providing and maintaining safe means of **access** to and **egress** from it.

plaintiff is a term that is reported to have been replaced by that of **claimant**.

planning helps to ensure, for example, effective safety management. It should:

    (a) be all encompassing, identifying all *reasonably* foreseeable events;
    (b) identify targets and objectives;
    (c) set performance targets for:
        (i) management;
        (ii) hazard identification;
        (iii) risk control;
    (d) base targets on:
        (i) **risk assessments**;
        (ii) legal standards as a *minimum*.

planning law has some application in the prevention or control of pollution, largely through granting or denying planning permission in the case of new development. The particularly relevant provisions are found in sections 55, 57 and 70 of the *Town and Country Planning Act 1997* (or the *Town and Country (Scotland) Act 1997*, sections 26, 28, 37 and 38).

plastics are organic materials, commonly petroleum based, which can be shaped or moulded under heat, pressure or both. They are widely used but the processes used during their manufacture and use creates toxic hazards and waste, and problems in disposal, since plastics deteriorate slowly, if at all.

plume is the emission of gases and particulate matter from a chimney that are not immediately dispersed but retain their distinct identity as they move away from the source. They, or their contents, can create havoc to the environment.

plutonium is an *actinide*, a silvery dense metal, produced as a result of nuclear reactions. Plutonium has a *half-life* of 24,000 years and the high level of radioactivity it emits during that time makes it one of the most hazardous elements known (neptunium, another *actinide*, has a *half-life* of 2.1 million years).

pneumoconiosis is the name of a chronic lung disease, caused by the inhalation of dust, almost inevitably over a long period. Commonly found amongst general miners, called silicosis or, with coal miners, termed black lung.

poisons unit provides information to **medical professionals** on toxins, possible effects and their treatment. It is **not**, repeat **not**, a general public inquiry point. The Unit for the UK is located at the Medical Toxicology Unit, New Cross Hospital, Avonley Road, New Cross, London SE14 5ER. Tel: 020 7955 5000 (tie line via Guys Hospital) or, for emergencies, direct line 020 7635 9171.

polluter pays is the principle adopted by the UK and some other countries (including the USA) whereby those who cause the pollution pay for its clean-up or prevention. The polluter can be the producer *and/or* the consumer.

The principle is an important part of the current UK environmental legislation, divided by the **EPA 1990** into providing two categories – A having full liability for the site as owner, occupier and polluter; B typified by a purchaser with limited liability. A 'Class A' group can transfer liability to 'Class B', for example, if sufficient remedial action is taken or if a site is sold complete with *adequate* information as to its contamination. 'Adequate' means sufficient to allow the purchasers to carry out their own investigation and evaluation of the site.

Persons who hold a *Waste Disposal Licence* for a site have special liability. It is important to recognise that the site owner/occupier will almost invariably be held liable for contaminated land.

pollution from vessels on the sea is controlled by the *Merchant Shipping (Prevention of Oil Pollution) Regulations 1996, Merchant Shipping Act 1995* (sections 128-151), *Food and Environment Protection Act 1985* (sections 5-15; dumping at sea).

Pollution Prevention and Control Act 1999 is an enabling **Act** which requires implementing regulations. The UK was very tardy in introducing such pollution legislation and did not achieve the EC deadline for implementation. However, the proposed ***Pollution Prevention and Control Regulations***, enabled by the 1999 **Act** may be implemented in late 2000. The current situation requires checking.

Polyvinyl Chloride (PVC) is the most commonly used plastic, a mix of the hydrocarbon (ethylene) with the addition of a chlorine atom. It is extremely versatile in use but in its powdered form inhalation can cause pneumoconiosis and if burnt releases hydrochloric acid gas and ***dioxins***. The acid gas can easily be removed through use of scrubbers, but ***dioxins*** are far more difficult to remove. ***Dioxins*** can cause the development of cancer, neurological problems and birth defects.

Portable Appliance Testing (or PAT) is used to determine the safety of portable electrical appliances, particularly their insulation.

See *Electrical Equipment (Safety) Regulations 1994* and the **HSE** leaflet **INDG236L**.

portable electrical appliance is usually defined as portable electrical equipment, with a plug and lead.

Dangers (preventive measures in brackets) with portable electrical appliances include: those arising from faulty leads and plugs (regular recorded maintenance, replace); unsuitable equipment (improve selection, change); 240 volt operation (substitute 110 volt or lower); metal fuses (replace with RCDs); misuse (instruct, inform and train); fire and explosion (regular recorded maintenance, unwind cables before and during use).

See **HSE** leaflet **INDG236L** and *Portable Appliance Testing*.

power is a measure of work done or energy expended per unit of time. The unit of power is the *watt*.

powers of enforcement officers are extremely wide ranging. They are generally associated with the *HSE* but there are others, e.g. Environmental Health Officers (EHOs), Fire Prevention Officers, etc., who are appointed to carry out inspections, ensure compliance with the relevant statutory provision and give advice. However, Enforcement Officers cannot inspect their own premises, for example the EHOs inspect *HSE* offices and vice versa.

Powers of Enforcement Officers, commonly called 'Inspectors', included:

(i)   enter any premises at any reasonable time, if necessary (e.g. in the event of refusal) utilising the services of the police;
(ii) be accompanied by any other person duly authorised by the enforcing authority, together with materials and equipment, which may be required;
(iii) direct that premises, or part of them, must be left undisturbed for so long as is reasonably necessary;
(iv) take measurements and photographs and make such recordings as considered necessary;
(v)   take samples of any articles or substances found on the premises, and of the atmosphere;
(vi) dismantle or subject to test any article or substance, which they think is likely to cause danger to health and safety;
(vii) take possession of, and detain, any article or substance for so long as is necessary. In such cases, a notice explaining the inspector's actions must be left at the premises;
(viii) question any person who may have information relevant to the investigations, and require that person to sign a declaration of the truth of the answers; If the evidence taken is *admissible*, persons who are a 'suspect' must be cautioned to comply with the **Police and Criminal Evidence Act**;
(ix) require the production of any books or documents, which are relevant to the investigations;
(x)   demand facilities and assistance as necessary to carry out their duties; and
(xi) assume such additional powers as are necessary to enable them to carry into effect the relevant statutory provisions.

Written responses, verified by signature as being truthful, are *not* admissible as evidence in any subsequent proceeding *against that person*. Furthermore, some documents may be protected by 'legal professional privilege'.

practicable means something that it is possible to do, taking account of 'current knowledge and invention' (per Parker J. in *Adsett v K. & L. Steelfounders and*

practical assessment

Engineers Ltd (1953)). Cost, time or trouble are not usually considered in the equation – if it can be done, it must be done. The test of practicality includes that of foreseeability and cannot be based on hindsight.

See also **reasonably practical**.

practical assessment is not to be confused with **(risk) assessment.** A practical assessment is very wide and sometimes used for examination purposes. However, it is a very useful technique for a fairly in-depth study of a health and safety 'problem' in a workplace, section or undertaking. The process of carrying out a practical assessment commences with identifying **hazards** (virtually a **risk assessment**), describing breaches of legislation, proposing appropriate **control measures** and any **training needs**, consideration of necessary action and, most importantly, taking account of cost *and savings* (in effect, a **cost benefit analysis**).

The writing-up of a practical assessment should bear in mind the following:

(i)   its purpose is to convince management that action must be taken;
(ii) keep it clear, precise and as simple as possible;
(iii) the layout MUST be consistent and contribute to understanding, not crushed together, without paragraphs which would mean that a reader could not easily understand points made;
(iv) keep hazards and resultant dangers in one subsection, separate from suggested control measures and action to be taken *with cost*, e.g.:
　　(a) Paragraph 1 – Headed 'Electricity', sub-para 1.1. e.g. all electrical hazards, electrocution, briefly identify breach of (which) **Regulations.** Make sure you identify where hazard(s) are located.
　　(b) Para 1.2 – Control measures and action to be taken e.g. low voltage, RCDs, regular maintenance, inspection and testing, **training** for staff. Conclude this paragraph with cost *and forecasted saving/benefits.*
　　(c) Repeat for each separate 'type' of hazard, e.g. machinery, electricity.
(v)   provide 'Conclusion' presenting simple list of hazards/action required *in order of priority,* and summarise in one short paragraph **relevant** points.

The person who reads and takes the decision to action the assessment may not have any great understanding or knowledge of health, safety or environmental matters. In fact, they may only be interested in complying with the law and avoiding penalties (not usually admitted, but regrettably sometimes true).

Therefore conciseness, simple terms and clarity are essential. The objective of a practical assessment is not to demonstrate the great knowledge or cleverness of the compiler but to get something done.

precedent comes in many forms or 'levels'. Concentrating on implications for health and safety, one 'type' of precedent is a judgment or decision that is referred to (*cited*) to justify a *decision* in a later, apparently similar, case. There are *authoritative precedents*, which are generally binding and **normally** must be followed; *persuasive precedents* which need not be followed; *declaratory precedent* which applies an existing rule of law; and an *original precedent* which creates and applies a new rule of law. Decisions on questions of fact must not be cited as precedents. The 'level' of precedent is related to the 'status' of the court where the precedent was established, in simple terms, the higher the court the higher the precedent. It should be noted that the Lord Chancellor in 1966 declared in the House of Lords that if 'too rigid adherence to precedence may lead to injustice . . . (departure) . . . from a previous decision . . . (is allowable) . . . when it appears right to do so'.

preparation: a mixture or solution of two or more substances.

presbycusis is a term used to describe hearing loss induced following the onset of old age and consequential deterioration of the middle ear ossicles leading to a reduction in their ability to transmit higher frequency vibrations.

prescribed industrial diseases are those industrially induced diseases, which are listed (i.e. prescribed), in the Benefit Agency's leaflet *NI 2*; benefit (subject to proof) is an automatic entitlement. Examples include **industrially induced** *asbestosis, asthma, deafness* and, subject to different rules, '*tennis elbow*'. After a claim has been made, an *Insurance Officer* (who is independent from but usually based at a *Benefits Agency* office) determines entitlement. A *medical tribunal* (meaning at least **two** doctors) assesses the significance of the prescribed disease, the percentage of disability and how long the disability will last. Claims are made through use of Form *BI 100B*. There is a 90-day waiting period before benefit is paid. There is also a *review* and *appeal* procedure.

See *BI 95*.

preventive and protective measures, according to the *MHSWR,* are those '*measures which have been identified by the employer or by the self-employed in consequence of the assessment of the measures he* (sic) *needs to take to comply with the requirements and prohibitions imposed upon him* (sic) *by or under the relevant statutory provisions and by Part II of the Fire Precautions (Workplace) Regulations 1997'.*

privilege, in short, and for the purpose of this dictionary, means that the *discovery* and inspection of certain documents can be withheld, on the ground of some special interest *protected by law*. For example, **communications** between an **employer** and his/her insurance company, would almost invariably be a privileged, non-discoverable document.

probability theory is used quite extensively in health and safety, although it may not be so termed. In technical terms, probability theory is a branch of mathematics that deals with measuring or determining quantitatively the likelihood that an event will have a particular outcome. Probability theory studies the permutations and combinations arising from an event, e.g. if a coin is tossed x number of times, probability theory will calculate the possible outcome. For example, as part of a health and safety risk assessment the probability of 'something happening' is often measured or quantified on a 1-10 basis (1 = almost impossible, with 5 = even chance, through to 10 = inevitable).

In health and safety, probability theory is a very useful tool because it can predict the likelihood of an incident occurring *and* the extent or type of injury, loss or damage likely to occur. However, it is only accurate (and therefore useful) if trained professionals are involved at all stages of its application and interpretation.

procurator fiscal is an officer of the Sheriff Court in Scotland (roughly equivalent to the English County Court, i.e. 'higher' than a **Magistrates' Court** of England and Wales). The procurator fiscal must be a qualified advocate or solicitor and therefore cannot be considered similar to the **Magistrate** of England and Wales.

producer can have various meanings in connection with health and safety. The term is frequently defined within specific legislation or through reference to *case law*. For example, under the **Consumer Protection Act 1987** a producer *liable for a defective product* includes the manufacturer, a person whose name or trademark is on a product, an importer of a product into the European Community, and a supplier who, when reasonably asked to do so by a person injured, must provide the producer's name and address.

product liability see *liability*.

prohibition notice is served where an enforcement officer (inspector) is of the opinion that continuing with an activity presents the risk of serious personal injury (sometimes termed 'imminent personal danger'). The prohibition notice must: (i) state the inspector's opinion; (ii) specifically state what creates the risk; (iii) if there is breach of or anticipated breach of statutory provisions, identify the relevant statutory provisions and give reasons why there could be a breach; and (iv) stop the prohibited activities until the actions required have been carried out. Usually prohibition notices takes immediate effect but can be deferred until a specified date – the 'deferred prohibition notice'.

There is no need for an inspector to believe that a statutory provision has been or is being contravened partly because prohibition notices are served 'in anticipation of danger'.

Failure to comply with a prohibition notice attracts the severest penalties, including possibly imprisonment. Appeals are made to an *employment tribunal*, with the notice staying in effect until the decision of the tribunal is reached.

propane see *liquid propane gas*.

prophylaxis means preventive treatment.

proton is a stable elementary or subatomic particle carrying an electrical charge equal to, but of opposite polarity to, an *electron*. The number of protons in a *nucleus* of an *atom* indicates its atomic number.

***Provision and Use of Work Equipment Regulations 1998* or PUWER** requires *employers* to ensure that all *work equipment*, new and secondhand, ranging from *machinery* to *hand tools*, from *abrasive wheels* to scissors, e.g. including pencil sharpeners, staplers, provided for use at work and taking account of its purpose, is safe to use, operate and *maintain* and suitable for the purpose for which it is provided. *Use* of machinery covers any activity relating to work equipment, including 'starting, stopping, programming, setting, transporting, repairing, modifying, maintaining, servicing and cleaning'. A review of selected salient points from **PUWER** includes:

> **adequate lighting** must be provided to allow safe use of work equipment (Reg. 21);

> **assessment must be carried out** and *significant risks* recorded where five or more are employed and drawn to the attention of *all employees;*

> **CE requirements** must be complied with, including displaying the CE mark, to demonstrate that the work equipment has satisfied the EC Directive;

> **consultation** should be carried out with regard to health and safety of work equipment with *Safety* and/or *Elected Representatives;*

controls which start, stop 'or make a significant change in operating conditions' by deliberate action must be provided in a suitable position;

guarding and hierarchy of control measures (machinery), which are suitable and allow safe maintenance required by **PUWER** (Reg. 11(2)) following: (i) fixed guards; (ii)other guards or protective devices, e.g. mechanical, trip, pressure mats etc.; (iii) *protection appliances*, e.g. jigs, push-sticks; (iv) provision of *information, instruction, training* and *supervision*;

high and very low temperature where work equipment is produced, used or stored must have protection to prevent any injury (Reg. 12);

information, **instruction and training**, which are suitable and sufficient, must be provided to operators, supervisors and managers (Reg. 8 and 9);

inspection of work equipment before use where its safety depends on installation conditions *and* if work equipment is exposed to conditions causing deterioration (Reg. 6);

maintenance must be carried out and, where logged/recorded, the log must be kept up to date (Reg. 5);

marking equipment clearly for reasons of health and safety, for example, to identify operational parameters, such as pressures (Reg. 23);

particular precautions must be put in place to ensure that maintenance operations do not give rise to risks to health and safety, e.g. machinery normally safe to operate may be highly dangerous to maintain;

risks, specific, associated with use, modifications or maintenance of work equipment, must be taken into account (Reg. 7);

selection of equipment must take account of the working conditions and risks found in the premises, together with consideration of the health and safety of persons through the use and location of the work equipment (Reg. 4);

stop and emergency stop controls, must be easy to identify and *access,* safe to use and be designed to ensure health and safety, including (where appropriate) the possibility of isolating machinery from its power source (Reg. 15 and 16);

suitability of work equipment for its purpose and used only for that which is suitable (Reg. 4);

warnings must be fitted or used where necessary, e.g. notices, flashing lights, etc. (Reg. 24).

Part III of the **PUWER** 1997 refers to *mobile work equipment*, which includes forklift trucks. **Employers** who have mobile work equipment provided for use before 5 December 1998 have until 5 December 2002 before **PUWER** 1998 applies. Part III also includes: **employees** carried on work equipment; rolling over of mobile work equipment (Reg. 26); overturning of fork lift trucks (Reg. 27); self-propelled work equipment (Reg. 28); remote-controlled self-propelled work equipment (Reg.29); drive shafts (Reg. 30).

Part IV of **PUWER** covers power presses and in particular press exemptions, the examination of power presses, guards and protection devices (Reg. 32); inspection of guards and protection devices (Reg.33); reports (Reg. 34) and keeping of information (Reg. 35).

Part V provides for exemptions and transitional provision.

Schedule 1 identifies instruments which give effect to Community Directives concerning the safety of products.

Schedule 2 refers to power presses to which Regs. 33 to 36 do not apply.

psychology is a discipline very useful for health and safety introduction, application, monitoring, review, improvement and maintenance. It falls within the discipline of *social science* and only an outline is provided. However, inspection of psychology suggests that unless you have 'done the course' it can prove daunting and its usefulness in health and safety overlooked. In brief, the important 'types,' 'perspectives' or 'schools' of psychology include:

Behavioural scientists consider that psychologists should only study observable behaviour for it to be a science. See *behavioural science*.

Biopsychological which suggests that for every behaviour, feeling and thought, there is a corresponding physical event in the brain. Biopsychology tries to identify and understand this relationship. Sperry, who was awarded the Nobel Prize for his work on the split brain, is an example of a biopsychologicalist.

Cognitive perspective refers to the many ways that we process or transform information. It includes the mental process of thinking, knowing, perceiving, attending and remembering. In health and safety, cognitive psychology is useful in assisting people to identify danger and hazards and to resolve the dangers they face. Neisser and Duncker are two important proponents of cognitive psychology, with Kotovsky and Simon, as early as 1973, using computers to attempt to demonstrate how the human brain solves problems.

Humanistic approach places emphasis on the 'whole person' and in particular the individual's subjective experience. Humanists declare that persons can choose and, provided they are given the opportunity, welcome accepting responsibility for their own lives. Leading humanists included Carl Rogers (encounter groups) and Abraham Maslow (hierarchy of **motivation**).

Psychodynamic assumption is that unconscious forces are important influences on human behaviour. Catharsis and free association, used by Freudians and non-Freudians, are examples of the psychodynamic perspective.

The above perhaps well illustrates how understanding of psychology is not helped by the differences and even disagreements (which are more often key debates) between the multi-method approaches to issues or within the 'schools' of psychology. On the other hand, such differences (and debate) *are* constructive in developing knowledge, understanding and advancing the science. Nevertheless, confusion is compounded by national differences influencing approaches to the same discipline; e.g. US psychologists frantically scramble for solutions; German psychologists march in straight lines towards a solution; British psychologists wander towards a solution, taking care not to give offence.

In fact, we all use psychology throughout our lives. If you have a partner, a truly successful relationship, even maintain a poor relationship (for whatever reason) or bring up children, you use just about every psychological technique in existence. In short, you manipulate a person or a number of persons.. Manipulation of **employees** through use of psychology by professionally trained and qualified persons is a very inexpensive, effective way of installing, improving and ensuring high standards in overall health and safety. Indeed in some European countries (such as the Netherlands), it is a significant part of the legal framework and approach to health and safety.

See also **human factors**.

Public Health Act 1936 covers buildings and sanitation largely through bylaws, but local authorities are not obliged to make or introduce them.

Public Health Act 1961 gives the Minister powers to make building regulations. Local authorities can relax or not apply building regulation requirements considered unreasonable.

See *Building Regulations 1991 (and 1984)*.

puisne judges are inferior or junior judges. For example, High Court judges are styled puisne judges.

PUWER see *Provision and Use of Work Equipment Regulations 1998*.

PVC see *Polyvinyl Chloride*.

pyrethrum is a brown oil or solid, used as an insecticide and on crops. Hazardous to the respiratory system, skin and central nervous system, toxic by inhalation, ingestion and contact, symptoms include erythema, dermatitis, asthma, etc.

Q

qualitative differences are of actual and potention outcome, such as injuries, ill health or damage.

See also *risk assessment.*

quantitative differences in outcomes include those from minor or major injuries or damage.

See also *risk assessment.*

quantum: the smallest indivisible quantity of radiant energy, a *photon.*

Queen's Bench Division (QBD) is a division of the High Court, consisting of two to three judges presided over by the Lord Chief Justice with a staff of *puisne judges.* It possesses civil, criminal, original, appellate and supervisory powers. The QBD exercises the most *jurisdiction* of all the *Divisional Courts,* provides judicial review, hears appeals by way of *case stated* from *Magistrates' Courts* (in family law) or from the *Crown Court* and hears applications for *Habeas Corpus* (a prerogative writ to determine validity of a person's detention); it also deals among other matters with claims in *tort* or *contract.* It includes the *Commercial* and *Admiralty Courts.*

Quinone is a yellow solid with an acrid odour, derived from *benzene,* used, for example, in the following industrial processes: insecticides and fungicides, polymers, resins, tanning, etc. Hazardous to the skin and eyes, toxic by inhalation, ingestion and contact, symptoms include conjunctivitis, eye and skin irritation.

R

Race Relations Act 1976 covers discrimination with regard to colour, race, nationality, ethnic or national origins. The RRA could apply in health and safety if, for example, one ethnic group was favoured over others (unfairly) for a particular task.

radiant energy is energy transmitted in the form of *radiation*, for example as rays, waves or streams of particles.

radiation is the giving off of energy, rays or waves. It is the emission and propagation of energy in space or through a material in the form of waves, the transfer of heat or light by waves of energy, usually refers to electromagnetic radiation but can also be applied to sound waves and emitted particles. Radiation is **non-ionising** or **ionising**, the former of lower frequency than the latter.

radiation measurement is carried out, for example, using a *Geiger Counter*, a form of **grab sampling** (e.g. sucking air through a tube across a sensitised diode).

radiation sickness is caused by exposure to a sub-lethal dose of ionising radiation (between 100-300 **rem**). Symptoms include nausea, vomiting, diarrhoea, hair loss, haemorrhaging and damage to the bone marrow, miscarriages and stillbirths. Long-term effects include increased risk of leukaemia and other forms of cancer.

Radioactive Substances Act 1993 or RSA requires premises that keep radioactive material to be registered through an application to the Chief Radiation Inspector, with the registration certificate on display and available for inspection. The RSA also covers radioactive waste disposal (e.g. the waste cannot be directly disposed of from trade premises without authorisation from the Chief Radiation Inspector).

radioactivity is emitted from the decay of atomic nuclei of *radionuclides*. Exposure to radioactivity can have harmful or positive effects, e.g. in treating certain cancers.

radionuclide is a spontaneously disintegrating nucleus of an *atom*, which releases radioactivity in the process, e.g. *uranium* and *radium* atoms are radionuclides.

radon gas is a naturally occurring colourless and tasteless radioactive gas formed by the delay of radium in the soil and enters buildings through cracks and other openings. If trapped, radon can accumulate to hazardous concentrations. Hazardous to the respiratory system, kidneys and blood, radon is toxic by inhalation. Symptoms include cancer and non-neoplastic diseases, silicosis, chronic obstructive pulmonary disease, fibrosis, emphysema, lung cancer, etc.

RCD see *Residual Current Device.*

reasonably practical is often described by association with a pair of scales, one scale carrying 'risk', the other the 'time, cost, trouble and physical difficulty'. If the scale containing 'risk' goes down, then injury, damage or loss is highly likely; if the other scale goes down, the probability of injury, damage or loss is low.

In legal terms, if the quantum of risk exceeds the time, trouble, cost, technical knowledge and physical difficulty of carrying out the duty then the control or protective measure must be carried out or installed, irrespective of the financial position or size of the *employer's* company or undertaking (*Edwards v National Coal Board [1949] 1 AER 743 CA; Marshall v Gotham and Co [1954] 1 AER 937*). See also HS(G)65L p. 42).

reclamation or improvement of land see *derelict land.*

recognised trade unions are those recognised by an *employer* for the purpose of collective bargaining, including health and safety. For example, trade union Safety Representatives (SR) are not legally recognised as complying with the SRSC *Regulations*, until a 'letter of appointment' including health, safety and welfare has been received by the *employer* from the *independent and recognised* trade union concerned.

If an *employer* does not *recognise* a trade union, even if that union has members working for the *employer*, that trade union may have no rights as a negotiating body e.g. for the appointment of **SR**s. Incidentally, an *employer* would find it difficult to 'de-recognise' a trade union it had previously recognised: in the case of *Griffith v South West Water Services (1995) IRLR* the court held that despite the fact the *employer* had de-recognised the union and established a works council, the union remained the legitimate representative body for the workers.

recorder is a *barrister* or *solicitor* appointed as a part-time judge. A recorder must agree to be available regularly for at least four weeks per year. Recorders usually sit in the Crown Court, but may also sit in the **County** or **High Court**.

Red List is a *British list,* currently comprising some 23 substances, named in

European Directives, which have minimised discharge levels because they are dangerously pollutant. They include **DDT**, **mercury** and its **compounds**.

reference doses are an estimate of the daily exposure of the population to a potential hazard that is likely to be 'taken in' without risk of deleterious health effects during a lifetime.

Regulations are *statutory instruments*, which have been laid before (but not necessarily debated in) and approved by Parliament. *Regulations* are termed *delegated* or *subordinate* legislation. For example, Secretaries of State may be 'enabled' under an Act of Parliament (such as by the **HSWA** s.15) to draft, publish and thereby introduce *Regulations* in health and safety, often (but not always) following proposals from the HSC. While *Regulations* do not need to be debated or voted upon, they can be vetoed by a vote within forty days of being laid before Parliament.

See also **general duties** and **goal setting**.

Regulations, similar to the **HSWA**, are generally goal setting – what must be achieved rather than how it must be done – leaving **employers** the right to decide how to control identified risks. There are exceptions however, some *Regulations* (and requirements) *are* prescriptive and spell out in detail what must be done. Such *Regulations* place an **absolute duty** on **employers** to do certain things either specifically, e.g. during the removal of asbestos, or identifying mandatory duties, e.g. assessments **must** be carried out.

relevant agreement has its literal meaning but it is a concept not widely known or used in the UK. However, in the **Working Time Regulations** the concept is a key element, referring to a **collective agreement** or a **workforce agreement**.

relevant training is defined within the *Health and Safety (Training for Employment) Regulations* 1990 as work experience provided pursuant to a *training* course or programme, or *training* for *employment*, or both. All persons receiving *training* or work experience, including school children on work experience and college students on sandwich courses, and government *training* schemes, are **employees** and, incidentally, covered by health and safety legislation. **Employers** (and *training* establishments) should note that a higher degree of care, supervision and *training* almost invariably will be necessary to take account of relative inexperience and any immaturity (see *Carmichael (Procurator Fiscal, Airdres) v Rosehall Engineering Works Ltd. (1983) IRLR 480*).

See also **employment**.

rem is an acronym for the *Roentgen Equivalent Man,* an old measure of the biological effect of radiation on the human body. The term rem has been replaced by the *sievert* (Sv), with one Sv being equivalent to 100 rem.

remedial notice is issued, after a consultation period of up to three months, to a person responsible for doing any necessary clean-up work for **contaminated land** and paying for it, or to the owner and/or occupier of **contaminated land.** The **EPA 1990** requires the enforcing authority to identify in the notice what is required, with cost a consideration. If a remedial notice is *not* complied with then the enforcing authority may carry out the work itself and recover reasonable costs from the **appropriate person.**

renewable energy is energy from natural sources – e.g. wind, flowing water, the sun – that can be replaced as it is used or relatively quickly. Environmental concerns have led to increased consideration and use of renewable energy sources but they may not be without problems. For example, unrestricted or unplanned hydroelectric development can have a detrimental effect on the *ecosystem.*

repeals (of Acts of Parliament) can be total (the whole Act) or partial (just referring to a sentence, phrase or single section).

See also *revocations of Regulations.*

repetitive strain injuries see *work related upper limb disorders.*

Reporting of Injuries, Diseases and Dangerous Occurrences Regulations 1995 or RIDDOR cover all places of *employment* and place duties on *employers, self-employed* and those in control of work premises concerning the reporting of injuries (following three days or more absence from work), diseases and specified dangerous occurrences.

Under RIDDOR a *responsible person* has the duty to report to the relevant enforcing authority any of the following, which arises from 'or in connection with work', including those resulting from violence at work *and* members of the public killed or taken to hospital following an injury received from an *accident* occurring at work. Selected salient points are:

    Dangerous gas fittings (and equipment) installed or maintained by persons approved under the *Gas Safety (Installation and Use) Regulations 1994* **must** be notified to the **HSE.**

    Dangerous occurrences include: the failure of any load-bearing part or overturning of any lifting machinery; fire or explosions associated with electrical short circuits or overloads, requiring the plant to be shut down for 24 hours or having the *potential* to cause death; the release or escape, or *potential* release or escape, of a biological agent likely to cause severe human infection or disease; the malfunction of breathing apparatus *while in use* **or** *during testing before use* which could have resulted in danger to the health and safety of the user. Malfunctions found during routine maintenance are excepted.

Death as the result of an *industrial accident*. In addition, if an *employee dies within one year as a result of a reportable accident employers* must notify the enforcing authority as soon as they know of the death.

Gas, certain matters associated with suppliers of flammable gas through a fixed pipe system and those who import, fill or supply liquid petroleum gas must report any death or major injury associated with their activities.

Injuries causing more than three-day absence must be reported and *include* those resulting from 'violence to staff'; the day the *accident* happened **not** being included but non-working days (i.e. Sunday) *are* included.

Major injuries *under RIDDOR* include amputation; fractures (other than those to fingers, thumbs and toes); dislocation of the shoulder, hip, knee or spine; electric shock leading to unconsciousness *or* requiring resuscitation *or* requiring admission to hospital for more than 24 hours; loss of sight (temporary or permanent); chemical or hot metal burn to the eye; any penetrating injury to the eye; acute illness requiring medical treatment or loss of consciousness arising from absorption of *any* substance by inhalation, ingestion or through the skin; acute illness requiring medical treatment *where there is reason to believe* that this resulted from exposure to a biological agent, its toxins or infected material.

Reportable *work-related* **diseases**, as provided in Schedule 3 of RIDDOR include those from: (a) exposure to physical agents: i.e. cataracts due to electromagnetic radiation, decompression illness, lung, or other organ damage, etc.; (b) from physical demands of work: i.e. carpal tunnel syndrome, tetanus, etc.; (c) arising from substances: i.e. cancer of the urinary tract or bladder, occupational dermatitis or asthma, pneumoconiosis (excluding asbestosis), extrinsic alveotis (including farmers' lung).

Responsible person reports to the enforcing authority deaths, *major accidents* and conditions and *dangerous occurrences by the quickest possible*

Residential Care Homes

means, usually the telephone, following which a form F2508 must be sent to the enforcing authority within ten days. In the case of a more than three-day absence of an *employee* due to a work-related injury, the responsible person sends a F2508, to the enforcing authority within ten days.

Residential Care Homes see *Nursing Homes and Mental Nursing Homes.*

Residual Current Device (commonly called a RCD) is a mechanical switching device or association of devices, which cause the opening of contacts when a given value of residual current exceeds a predetermined value. It is fast, and protects the *user* of equipment. Strictly speaking an RCD is *not* a *fuse* (see *fuse*), although it has the same effect in disconnecting the circuit but with significantly less danger to the user. It is essential to check what caused the RCD to trip before reconnecting the electrical supply.

respiration is the process by which *aerobic organisms* take oxygen from the air and use it to produce energy. Process by-products include *carbon dioxide* and water.

respiratory defence mechanisms against toxic substances *after* they have entered the body, as an example those against dust, typically include: the nasal hairs and sneezing which remove larger particles; mucous coated cilia (hairs) which remove medium sized particles; those particles which reach the bronchi are removed by coughing due to irritation; smaller particles reaching the alveoli are trapped and may be attacked by anti-bodies or cells (the process of phagocytosis).

respiratory protective equipment or RPE are an essential last resort and only provided and/or used after all other possible methods and/or controls **(ERICPD)**, have been considered and applied and/or adopted as legally required (see *asbestos*). The comprehensive **British Standard BS** 4275 *Recommendations for the selection, use and maintenance of respiratory protective equipment*, together with the **HSE** '*approved list*', which identifies and describes RPE considered by the **HSE** to satisfy legislation must be consulted before purchase and use of RPE.

Adequate and suitable training must be provided by *employers* to their *employees* in the use, maintenance and minor repairs necessary to maintain the RPE in good order.

After use and during maintenance, RPE must be cleaned *and* disinfected, following manufacturer's instructions.

Checks on RPE *must* always be made *before* issue and *before* use.

Classes of RPE depend on the *principle* by which protection is provided to the wearer. Within these classifications, there are many different types even some combining features found in each class.

Class 'a' respirators must **NEVER** be used in an oxygen-deficient atmosphere. They can be categorised in five basic types, which are:

(i)   Filtering facepiece, which removes respirable size particles. The facepiece covers the whole of the nose and mouth. *Not to be confused with* the type of dust mask which prevents fairly large particles from entering the nose or mouth.

(ii)   Half mask with a replaceable filter cartridge, a rubber or other non-permeable material facepiece, covering the nose and mouth.

(iii)   Full face, similar to (ii), but with the facepiece covering the eyes as well as the nose and mouth.

(iv)   Powered air purifying where air is drawn through a filter and then blown into a half mask or full facepiece at a slightly positive pressure to prevent inward leakage of contaminated air.

(v)   Powered visor using a fan with filters fitted inside a helmet so that purified air blown is down behind a protective visor past the wearer's face.

Class 'b' respirators basically comprise:

(i)   Fresh air hose where the breathing action of the wearer (unassisted) or use of bellows or pump (assisted), brings air from an uncontaminated area.

(ii)   Compressed air line using a flexible hose attached to an airline with in-built filters and pressure limiting or reducing valves. The air is supplied to the wearer, who may be fitted with half-mask, full facepieces or hoods.

(iii)   Self-contained breathing apparatus, which is a cylinder (containing air or oxygen) carried on the back, fed into a facemask. Mainly used for rescues and/or escapes.

Decontamination equipment and decontamination areas must be provided *at the exit* to the contaminated area. This is **IN ADDITION** to normal cleaning and maintenance.

Duties placed on *employers* include ensuring that 'RPE used in compliance with the legislation is: (a) suitable, i.e. capable of exposure in the

231

particular circumstances of use; and (b) either of a type approved by the *HSE* or conforms to a Standard approved by the *HSE*'.

Factors, which can affect wearers of RPE, include length of time it is worn, type of equipment. High work rate or extreme effort may cause psychological and physiological problems; restricted mobility; poor visibility and/or *communication*. Remedies are legal requirements, notably good fit and suitable for the purpose *(PPER)*.

Inspection and maintenance checks must be carried out on RPE at least once per month. **COSHH** 'recommends' a thorough examination of RPE at the very least once a month, more often in high toxic situations. In areas of low toxicity and/or infrequent use of half-mask respirators, the *competent person* maintaining equipment can decide on examination intervals, but these must be never longer than at three-month intervals. Maintenance includes cleaning; disinfection; examination; repair; testing; and record keeping.

Malfunctions of breathing apparatus where the wearer is likely to be either (i)deprived of oxygen or (ii) exposed to contaminated atmosphere where and/or when the RPE is being used *at work*, must be reported **immediately** as a 'dangerous occurrence' under the *RIDDOR*.

Problems for wearers of RPE must be taken into account, eliminated or minimised; these may include facial hair, physiological differences and perspiration.

Rescue equipment must always be readily available.

Storage for RPE should be separated from anything that might harm it, such as heat, sunlight, excessive moisture, corrosive substances or contaminants.

Tests for efficiency must be carried out and results of the test and examination recorded (written or computerised) and available for inspection by those who ask to see them, including *employees*, their representatives, enforcing authorities, etc. The records should be kept for not less than five years.

Training for RPE must include theory, followed by practice.

Users and potential users of RPE must be medically fit. All checks carried out by manufacturers of RPE on the effectiveness of their products are based on the user being an average healthy person. Persons who suffer from persistent catarrh or asthma may be unsuitable where full masks or hoods are worn, or where RPE used depends on 'lung-power' for operation.

In summary:

(i) The correct **HSE** approved equipment must be selected by the **employer** for the task and environment.
(ii) Users must be fully trained in the use of RPE, health and safety legislative duties and requirements and understand the hazards they face.
(iii) Users must check the RPE before, during and after use.
(iv) High quality and standards of systematic, recorded maintenance must be in place and operated.
(v) A safe system of work must be in operation.

respiratory system, in absolute simplest terms, includes the mouth, throat and nasal passages, the passage (including the pharynx, larynx and trachea) leading into the bronchi and the lungs, with the *alveoli* transferring and filtering oxygen into the blood. For non-medical professionals the respiratory system can be crudely represented visually as comprising two partly filled sacks (the lungs, one each 'side' of the body), dangling from hooks (the bronchi) suspended by a rope (passageway) ending in the head, divided at the top end into two parts (passages to and the mouth and nose). The whole comprises some of the *routes of entry* to the body and can provide a passageway for *toxins.*

responsible person is a person who satisfies the requirements of the **RIDDOR.** Examples include: mine or quarry manager (mines or quarries); mall owner (shopping mall); manager (shops within a mall or anywhere); pipeline owner (pipeline); registered keeper (vehicles with no operator's licence) and operator. The responsible person has the duty to maintain and keep various records, e.g. as required by **RIDDOR.**

review (*examination term*) requires an examination of something including a brief *critical* account of it.

review (*in industrial injury benefit terms*) is a procedure which can be used by claimants to request a reassessment, if they consider that their claim has been 'wrongly rejected' or, if in the opinion of the claimant or their advisors, they have been 'awarded' an inadequate percentage disability, or at any time during an award their disability (or disease) may have worsened since the 'award' was made. Although strictly speaking a *review* forms part of the *appeal* procedure, it is nevertheless effectively separate from and different to what is termed an *appeal*. Failure to 'win' a review still allows an appeal to be entered. An *Insurance Officer*, often with advice from a *medical tribunal*, determines entitlement.

review (*in occupational health and safety terms*) is carried out to: (a) ensure standards and objectives are being achieved; (b) provide information to justify either changing or retaining current *policies*, plans or *strategies* (see *planning*); (c) identify deviations from required or agreed *standards*.

revocations (of legislation) apply to the *annulment* of the whole or part of a Regulation through a 'succeeding' Regulation e.g. made under powers of the *HSWA*.

revoked see *revocations (of legislation)*.

RIDDOR see *Reporting of Injuries, Diseases and Dangerous Occurrences Regulations*.

Ringlemann Smoke Charts are six in number, ranging from 0-5, shaded from white to black, which are used to determine the density of smoke.

See also **Clean Air Act 1993**.

riparian owner is a term of particular use in *environmental law* and means 'relating to the bank of a river or stream'. A riparian owner has (**common law**) right of use of the water, provided it is not altered and restored to the stream or river.

risk is the *chance or probability* that a hazard is likely to result in an *accident*, *taking account of the severity of outcome*, e.g. 'how' the tool or (*hazardous) substance,* machine, *work equipment*, system of work etc. can cause 'what' *harm*.

risk assessment is the commonly used expression for what is often termed in legislation as an *assessment* or *analysis*. **An assessment is a mandatory requirement**. It has been an implicit (and generally ignored) requirement of all UK health and safety legislation since the *Health and Morals of Apprentices Act 1802*. The 1802 Act required the windows in textile mills to be cleaned as *frequently as required*; checking the state of the windows meant carrying out an assessment or inspection. Inspections were not formally called assessments until 1988 (**COSHH**).

The **MHSWR** and other legislation demands that a *suitable and sufficient* assessment be carried out in all workplaces by a *competent person*. Those appointed by the *employer* to carry out the assessment must be provided with sufficient time to complete it and adequate means carry it out – pressurised assessments with time constraints are *not suitable and sufficient assessments*. In summary, a **risk** assessment is *a competent person's judgement based upon the potential **hazards** and circumstances of use*.

A *suitable and sufficient* risk assessment is one that:

(a) correctly and accurately identifies all hazards;
(b) disregards inconsequential risks and those trivial risks associated with life in general;
(c) determines the likelihood of injury or harm arising;
(d) quantifies the severity of the consequences and the numbers of people who would be affected;
(e) takes into account any existing control measures;
(f) identifies any current specific legal duty or requirement relating to the hazard;
(g) identifies and proposes any appropriate control measures;
(h) will remain valid for a reasonable time;
(i) provides sufficient information to enable the *employer* to decide upon appropriate control measures, taking into account the latest scientific developments and advances;
(j) enables the *employer* to prioritise remedial measures.

In addition to identifying the **preventative** or **protective or control measures** that need to be adopted, assessments are an invaluable source of information concerning actions and areas of concern. An assessment is a *pro-active* aid and also **monitors** and/or **reviews** the effectiveness of measures taken, including **systems of work** and, incidentally, the quality and effectiveness of **health and safety management** within an organisation.

Significant assessment findings **must** be **recorded**, including what (prioritised) action is required to be taken, monitoring systems for establishing effectiveness, and reviewed when necessary.

Generic risk assessments may be carried out and considered *sufficient and suitable*. When conducting a generic risk assessment great care must be taken to ensure everything is exactly the same, e.g. everyone is carrying out the same task, each sitting at the same type of desk, with the same chair, etc. However, lighting (illumination) may vary, depending upon the distance from windows or glare, or there may be ergonomic variations due to physiological differences, such as height.

risk assessment

A risk assessment establishes the *likelihood of occurrence* (chances that a hazard realises its potential to cause harm) and the *severity of outcome* (extent of injury, damage etc.). One method is to take measurements and present them *quantitatively* (numerically), e.g. 1-5 in ascending likelihood/severity of outcome, or *alphabetically*, e.g. L (low likelihood/severity), M (medium) or H (high) or qualitatively (literally, depending on quality). How many members of staff are exposed to risk influences rating, e.g. a defective step on a seldom used stairway may receive a lower rating than a similarly damaged step on a stairway in constant use or by large numbers of people. The names of groups and numbers of workers exposed to high risk should be recorded separately.

A simple formula for calculating risk assessments may clarify:

$$\text{RISK} = \text{SEVERITY OF} \times \text{LIKELIHOOD OF}$$
$$\text{OUTCOME} \qquad \text{OCCURRENCE}$$

By multiplying one factor with the other, a risk rating can be achieved from 1 (nil severity and unlikely to happen) to 25 (just waiting to happen and with disastrous widespread results). A worked out example illustrates: to obtain the *risk* rating, with a minor injury severity (e.g. abrasion) recorded at 2 or L, but one very likely to occur (say, once a week) at 4 or H the resulting equation would be:

$$\text{RISK} = 2 \times 4 = 8$$

If the alphabetical L M H is used, then:

$$\text{RISK} = \text{L} \times \text{H} = \text{M}$$

Following inspection of the derived ratings (in the examples, 8 or M), a 'cut-off' number is chosen by the **competent person** in consultation. Risks that are on or above the chosen number are called 'significant risks' and **must** be recorded if five or more are employed, and **must** be the subject of action and control measures to reduce the rating. Once action has been taken, or the control measure installed, a review risk assessment is conducted. In other words, *without reference to any earlier assessment*, a further assessment is carried out.

It is essential, not merely desirable, to carry out the 'likelihood' and 'severity' measurements **independently**. If carried out together research has found that persons tend to let their judgement of the probability of events be subconsciously influenced by the anticipated seriousness of the outcome.

Employees must be provided with comprehensible, relevant and up-to-date information on all significant risks, measures taken to prevent and protect against the risks and provided in the Safety Policy, the named responsible person to contact, what they do and their location.

Risk assessments are not a once and for all exercise, they must be reviewed by the *employer* or the *competent person* if there is reason to suspect they are no longer valid or there has been a significant change in the matters to which they relate. The *Health and Safety (Display Screen Equipment) Regulations* and the *Manual Handling Operations Regulations* present useful pro-forma providing what is required or what should be done regarding assessments. There are also excellent *HSE* free publications describing assessments and procedures, such as *INDG163Rev. 5 Steps to Risk Assessment*.

risk assessment records must be completed and held where five or more persons are employed. The records should include:

    (i)   significant hazards;
    (ii) significant risks;
    (iii) details of existing control measures;
    (iv) effectiveness of control measures;
    (v) details of people at risk;
    (vi) prioritisation of risks and action;
    (vii) details of preventative or protective action required.

risk management, simply, is the identification, analysis and degree of control exercised, of risks, which have the potential to threaten the assets or well being of an enterprise. Within every organisation hazards exist, the objective of risk management is to eliminate or control all risks from whatever source, not just health, safety and environment. See **BS 8800**, HSG65 (current edition) *safety management, total loss control* and *total quality management*.

risk phrase is a labelling requirement for certain *dangerous substances* or preparations, in specified concentrations. The letter R is followed by a number and what is termed a warning risk phrase, e.g. 'R34 causes burns' or 'R49 may cause cancer by inhalation.' The complete list is shown in Part III of the *Approved Supply List*.

road transport health and safety requirements placed on *employers* and *employees* are found in general health and safety legislation, e.g. **HSWA 1974** and in specific road transport legislation, e.g. *Carriage of Dangerous Goods by Road Regulations*. However, road transport *employees* are excluded from cover by some health and safety legislation, e.g. the *Working Time Regulations*. The entries outlining the salient points of legislation usually identify any exclusions.

roentgen is an old term for a measurement of X-ray or gamma radiation. Still found in older texts, it has been replaced by *coulombs per kilogram of dry air* in the **SI Units** system.

root cause of an *accident* is factor y, not necessarily readily apparent. For example, if an *employee* trips over a pallet located on the factory floor, then some person had been careless – the *immediate cause* is the pallet being left on the floor. However, *root cause(s)* may be lack of *training, supervision, poor housekeeping, failure to comply with legislative demands.*

See also **HSWA** and *Workplace (Health, Safety and Welfare) Regulations.*

routes of entry (into the body) by *chemicals*: in the majority of cases, the *toxin* searches for a *target organ*. The principle routes are via: (i) *inhalation* via the nose or mouth (this represents the greatest probability and therefore risk); (ii) *ingestion* via the mouth; (iii) *absorption* through the skin; (iv) *injection* via punctures in the skin from sharp objects (the least common). The routes of entry are sometimes described more technically by industrial or occupational hygienists as via the: (a) respiratory system; (b) skin; (c) gastrointestinal tract. Generally of less importance are the routes of entry via the: (d) mucous membranes; and (e) open lesions.

Royal Society for the Prevention of Accidents (*RoSPA*) was established in 1916, being formed from the members of the *Safety First Council*. In 1941 RoSPA received the royal accolade and in 1976 RoSPA moved its headquarters from London to Birmingham, where it remains today.

The involvement and commitment of RoSPA to safety is at all levels (e.g. industrial, home and road) and includes *training*, research, publications, pressure group activity, etc. There are RoSPA safety groups throughout the UK and they act as a useful forum for safety practitioners, particularly those who are not members of any other professional safety institutions. The Headquarters address of RoSPA is: Edgbaston Park, 353 Bristol Road, Birmingham B5 7ST (Tel: 0121 248 2000; web site http://www.rospa.co.uk).

RSI (Repetitive Strain Injury) see *work related upper limb disorders.*

S

safe person approach in health and safety is where the individual worker's perception of *risk* is significantly increased, often through high levels and quality of *training*, to encourage and improve self-awareness and self-discipline regarding safe working. For example, a *safe person*, where appropriate, would *always* wear safety goggles, facemask or ear protectors without being reminded. A problem with this approach is that humans are individuals, each one different, therefore individual perception of the same *danger* or *risk* may differ, one reason why the prime *duty of care* and the duty to carry out *risk assessments* is placed on *employers*. It is easier and arguably more effective to eliminate or minimise *risk* in the *workplace*.

safe place of work is a requirement of the *HSWA 1974*, under which *employers* have a *duty*, so far as is *reasonably practicable*, to provide a safe place of work. Its provision is the most effective *accident* prevention measure that can be achieved. The purpose of *risk assessments* includes that of identifying risk and danger in the workplace, as well as task and process. Legislation identifies what is required, sometimes as an *absolute duty*, with *Approved Codes of Practice, Guidance Notes* or *British Standards* presenting *quasi-legal* information on how standards can be achieved.

safe system of work is a formal, systematic procedure, to ensure a specific task or work activity is carried out safely and without risk to health. After it has been applied, it is monitored and reviewed. All *employers* have a duty, so far as is *reasonably practicable*, to provide and maintain a safe system of work (*HSWA* s. 2(2)(a)). *Employees* have a duty to co-operate with their *employers* regarding health and safety, and use or apply such safe systems of work (*HSWA* s.7).

To establish a safe system of work includes:

(i)   an assessment of the task;
(ii) identification of hazards and assessment of risks;
(iii) identification of safe methods;
(iv) implementation of the system;
(v)   monitoring the system of work;
(vi) reviewing the system, when necessary.

safety is the converse of *danger*, e.g. where there is virtually no likelihood of exposure to risk of death, injury or disease.

safety audit is a systematic, critical, detailed assessment and examination of the health, safety and environmental aspects of a company, paying particular attention to health, safety and environmental management. An audit has the prime objective of determining the true state of safety at a particular moment in time within a company, thus minimising the potential for loss to occur.

There are two major 'types' of safety audit, the internal and the certification. The internal safety audit may be carried out to see where improvements can be made or an assessment of the actual situation regarding all aspects of safety within an organisation, e.g. as a preliminary to compiling a safety policy. The certification audit may be for an independent assessment, e.g. as part of an ISO programme.

An audit is carried out by competent persons, and a formal report is compiled. *Every* component of a total safety system is included in the audit, e.g. management policy; safety *attitudes*; safety *training*; processes; plant layout and design; systems of work; operating procedures; emergency plans; personal protection standards; *accident* records and analysis methods, etc. In summary, the safety audit is primarily a measurement of *management's*, *employees'* and company's effectiveness concerning health and safety, *to enable improvements to be made*.

safety committees have the purpose and function to provide a forum for discussion, identify appropriate courses of effective action, ensure that action is taken and disseminate information concerning matters of health and safety throughout an organisation. It is authoritatively considered that an effective safety committee, chaired by a *competent person* (see e.g. Citrine *ABC of Chairmanship* (sic)), can make a very significant contribution to standards of health and safety and towards achieving a positive *safety culture* throughout an organisation. If two Safety Representatives (SR) make a written request to an *employer* for the formation of a safety committee, the *employer* has the legal duty to comply within three months.

The guidance notes (GN) associated with the *Safety Representatives and Safety Committee Regulations 1977* (as amended) provide various 'recommendations' concerning the formation and operation of safety committees. They include: recognising that safety committees should consider and deal with health, safety and welfare (GN 35); taking account of the needs of the workplaces (GN 36); ensuring that the safety committee is the only committee within an organisation dealing with health and safety matters, e.g. health and safety is not included in the agenda of other committees (GN 37); preferably having committees restricted to a particular premise, rather than dealing with a number of different locations through *one* central committee, except in the case of large companies where the *addition* of a central committee may prove useful (GN 38); reviewing 'measures taken to ensure the health and safety at work of . . . *employees*' (GN 39). Other guidance notes are categorised under the following headings: Objectives and functions of safety committees (GN 39-42); Membership of safety committees (GN 43-53); The conduct of safety committees (54-59).

safety culture is very similar to *organisational culture*. It includes the philosophical underpinnings of *attitudes* to health and safety, as well as the planning, organising, implementation and control of hazards, within a workplace or organisation. If the safety culture is positive, then there is a strong probability that the workforce will be safety conscious, work safely and have a low *accident*, damage, loss, personal injury and ill-health ratio.

Positive (or negative) safety culture begins at the top, with management example having a tremendous influence, For example, the director or manager who crosses a **construction** site without wearing a safety helmet, despite legislative duties and signs requiring safety helmets to be worn, is **not** protected by the invisible hand of God over head. Even worse, the bad example provided by such persons, in part because of their position in the company, can quickly become the safety norm and form part of the safety culture of the company. The 'he is not wearing a helmet, why should I?' permeates throughout all *employees*.

safety data sheets (also known as *hazard data sheets*), updated as and when necessary, are required to be provided by *suppliers* to all recipients of dangerous substances or preparations intended for use at work.

The safety data sheets supplied in the countries of the EU must be *free of charge* and in the language of the country of *supply* (**Note: NOT** country of manufacture), i.e. English for substances/preparations *supplied for use in England*.

safety inspection is a routine, regular, scheduled inspection of a workplace, department, section or undertaking – for example, at monthly intervals. A safety inspection is sometimes, in error, called a *safety audit*. As opposed to a *safety audit*, a safety inspection can be a snapshot or wide-ranging but with less depth than an audit.

safety management is the term commonly used for *health and safety management*. Safety management is part of the 'normal' functions of management. An **HSE** study, published in 1993, stated 'the cost of failures in health and safety management are high,' with '30 million days lost in a year from work-related injuries and ill health,' and 'uninsured losses from *accidents* (whether they result in personal injury or not) can cost between 8 to 36 times what an organisation normally insures for; . . . '

241

safety policy

There are three fundamental reasons why high quality safety management is essential. These are: (i) **moral** (which is good *employment* practice); (ii) **legal** (following relevant legislative demands minimises *accidents*, *damage*, injuries, loss, insurance costs, fines and *penalties*, thereby *benefiting* the *employer*, manager *and* the *employee*); and (iii) **financial** (increased productivity, lower sick absence rates and minimal damage to humans and machines).

The successful and efficient *manager* (and *employer*) commences with the use effective selection methods, providing *comprehensible* health and safety *training*, information and **instruction**, not merely during the induction of new *employees* but regularly updated throughout their career (**all** legal duties). However, there are several 'types' of, or approaches to, safety management. These include total quality management (TQM), **total loss control** and **risk management**. Each has its devotees, although all have the common basis of a systematic approach and application. The basic principles and practice of health and safety management systems are described in the **HSE** *Successful Health and Safety Management* HS(G)65L and BS 8800 *Health and Safety Management*.

Every component in a safety management system should be audited, initially almost continuously, later perhaps bi-annually or as perceived to be necessary. Continuous flow feedback loops, both formal and informal, monitor progress and allow for necessary changes to be made quickly during the developmental stages and thereafter. The components or stages include:

(a) policies;
(b) organising;
(c) planning;
(d) measuring performance; and
(e) auditing and reviewing performance.

These objectives form the acronym, POPMAR, mnemonically represented as *Please Operate Perfect Management Always Rapidly*.

safety policy see *health and safety policy document*.

safety professionals, also termed *occupational health and safety professionals*, are those persons who conduct themselves within high moral and ethical standards, usually (but not invariably) belonging to a professional association, institution or body and having achieved a high standard of professional *training*, education and experience in the field of what is termed *occupational safety and health* (although 'health' is seldom at professional medical level).

In *occupational health and safety* in the UK it is virtually impossible, outside a specialist text, to provide a full list of the various disciplines (in their own right) required and used by *occupational health, safety and environmental professionals*. In other countries, such as the Netherlands and the Philippines, the disciplines required are identified by legislation. In the UK a non-exhaustive list includes: law, engineering, agronomy; medicine (provided only the practitioner has received specialist *training* and is qualified in *occupational health*); hygiene; ergonomy, biology; chemistry, psychology; behavioural science; toxicology; social science; environmental science; and health and safety generally.

Those managers who have a clearly identified role function with responsibility for health and safety within their organisation and who have received *adequate and suitable professional occupational health and safety training* and become qualified can also be included. However, managers **without** *occupational health and safety training* and with responsibility for health and safety as part of their normal managerial role and function, or appointed to a health and safety responsibility by an *employer*, neither comply with legislative requirements nor are they *competent persons* or safety professionals.

Safety Representatives or SRs are *appointed* by *independent and registered recognised trade unions* to represent their members restricted to the workplace. Identified in the letter of appointment (from the trade union) SRs have considerable 'legally defined rights and privileges' and should **not** be confused with *Elected Representatives*. There is no limit on the number of SRs who can be appointed by trade unions for each workplace, even by reference to the number of *employees*.

The manner of selecting potential SRs varies from trade union to trade union. For example, some trade unions require that candidates for appointment of Safety Representative **must** already be shop-stewards in their trade union, other unions allow any member of their union to be put forward for appointment. In both cases SRs may be elected by the whole workforce membership or chosen by the branch committee and then their names put forward to the trade union. In all cases until the letter of appointment is provided by the trade union and received by the *employer*, the person selected is **NOT** a Safety Representative as defined in the *SRSCR*.

Safety Representatives and Safety Committees Regulations 1977 **(as amended)** cover the appointment, rights and duties of Safety Representatives. The reason for the appointment of SRs is to provide representation of their member's interests in health and safety matters related to the workplace. The *Regulations* advise that those appointed as SRs should be *employees* (except in the case of the Musicians Union and Equity) and, *so far* *as is reasonably practicable,* have at least two years' **employment** with their present **employer** or at least two years' experience in similar **employment**. The **HSE** booklet *Safety Representatives and Safety Committees* includes the **Regulations,** Code of Practice and Guidance Notes and is an exemplar of its kind.

After appointment, the **SRSCR** give safety representatives the following rights:

(a) to represent their fellow **employees;**
(b) to carry out investigations and inspections;
(c) to deal with information;
(d) to consult with their **employer** on health and safety matters related to their area of appointment.

Subject to notifying an **employer** in writing in 'good time,' SRs may investigate (or inspect) potential hazards in their area of appointment, members' complaints about health and safety. SRs may investigate the causes of an **accident** or incident in their area of appointment, inspect the **accident book** and other documents (except identifiable personal health records) that an **employer** is required to keep relevant to the workplace, *so far as is reasonably practicable* and with prior written notice.

The **SRSCR** gives SRs consultation rights with the various Inspectorates on health and safety matters concerning the workplace where they represent members. SRs have a degree of legal immunity, subject to their carrying out their activities in a lawful manner. For example, according to the **SRSCR** a SR cannot be 'victimised' for carrying out legally specified health and safety duties and activities.

An **employer** 'shall provide such facilities and assistance as the Safety Representative shall require' (**SRSCR** Reg. 5(3)). The facilities that should be supplied by an **employer** are not defined in the **Regulations,** but are subject to negotiation. The **TUC** offers a suggested list of facilities required by SRs, which includes:

(i) a room and a desk at the workplace;
(ii) facilities for storing correspondence;
(iii) inspection reports and other papers;
(iv) ready **access** to telephones;
(v) other facilities, including the provision by the **employer** of copies of all relevant legislation, **ACOPs** and GNs and legal standards applicable to the workplace.

If two or more SRs request in writing to their **employer** the formation of a *Safety*

Committee, the *employer* must comply and form a committee within *three months* of the request being made (SRSCR Reg. 9). If the *employer* does not form *a Safety Committee* within three months, the SRs may appeal to an industrial tribunal. SRs have the right to attend **Safety Committee** meetings (**SRSCR** Reg. 4 (1), as amended by the **MHSWR**). The **MHSWR** further amended the **SRSCR** through inserting Regulation 4A(1) placing a duty on *employers* to consult with SRs 'in good time' of certain subjects *relating to the workplace* (area of appointment), namely *before*:

(i) **the introduction of any new measures** at a workplace which may substantially affect health and safety;

(ii) **arrangements for appointing** *competent persons* to assist the *employer* with health and safety and implementing procedures for imminent risk;

(iii) **any health and safety** *information* the *employer* is required to provide; and

(iv) **the planning and organisation of health and safety training** and **health and safety implications** of the introduction (or **planning) of new technology.**

SRs as *employees* (s. 7 *HSWA*) still have the duty to co-operate with *employers* in helping them to comply with health and safety legislation and assisting in raising health and safety standards throughout their place of work.

safety sampling is a regularly conducted technique intended to assess *accident potential* in the workplace. Trained observers record the number of defects or hazards (those with *accident* potential) observed against a prepared checklist following a pre-determined route. Sampling takes very little time, typically around 15 minutes and at weekly intervals *but* varying the day of the week *and* time of day, to reflect the different conditions, activities and staff and thereby variations in *accident* potential. The results of the sample can be used to indicate trends within a department, section or even a company as a whole.

safety signs see the *Health and Safety (Safety Signs and Signals) Regulations 1996* and *warning symbols*.

safety survey is a detailed examination (although not as comprehensive as a *safety audit*) of administration, environmental approaches, industrial safety and fire protection. Surveys are carried out as and when required, on a company wide or departmental basis, perhaps alternating with a safety audit. The survey is useful to make a safety check on new or refurbished premises or following the installation or modification of a plant.

safety tour is a simple, unscheduled tour of a workplace, carried out by a range of staff from the Managing Director to members of the safety committee at three-monthly or so intervals. Its objectives include that of demonstrating the commitment of senior management and the company towards safety in the workplace and ensuring that safety standards are being observed and maintained at an acceptable level.

safety training is a key component in successful *Health and Safety Management*. The first step should be to carry out a *training* need analysis. In an organisation safety *training* is required both to satisfy legislative requirements, taking account of organisational demands and *be suitable for the persons attending the course* – otherwise resources will be wasted.

For example, the course content for a manager may be organisationally oriented, with the establishment, monitoring and reviewing of the effectiveness (or otherwise) of safety procedures, such as *safe systems of work*, safety policy organisation and arrangements, being of priority. Operators would require information on those factors, and how to carry out their tasks within the company (and legal) requirements. In summary, safety *training* may be technical (relating to the task) or procedural (relating to managing health and safety).

***Sale and Supply of Goods Act 1994* or SSGA** covers the sale of goods, hire of goods and redemption of trading stamps for goods. Various terms and conditions in the *Sale of Goods Act 1979* have been replaced or changed by the SSGA, including:

(a) 'merchandisable quality' has been replaced by the implied term 'satisfactory quality';
(b) the examination of goods before acceptance is now a right;
(c) a buyer can accept part of a consignment and reject the defective remainder.

sale (of goods), in the health and safety sense of the term, is frequently associated with specific legislative definitions or requirements (see **PUWER**, *liability* and *supplier*).

***Sale of Goods Act 1979* or SGA** contains a number of implied conditions, some of which have been changed, altered or replaced by the *Sale and Supply of Goods Act 1994*. In selective brief, the SGA still includes cover:

(i) goods sold by description must correspond with that description, commercial and private sales are both included (SGA s.13);
(ii) obligations regarding merchantability and fitness for purpose (SGA s.14) applies generally, but not in the case of private sales;

(iii) if a seller sells something which he/she does not own, e.g. it is subject to hire purchase, then the hire-purchase company can recover the goods from the new purchaser *and* retain the right to payment of outstanding instalments from the defaulter.

salmonella is a common bacteriological cause of food poisoning. The incubation period for salmonella is 12-36 hours, duration of illness ranges between one to eight days; the source of the infection includes raw meat, especially poultry; foods usually involved include meat and meat products. Adequate cooking can destroy the salmonella bacteria.

sanitary conveniences, according to the **WHSWR** and the **CHSWR**, in workplaces generally and on building sites must be of 'suitable and sufficient . . . (numbers) . . . provided at readily accessible places'. Washing facilities should be in a room sufficiently ventilated, lit, kept in a clean condition, with separate facilities for men and women (or in a locked cubicle), and include a 'supply of clean hot and cold (or warm) water (ideally running water) and soap, towels etc.'. The washing facilities must be provided within 'readily accessible places', *so far as is reasonably practicable*, in the immediate vicinity of sanitary conveniences.

The numbers of WCs which should be provided vary according to the numbers of persons at work and whether or not the work is 'dirty', resulting in heavy soiling of hands, arms and forearms. For 'normal' work the number of facilities are as follows:

Persons at work	Number of WCs	Number of wash stations
1-5	1	1
6-25	2	2
26-50	3	3
51-75	4	4
76-100	5	5

For every 25 persons above 100 an extra WC *and* wash station should be provided. However in the case where WCs are used only by male workers, an additional WC per 50 *above* 100 is sufficient, with an equal number of urinals supplied. The requirements for WC/urinals for male workers is as follows:

Number of men at work	Number of WCs	Number of urinals
1-15	1	1
16-30	2	1

savings

31-45	2	2
46-60	3	2
61-75	3	3
76-90	4	3
91-100	4	4

Where work results in heavy soiling of hands, arms and forearms, there should be one wash station for every ten persons at work, up to 50 workers, with one wash station for every 20 persons at work thereafter. Where members of the public and persons at work use the same facilities, suitable arrangements must be made so that workers are not delayed.

savings achieved through applying good standards of health and safety see *cash benefits*.

scaffold towers see *tower scaffolds*.

scaffolds are generally covered by the **Construction (Health, Safety and Welfare) Regulations 1996**, more specifically various *Schedules* within those *Regulations* (e.g. Schedule 1 refers to guard rails and toeboards). Please note that *tower* and *mobile scaffolds* types (many of which are of proprietary design and manufacture), are described separately.

The three basic types of general *access* scaffolds, all temporary in nature, are:

independent tied scaffolds which are independent of a structure to which *access* is required but tied to it for stability;

putlog scaffolds which depend on the building to provide structural support through placing the flattened ends of (transom) tubing into the wall;

birdcage scaffolds which are independent structures, usually erected for interior work, big in area and normally providing only one large working platform.

Scaffolds of all types must be erected by a *competent person* or under the close supervision of a *competent person*; be of sound design and materials; on sound foundations; maintained in good condition; with safe working platforms; inspected on completion, thereafter weekly and after inclement weather (e.g. storms or gales) by a *competent person*, with the details recorded.

Relevant British Standards which are applicable include BS 6037 *Access Equipment*, BS 5973 *Scaffolds, Code of Practice* and BS 5974 *Suspended scaffolds*, *temporally installed*. The **HSE** free booklet, CIS49 *General access scaffolds and ladders* obtainable from **HSE Books** (Tel: 01787 313995) is also very useful.

schedules, in effect, are an appendix to an **Act, Regulation** or other legislation that either refer to special areas or provides explanation on the main points, sometimes including suggestions as to how to comply, e.g. see **Control of Substances Hazardous to Health Regulations 1990**.

school health and safety is covered by general health and safety legislation, with an added extra duty of care concerning children and young persons. This identifies two concerns of the legislation, persons at work (e.g. s.2 **HSWA** or **HSWA**) and those who may be affected by work activities, which includes pupils and/or students (e.g. see ss.3and4 **HSWA**). All health and safety arrangements **must** be included in the arrangements section of the (mandatory) health and safety policy document for **individual** education establishments (each varying in some elements).

The health and safety legislation places prime duties and responsibilities, aside from the general *duty of care*, on the *employer*. For example, assessments **must** be carried out throughout the school, with significant findings recorded and actioned.

Unfortunately, pending *case law*, exactly who is considered to be the *employer* at schools can be difficult to establish. In broad terms, the allocation of *employer's* duties and accountability for health and safety in schools largely depends on the 'type' of school, e.g. whether or not it is a Local Education Authority (LEA), an aided or grant maintained school. In LEA wholly owned and/or controlled schools the LEA is effectively the *employer*; in aided schools such as Church Schools the governing body assumes at least part if not the whole of the *employer's* accountability and responsibilities, with advice and assistance obtainable from LEA or Diocesan bodies, in the carrying out of their health and safety duties. In grant maintained schools, city technology colleges and independent schools (all of which may be 'run' by a limited company, the Board of Governors (or the Board of Directors) effectively are the *employer*, with all the *employer's* duties and responsibilities (and accountability) concerning all aspects of health and safety legislative requirements.

In a limited number of cases, the school buildings may be owned separately by a private or public company. In such cases the person or company responsible for maintenance has certain health and safety responsibilities and accountability.

It is important to note that there is a duty (i.e. **must**) for the Board of

scrubbers

Governors, the head teachers and staff to co-operate and co-ordinate regarding matters of health and safety.

Some legislative duties are a specified **must** (e.g. the carrying out of *risk assessments)*, others at the *so far as is reasonably practicable* level. Only with the latter can cost, time, trouble etc., enter the equation. Obligatory health and safety duties cannot be delayed or avoided on the grounds that the school budget cannot afford it. If a legislative duty is not carried out than **criminal** charges may be brought against the offender (e.g. Board of Governors) and **criminal penalties** can be awarded to convicted offenders.

It is strongly re-emphasised that the *fact* that a school may be under-funded or even in debt is **not** an acceptable legal or valid reason for failing to take necessary action in health and safety matters. In short, providing goggles, gloves and/or hairnets for pupils using laboratories or during woodworking may be expensive but, subject to the findings of an assessment made by a *competent person* showing there to be a significant risk of injury without the use of goggles, gloves and/or hairnets (bearing in mind the age and experience of the pupil), it will be an expenditure which **must be made** or laboratory or woodworking school-work *stopped* until they are purchased *and in use*. Incidentally, pupils **must** be trained in their use, informed why they are essential for the task and of course, adequately supervised.

The various health and safety legislation entries (e.g. *HSWA, COSHH*) as well as general entries in this book, such as *access, accident prevention* etc., should be consulted. *HSE publications* (often drawn up in association with the *Education Service Advisory Committee*) also should be consulted, e.g. *The responsibilities of school governors for health and safety*, obtainable from *HSE Books*, PO Box 1999, Sudbury, Suffolk CO10 6FS, or from large booksellers.

scrubbers are 'structures' used to reduce acid gas and impurities from industrial plants, with the objective of preventing contamination, especially acid rain. Wet or dry scrubbers are used, with effective wet scrubbers removing 95 per cent of acidity from emissions.

Secretary of State is a person, who by convention is a *Member of Parliament,* appointed by the Crown (on the advice of the Prime Minister) to government office. He/she may be in charge of a department or a senior minister without specified departmental responsibilities. In summary, such persons may be termed a Minister or a Secretary of State.

self-employed, by legal definition, is someone who is gainfully employed in Great Britain, other than in employed earner *employment* or under a contract of *employment*. Basically the term *self-employed* means persons who works for themselves and who may contract their services to others. In health and safety terms it can mean that dual duties and responsibilities result, *both* as an *employer* and as an *employee*. Regulation 3(2) of the *Management and Administration of Safety and Health at Mines Regulations 1993* declares 'These *Regulations* shall apply to a *self-employed* person as they apply to an *employer* and an *employee* and as if that *self-employed* person were both an *employer* and an *employee*.'

However, should an injury ensue when a *self-employed* person is working for a company *under contract*, that company may be held liable for those injuries as if the *self-employed* person had been one of their own *employees* (*Lane v Shire Roofing Co [1995] IRLR 493*). Freelance (or occasional) *employees* are different, e.g. *Hall v Lorimer [1994] IRLR 171* where it was found that the plaintiff was a freelance worker, since 'he incurred expenditure and ran the risk of bad debts'.

severity rate is part of the process of accident statistics and calculates the number of days lost through number of *employees* at risk (e.g. in an industrial sector).

$$\frac{\text{Total number of days lost}}{\text{Number at risk in the particular industry sector}} \times 1,000$$

sewage is liquid or semi-solid waste from domestic or industrial sources. Predominantly organic, it includes human waste and residual industrial chemicals and heavy chemicals. Despite environmental legislation, especially in developed countries, pollution from sewage is widespread.

Sex Discrimination Acts, 1975, 1986 or *SDA* cover unlawful and *favourable* or unfavourable treatment, direct, indirect, or by victimisation, of a person by sex or marital status. As an example, the *SDA* would apply if during a job interview a sexual suggestion or approach is made prior to or as a condition of offering *employment* or *affording access* to promotion. Sexual discrimination can apply to health and safety, for example if instead of installing control measures an *employer* restricts a job to a particular sex.

Under the *SDA employees* who feel they have been sexually harassed may make a claim against their *employer*, if the *employer* takes no action or ineffective action to counter it after being informed of the sexual harassment or discrimination (*Bracebridge Engineering v Darby [1990] IRLR 3*); usually the claim must be made within three months of the incident.

The legislation concerning sexual harassment is not restricted to the *SDA*, for

short term exposure level

example, the *Employment Relations Act 1999* and associated legislation is relatively specific, allowing an *employee* to claim sexual discrimination if dismissed for not giving in to sexual demands, or conditions became intolerable because of sexual harassment, physically assault or rape. The penalties under the legislation are in addition to any civil action the harassed individual may pursue. Aware that many are reluctant to publicise such matters, tribunals have the power to protect the identity of parties or witnesses in sexual misconduct cases, either during the hearing or indefinitely.

short term exposure level is the maximum concentration of contaminants in the air, beyond which workers should not be exposed for more than a *continuous* exposure time period of 15 minutes.

short-wave radiation is that from the high-energy end of the electronic spectrum with wavelengths of less than $5^{\mu m}$, commonly applied to solar radiation consisting of ultraviolet and visible light rays.

show how (*examination term*) means making clear what something means or how something works.

SI units mean *Système International d'Unités*, an internationally accepted system of measurement. It is divided into basic and derived units. Examples include the following:

BASIC UNITS

metre	=	length
kilogram	=	mass
second	=	time
ampere	=	electric current
kelvin	=	temperature
mole	=	amount of substance
candela	=	luminous intensity

DERIVED UNITS

newton	=	force
joule	=	work or energy
watt	=	power
volt	=	electric potential
becquerel	=	radioactivity
sievert	=	dose equivalent (ionising radiation)

sick building syndrome occurs more commonly than diagnosed, due to a variety of factors. Symptoms include fatigue and headaches, mucous membrane irritation, including in some instances diseases caused by infection, hyper-sensitivity, all only reported by *employees* when they make the link between their ill-health and working in specific buildings and especially specific offices.

A major cause of sick building syndrome is poor indoor air quality. In the past, poor *construction* and relatively ill-fitting doors and windows allowed dusts and noxious fumes to escape into the atmosphere. Improved *construction* and design have saved energy and often improved working conditions but reduced escape of fumes and dusts. Improved ventilation, regular maintenance of air conditioning and control over the release of contaminants (e.g. from *photo-copiers* or laser-printers) mitigate the situation. Incidentally, the **HSE** have accepted sick building syndrome as an *occupational health* risk and have issued several publications on the subject.

The mandatory required assessment carried out by a *competent person*, when *employees* must be interviewed and sick records inspected, should give indica-tions of any problems, although it depends on the accuracy of records (many people do not report headaches, unless they become oppressive, no link is made with the building and a hurried NHS consultation with a non-*occupational health*-trained GP, not given background information by their patient, (nor having time to investigate fully), frequently results in the misdiagnosis 'migraine', with tablets as the panacea.

All relevant UK health and safety legislation applies. Once sick building syndrome has been identified, the *employer* must take the appropriate control and/or preventive measures, with the full co-operation of *employees.*

sievert is the SI unit for the dose equivalent of ionising *radiation*. It represents the unit of radiation dose delivered in one hour at a distance of one centimetre from a source of one mg of radium element enclosed in platinum 0.5 mm thick.

signallers are *trained competent persons* who direct the movement of a load or vehicle through the use of correct signals and/or relay instructions from a slinger to a crane driver. In brief, the signaller should stand in a safe position, facing the crane driver, where he/she can see, and be seen by, the driver. Each signal should be carefully executed and clear to understand. The **Construction Industry Training Board** (01485 577577) publishes a small plastic-faced card, which easily fits in a pocket or handbag, *Know your Crane Signals*, showing the recognised signals.

silicosis is the frequently used name for the chronic lung disease *pneumoconio-sis*, predominantly affecting (non-coal) miners.

Simple Pressure Vessels (Safety) Regulations 1991

See also *black lung disease*.

Simple Pressure Vessels (Safety) Regulations 1991 (and the Simple Pressure Vessels (Safety) (Amendment) Regulations 1994) require certain written information to be supplied (concerning its design, **construction**, examination, operation and maintenance), if the simple pressure vessel was supplied **before** 1 July 1992.

six pack or 6 pack is a term commonly used to identify the following *Regulations*, all directly derived from *EU Directives*. The 6 pack includes one from the 'mother' directive, the **MHSWR**, and five from the 'daughter' directives, the **MHOR; DSER; PPER; PUWER**; and the **WHSWR** (or *Workplace Regulations*).

sketch (*examination term*) requires the provision of a *simple* line drawing, with key elements (or parts) identified.

skin cancer is the alteration of and subsequent damage to the genetic make-up of skin cells. General symptoms are the appearance of patches of discoloration on the skin, which change in shape and size, prove painful or irritant and may bleed. Professional medical opinion and advice should be immediately obtained. If detected early, the cure rate for skin cancer is extremely high.

It is considered exposure to ultra-violet radiation is the major cause. Current thinking is that the thinning of the *ozone layer* has led to an increase of the levels of ultra-violet radiation, although it is also suggested changes in social factors have promoted greater exposure of the skin to the sun. Skin cancer can prove fatal. The most recent edition of the **HSE** *Keep your top on* is extremely useful with regard to information on skin cancer.

There are several indicators, which identify those with a propensity for suffering from skin cancer. They include:

Skin	at high risk are those whose skin burns easily and who have freckles; low risk persons are those with brown or black skin;
Hair	at high risk are those with red and fair hair; the darker the hair, the less the risk;
Eyes	at higher risk are blue-eyed individuals; the darker the eyes, the lower the risk;
Moles	at greater risk are persons with a large number of moles on their skin (e.g. 100 for young persons, 50 in older people);
Family history	there is an increased risk of skin cancer if a close family member has suffered a malignant melanoma.

Changes in the skin tissue are due to ultra-violet radiation, most commonly from solar radiation. A burning sensation is **not** necessarily felt, so it is possible that the change can take place with the sufferer unaware.

Prevention includes keeping out of the sun or reducing exposure time, wearing effective clothing, avoiding exposure during maximum sun, applying skin protective creams or lotions (factor 15 or above).

slingers are *trained competent persons* who: attach or detach a load from a crane; know and use the correct lifting appliances; secure loads before movement, lifting or lowering; and direct the movement of the load through the use of correct signals.

smog is a polluting combination of smoke and fog. It can be the result of burning coal or photochemical pollution (including exhaust fumes).

smoke is air that includes incomplete combustion particles, the sizes of which range between 0.01 and 0.3 microns (micron = one millionth of a metre), e.g. particles from burning rubber. More people die from smoke inhalation than from burns, partly because smoke and other deadly gases spread more widely and faster than flames or heat from flames.

smoking is initially covered by the **HSWA 1974,** which states that *employees* must provide a safe and healthy place of work. The **WHSWR** requires *employers* to 'make suitable arrangements to protect non-smokers from discomfort caused by tobacco smoke', e.g. ban smoking. On the other hand, there is **no** requirement for *employers* to provide smoking rooms or protect those who stand outside a building while smoking, from bad weather (although the company may ban smoking entirely within the factory boundaries, not just within their buildings). The free booklet **HSE INDG63** *Passive Smoking at Work* is very useful, obtainable from **HSE Books.**

so far as is reasonably practicable means calculating the risk against sacrifices which would be made to behave reasonably under the circumstances. It extends far beyond cost.

See *practicable.*

Social Security (Claims and Payments) Regulations 1987 detail many requirements of recording an injury and obtaining a *declaration of industrial accident* (use DSS Form BI95), whether sick absence was involved or not, as the result of an **industrial accident** (*vitally important – see also* **back injuries**) as an essential prerequisite to obtaining benefits. The **employer** has the duty to draw the attention of injured *employees* to the DSS 'requirements' when the entry is made in the *accident book* (BI510A or *approved* book).

Social Security Industrial Injury and Disease Benefits are covered by an extensive range of legislation, far beyond the scope of this text. The basic objective of *industrial injury* and industrial disease legislation is to ensure those in 'insured *employment*' obtain monies via the national insurance scheme for serious injuries or disease arising from work. Certain work-related diseases or illness are, on proof of a connection with work, *prescribed* (in effect, automatically compensated). In addition to benefits obtainable through application of the state scheme, compensation may be obtainable through *tort* via the courts. Sometimes the amount awarded in a court settlement is deducted or recovered from benefit payments (see *Social Security (Recoupment of Benefits) Act 1997*). All *employers* must hold **Employers' Liability Insurance** to ensure compensation payment is covered.

solution a mixture formed when substances in different states (e.g. solid, liquid or gas) combine together and the mixture takes on the state of one of its constituents. For example, when a solid is dissolved in a liquid, the solution is liquid.

solvent is a liquid capable of dissolving other substances and incorporating them into a solution. Some solvents are hazardous and their use is covered by **COSHH**. The hierarchy of action includes: (i) eliminate use; (ii) substitute; (iii) eliminate exposure; (iv) minimise exposure to 'safe' limit; (v) only after (i) – (iv) have been implemented, provide PPE (**ERICPD**).

Solvent fumes can be inhaled or absorbed through the skin. Adverse symptoms following exposure to dangerous solvents include: headaches; dizziness; nausea; eye, lung or skin irritation; unconsciousness. Long term exposure can lead to loss of concentration, memory and significant mood swings; dermatitis, liver and kidney damage; cancer.

Safety data sheets must be provided with hazardous solvents by manufacturers or suppliers (see **CHIP**). Workers who are exposed to hazardous solvents must be provided with *information, instruction* and *training* and *health surveillance*. The 1998 **HSE** publication *Working with solvents: A Manager's Guide* obtainable from **HSE Books** is useful; reference to the **EH40** is essential.

sound is the sensation experienced through reception of vibrations transmitted through the air in the form of waves, somewhat similar to that seen when a stone is thrown into still water. Sound is measured through the use of electronic instruments. Incidentally, *noise* is unwanted sound (see *noise* for a further explanation).

sources of ignition include the following:

(a) static electricity;
(b) discarded smoking materials;
(c) hot surfaces, friction;
(d) radiant heat;
(e) accumulated rubbish (poor housekeeping);
(f) some dusts, e.g. flour;
(g) chemicals;
(h) sunlight through bottles (and some contents);
(i) faulty electrical appliances, plugs and wiring.

space see *work space*.

spark erosion is an electromechanical metal machining process where an electrode is placed very close to a workpiece, both submerged in a dielectric liquid. A current is passed through the gap, producing very high local temperatures which from the workpiece detaches particles following a 'pattern'.

Special Waste Regulations 1996 replaced the 1980 *Regulations* and are associated with the *Environmental Protection Act 1990*. The definition of special waste in the 1996 *Regulations* includes the most dangerous wastes, the majority of which are hazardous or toxic wastes, listed in the *Regulations*. The 1996 *Regulations* do **not** include domestic waste but are limited to the disposal, carriage and reception of *special* wastes. The 1996 *Regulations* include cover of special wastes going into storage, treatment, recycling or for disposal. See various *Waste Regulations*.

If the waste is 'special' the Environment Agency for England and Wales, or the Scottish Environment Protection Agency (the *Regulators*) must be informed **before** – *pre-notification* – the special waste is removed (except for waste taken off ships, or for materials that do not meet the specification being returned to manufacturers), through sending to the Regulators a *consignment note* which can be obtained from the Regulators – replacing the duty of care transfer note – at least three clear working days before the waste is removed. The *Regulations* **do not** say how the waste should be packaged and handled, but the *duty of care* requires a clear description to be given, to enable the waste to be managed safely. Examples of special wastes include acids, alkaline solutions, batteries (except automotive lead-acid batteries, which **do not** require *pre-notification*), fly ash, industrial solvents, oily sludge, pesticides, pharmaceutical compounds, photographic chemicals, wood preservatives.

Waste **must** always be transferred to an *authorised person*, e.g. a registered carrier or a licensed waste manager. Carriers and consignees **must** keep a register of consignment notes for at least three years, and consignees keep copies of consignment notes *until they surrender the licence for the site they manage*. In simple terms, *consignors* are those getting rid of the waste; *carriers* are those who carry the waste; *consignees* are those who receive the waste. Fees will be charged by the environmental agencies. Failure to comply with the **Regulations** could result in a fine of up to £5,000 and/or two years in prison.

specify (*examination term*) means to itemise, in summary form.

spores are bacteria with a rounded body, found inside the microscopic host bacteria. Some *pathogenic* bacteria produce spores. The spores have the ability to resist high temperatures (e.g. boiling water) for several hours and survive for years without food or moisture. When conditions once again become favourable for growth, spores return to their vegetative state and grow and multiply. Spores can be destroyed or killed by cooking *under pressure* at **120c** or above.

standard of proof in *criminal law* is where guilt is found to be 95 per cent *beyond reasonable doubt*; in **common law** guilt is where it is likely to be at least 51 per cent 'certain' on the *balance of probability*.

standard scale provides for five levels of fines on *summary conviction* (at *Magistrates' Courts*). The levels are 1 = £200; 2 = £500; 3 = £1,000; 4 = 2,500; and 5 = £5,000 (*Stones Justices Manual*). However, health, safety and environmental convicted offenders nay be subjected to fines greater than the *standard scale* and in the Crown Courts (and above) there are no maximum.

staphylococcus: non-mobile bacteria, looking like (microscopic) bunches of grapes. Staphylococcal food poisoning is caused by contaminated food handled by carriers, it is *not* directly transmitted person to person. Symptoms are severe nausea, vomiting, diarrhoea. Control and prevention is by good hygiene, cooking and heating of food.

state (*examination term*) means a clear and succinct description of something, in a few short sentences.

statement is any representation of fact, whether written, given verbally or otherwise. **NB** If ever a statement is given to an enforcement officer (including to the police) ask for a copy **before** making and especially before signing it, otherwise it may prove difficult to obtain one.

static sampling is where a 'sampler' is placed at a location to determine, for example, the particle size distribution of airborne dust in a specific area. Sometimes static samplers are used with *personal sampling* to obtain an answer. Fixed or static sampling is useful to identify the effectiveness, or otherwise, of emission control measures, such as *local exhaust ventilation systems.*

Statute Law is the written law of the land and consists of *Acts* of Parliament, *Regulations* and *Orders in Council.* Statute law includes statutes (primary legislation) which provide the framework and Statutory Instruments (subordinate legislation) which provide further details. Each year around 80 new Acts of Parliament are passed, many of which 'replace' existing statute.

Where there are conflicts between statute and *common law*, statute (should) take precedent because Parliament is legally sovereign. However, since judges interpret the law, they can in reality, change statute or minimise the effect of a law. As an example, Lord Denning, when Master of the Rolls, consistently defied the intention of Parliament as expressed in the relatively clear wording of the Sex Discrimination Act.

statutes are *Acts of Parliament*, which lay down the framework of a system and are part of the written law of the land, are 'laid' before (i.e. presented to), and debated in, Parliament and after receiving Royal Assent become law at a date specified. Judges in their courts may interpret the meaning of terms and phrases within *Acts* (and *Regulations*) thereby, in effect, changing their meaning and application.

Statutory Instruments, in outline terms, are 'any delegated legislation …. to which the *Statutory Instruments Act 1946* applies'. They are made by a Secretary of State or Minister of the Crown under a parent Act (an enabling Act) and are made by the person or authority specified in the enabling Act. They have to be numbered consecutively and dated, e.g. SI 2000 No 1, and *published* by the Queen's Printer. The term *published* is a key term, since everyone is presumed, at law, to be aware of the contents and requirements of Statutory Instruments – hence 'ignorance of the law is no defence!' Nowadays, Statutory Instruments are seldom considered in detail by Parliament although they must be 'laid' before Parliament.

Statutory Instruments Act 1946 enables a Regulation or Statutory Instrument which is within the scope of a 'parent' or enabling Act, to become law after a period of 40 days of being laid before Parliament (in effect, put in a room in the House to allow MPs and Members of the House of Lords to look at it), provided no resolution is passed against it in either House. A breach of the Statutory Instrument or Regulation is actionable, even though there may be no mention of this in the Statutory Instrument or Regulation.

statutory nuisances include dust, steam, smells or other effluvia emitted from industrial or trade premises. They must be either prejudicial to the health, safety, comfort or property of the public at large (known as a 'public *nuisance*' which is a *crime*) or 'an activity' which, for example, 'interferes with the use, enjoyment or rights over land' (private *nuisance*, a *tort* or civil matter); both *nuisances* are 'defined' by statute.

STEL see *short term exposure level.*

stress can be defined as the psychological, physiological and behavioural response on the part of a person to a situation in which that person is unable to cope with the demands placed upon him/her, leading eventually to incapacity and ill health. The **HSE** report that every year 250,000 *employees* suffer from work-induced stress and over five million working days lost. This means that the effects of stress costs UK businesses around **400 million pounds** per annum.

Unfortunately obtaining accurate reports and records of stress is difficult because *employees* are often reluctant to, as they (wrongly) see it, 'admit' to being personally unable to cope, which in error is commonly considered to be the prime cause of stress. Stressors can be personal but are more likely to be environmental or organisational. However, stressed *employees* should first consider *external-to-self* causes of stress, e.g. poor job design, bad work environment, poor lighting or ventilation, inadequate training, unsuitable equipment, role conflict or other factors.

Stress which is thought to be occupationally induced *by the employee affected* should be entered into the **Accident Book** and the employer must take action. If incapacity and ill-health due to stress result from the **employer's** breach of the general *duty of care* (**HSWA**) towards *employees* and if the stressor(s) had been drawn to the notice of an *employer*, who failed to take reasonable steps to mitigate a foreseeable situation (*Walker v Northumberland County Council [1995] IRLR 35*), then *very* substantial compensation may have to be paid.

However, not all stress is dysfunctional or bad. Some persons, particularly those known as *Type A*, appear to thrive on stress, apparently without ill effect – at least for some time.

A 1998 **TUC** study reported that of those employed in education, 88% suffer from stress; financial sector 84%; health services, 82%; local government, 81% and 90% of safety representatives in the voluntary and local government sectors reported being stressed. The same study identified the main causes of workplace stress to be workloads and staffing levels (reported by 60% of respondents); new management techniques (40%); long hours (28%); shift-work (21%) and bullying (21%).

A risk assessment should consider and identify stress and stressors, following which removing, monitoring, revising, reviewing, or 'changing' the cause of stress (the stressors) should be carried out. It is no use calling in professionals, such as stress counsellors, until the magnitude and true causes of the stress problem are accurately known. Simply providing **employees** with training in coping strategies to deal with stress and not removing the stressors not only is ineffective, it is wasting money. A useful introduction to stress is the **HSE** publication INDG281 (single copies free) obtainable from **HSE Books**.

strict liability see *liability*.

strip mining see *open cast mining*.

structure: its definition provides a good example of the way that compilers of legislation attempt to cover every eventuality and deserves reporting in full to illustrate the point.

According to the definition of structure provided in the **construction** health and safety legislation a structure is 'any building, steel or reinforced concrete structure (not being a building), railway line or siding, tramway line, dock, harbour, inland navigation, tunnel, shaft, bridge, viaduct, waterworks, reservoir, pipe or pipeline, (regardless of actual or intended contents), cable, aqueduct, sewer, sewage works, gasholder, road, airfield, sea defence works, river works, drainage works, earthworks, lagoon, dam, wall, caisson, mast, tower, pylon, underground tank, earth retaining structure or structure designed or used to provide support or means of **access** during **construction** work, and any fixed plant in respect of work that is installation, commissioning, decommissioning or dismantling and where that work involves the risk of falling more than two metres'.

substance, in *occupational health* and safety terms, means any natural or artificial substance (including micro-organisms) intended for use (whether exclusively or not) by persons at work.

suitable see *adequate and suitable* and *suitable and sufficient*.

suitable and sufficient has not been provided with a *universally* applicable definition, it commonly means 'suitable and sufficient for the circumstances'. Because of this difficulty, health and safety texts (understandably) are unable to provide a definitive definition. In fact, the courts often decide what is considered to be 'suitable and sufficient', only after an **accident** or **incident** has occurred, *taking account of all the circumstances*. This 'after the event' situation may seem unfortunate for **employers** and **employees**, but conversely has the advantage that it assists competent **employers** to take account of varying circumstances. In the event of doubt, firstly, see if it is defined in the beginning of the relevant legislation under 'interpretation', if it is not shown, consult an authoritative comprehensive text, or obtain advice from the **Health and Safety Information Centre and Public Enquiry Point** (Tel: 0541 545500), a Trade Association or Union or a professional safety advisor/consultant.

summarise (*examination term*) requires, using a few concise highly relevant sentences, the salient points of something, without going into details or providing examples.

summary conviction is a conviction by magistrates on a simple majority in a *Magistrates' Court*.

See also *magistrate* and *Magistrates' Court*.

superior legislation (or dominant legislation) is where (apparently or in reality) two or more *Regulations* are applied to the same 'thing', but one is superior. There are many examples, one being asbestos whereby it may appear to be that for a hazardous (or dangerous) substance only **COSHH** may apply, however, more specific *Regulations* and associated **ACOPs** (or *Guidance Notes* on how to achieve the objective) also apply. However, the **HSWA** is the prime superior legislation: firstly, it is a unique piece of legislation as an enabling Act; secondly, prosecution of offenders is almost invariably 'looped back' to a section or sub-section of the **HSWA**. In simple terms, in effect all health and safety legislation 'stems' from or through the **HSWA** – the **HSWA** places a duty on **employers** to provide a workplace without risk to safety and health, the **MHSWR** requires *risk assessments* to be conducted to identify such risks.

supplier is someone who supplies goods or services and has many duties under a variety of health and safety legislation. Purely as examples, the *Supply of Machinery (Safety) Regulations 1992* (and **1994 amendment**) cover what the title suggests, **CHIP** covers the supply of hazardous substances (particularly the provision of Data Sheets which, *within the EU*, must be supplied in the language of country of destination) and **PUWER** work equipment. Where required, goods, machinery and work equipment **must** satisfy CE *Marking Regulations*. Incidentally, the supply of hire equipment is also covered. Clients have the right to examine the supplier's health and safety systems and procedures.

Supply of Machinery (Safety) (Amendment) Regulations 1994
see **Supply of Machinery (Safety) Regulations 1992**.

Supply of Machinery (Safety) Regulations 1992 or *SMSR* and the

Supply of Machinery (Safety) (Amendment) Regulations 1994 or SMSAR will be generally treated as one, and they apply to all powered machinery. They cover *relevant machinery* as defined in SMSR Reg. 4 but excluding that listed in Sch. 5 of those Regulations, other than that covered by the Amendment. Machinery is defined by the SMSR (Reg. 4) as an assembly of linked parts, at least one of which moves, together with their controls and power circuits; assemblies of several machines arranged and controlled to function as one; interchangeable equipment that modifies the function of a machine, **UNLESS** the machinery is covered by other EU Directives (e.g., the Product Safety Directive). As usual, other relevant health and safety legislation also applies. Salient points include:

CE Mark must be *clear and distinct and permanently fixed*; only fitted if a Declaration of Conformity or Declaration of Incorporation is approved and the machinery conforms with other community directives that may apply (e.g. through complying with UK legislation) (Reg. 25).

compliance with SMSR requires machinery, in particular, to meet the specified *Essential Health and Safety Requirements* (EHSR).

conformity assessment procedures must be carried out by approved bodies and are detailed in Regs 17, 18, 19. The procedures are necessary for Sch. 4 machinery. Reg. 20 describes the Certificate of Adequacy and the EU Type Examination procedure.

Declaration of Conformity (or EU DoC) procedures, whereby a *responsible person* declares each piece of relevant machinery supplied within the EU is described in SMSR Reg. 22. DoCs (and Instructions) for machinery supplied to EU countries must be in the same language as that used in the EU destination country.

There is no obligatory pro-forma for the EU DoC and, provided they satisfy the **Regulations**, they can be designed by the manufacturer or his/her representative but must include as a minimum:

(a) full name and address of manufacturer *and* the responsible person;
(b) description of the machinery, including make, type and serial number;
(c) an indication of all provisions with which the machinery complies, i.e. specifics of machinery directive or other EU directions that apply;
(d) where Sch. 4 machinery has undergone an EU type examination, the identity of the approved body and the certificate number;

(e) where certain Sch. 4 machinery requires the drawing up of a technical file, the identity of the approved body holding the file or which drew up the Certificate of Adequacy;

(f) specification of the harmonised standards used (if any);

(g) specification of national standards or technical specifications used.

Declaration of Incorporation (DoI) applies to relevant machinery, which is intended for incorporation into other machinery or assembled with other machinery, but cannot function independently and is not interchangeable equipment. DoI procedures require a *responsible person* to declare each piece of relevant machinery satisfies SMSR Reg. 23. The DoI must:

(a) identify the responsible person and the person signing the declaration;

(b) contain a description of the machinery or machinery parts;

(c) with Sch. 4 machinery that has undergone an EU type examination, identify and display the approved body and the certificate number;

(d) with certain Sch. 4 machinery, confirm a technical file (see below) has been drawn up, identify the approved body holding the technical file or who drew up the certificate of adequacy;

(e) specify the harmonised standard(s) which apply;

(f) clearly state that the machinery to which the DoI relates **must not** be put into service until the whole machine has received the DoC.

enforcement is described in Regs. 28-31 Sch. 6 of the SMSR.

Essential Health and Safety Requirements (EHSR) are very wide ranging and include:

(i) an assessment of the risk to operators;

(ii) materials used in *construction*;

(iii) suitability of controls and lighting;

(iv) the effects of vibration;

(v) *noise*; and

(vi) the emission of dusts and gases.

Member states must presume that machinery bearing the CE Mark **and** accompanied by a *Declaration of Conformity* **or** *Declaration of Incorporation* satisfies the EHSR and must be allowed free circulation.

excluded from the provisions of the SMSR includes machinery for export outside the EU, certain machinery which is subject to other specific directives (Reg. 5-10).

Supply of Machinery (Safety) Regulations 1992 or SMSR

failure to comply with SMSR requirements is a *criminal* offence.

instruction books, *clear, understandable* (i.e. in the language of the country of use) *Instruction and Maintenance Handbooks*, which must draw attention to any foreseeable hazards, must be provided with all relevant machinery manufactured in the EU *or supplied* to EU destinations. In the case of non-EU sourced relevant machinery the supplier assumes the SMSR duties. *Instruction* handbooks can be typed or handwritten in block capitals (see Reg. 13).

lifting machinery carrying persons is covered by SMSAR Reg. 4 Sch. 2.

machinery cannot be supplied or put into service *(including by self-supply)* unless it complies with the following (Regs. 11 and 12):

(a) essential health and safety requirements, for example on its **construction**, moving parts and stability;
(b) appropriate conformity assessment procedures i.e.
    (i) in some cases, be subject to type examination by an approved body, and
    (ii) carry a CE Mark and other information.

machinery that complies with the **Regulations** may be *marked with the CE mark*. Machinery **not** complying with the SMSR or SMSAR cannot be sold in *any* member state of the EU.

maintenance must be carried out while the machine is at standstill. However, if for technical reasons this cannot be done, then maintenance must only be allowed if it is **without risk**, requiring safe *access*, with means of isolation, as much as possible maintenance should be possible without entering the machinery (SMSR Sch. 3).

modification procedures are outlined in Reg. 16.

non-mechanical hazards must be protected against, e.g. electrical, extreme temperature (high or low), risk of slipping, tripping or falling, entrapment, emissions of dust, gases, liquids and vapours (Sch. 3).

review of decisions made by approved bodies is possible through a procedure described in Reg. 27.

Schedule 4 machinery is of a more hazardous nature and described in SMSR Regs. 14-21, although other legislation **also** may apply (e.g.

HSWA, PUWER 1998). There are different procedures for machinery manufactured to harmonised standards from those for machinery manufactured to non-harmonised standards. Examples include:

- circular saws e.g. used for wood or meat;
- planers;
- power presses;
- specific types of lifting equipment (e.g. that which lifts people above three metres and vehicle servicing lifts).

Schedule 5 machinery includes:

- safety components e.g. detectors, logic units, non-material barriers and pressure mats (SMSR Reg. 5; Sch. 5 SMSAR);
- machinery/components for lifting or moving persons (Reg. 5 Sch. 5 as amended by SMSAR Reg. 4 Sch. 10);
- roll-over protective structures;
- industrial trucks.

suppliers of relevant machinery (i.e. that covered by the SMSR as amended), which can be foreign or domestic, must ensure that when such machinery or components are properly installed, maintained and used for their proper purpose, there is *minimal risk of them causing injury or death to persons or damage to property* (SMSR Reg. 2(2) amended SMSAR Reg. 4.2 Sch. 5). **NB** This requirement is additional to those of the **PUWER** and other relevant legislation.

suppliers, who may be a manufacturer, agent or wholesaler of EU and non-EU manufactured relevant machinery destined for use within the EU must issue with each machine:

- an EU declaration confirming the machine satisfies the 'necessary' health and safety requirements; or
- in the case of machinery to be incorporated into other machinery, a Declaration of Incorporation.

technical files will generally have to be kept available by the manufacturer (or authorised representative in the Community) for a minimum of ten years after the machinery was supplied (SMSR Reg. 24). A responsible person concerning the relevant machinery (other than Schedule 4 machinery) will draw up the Technical File. According to the SMSR (Reg. 13) the Technical File will consist of:

(a) an overall drawing, including control circuits;

(b) detailed drawings, calculations and test results *showing how the EHSR have been met*;
(c) the design parameters used, such as harmonised standards, other standards;
(d) a description of methods used to eliminate hazards from the machinery;
(e) where applicable, a technical report or certificate from an (author-ised) competent body;
(f) where conformity is claimed by manufacturing to a harmonised standard, technical reports and the results of tests;
(g) a copy of the instructions for the machinery as required by Schedule 3. The **MHSWR** should be complied with, i.e. *for destination countries* **within the EU,** *the instructions must be comprehensible to the user*;
(h) in the case of series manufacture, the documentation of the internal quality system used to ensure continuing conformity.

It will be seen that many of the items listed will have formed part of normal records and will not have to be specially written for the Technical File.

Supreme Court of Judicature is a court created by the Judicature Act 1873-75 and consists of the *Court of Appeal, High Court of Justice* and the *Crown Court.* The *Lord Chancellor* is President.

suspended access systems include working *cradles*, platforms or a *bosun's chair* (boatswain's chair) provided with means to raise or lower the system. The equipment should be erected and maintained by a *competent person*; capable of taking the loads possible to be placed upon it as shown by a working load indicator; working platforms should be suitably guarded and fitted with edge protection; adverse weather conditions, when operators must not use the equipment should be identified; suitable protective measures should be provided or taken for those working below and for members of the public.

symbiosis is a close and permanent relationship between organisms of different species. Symbiosis is subdivided into mutualism, whereby both organisms benefit; commensalism, where one benefits and the other is unharmed; and parasitism, where one of the organisms benefits at the expense of the other.

symbols, warning see *CHIP.*

system is an assembly of interrelated objects organised as an integrated whole. Systems are usually termed *open* or *closed.*

system of work

system of work is a formal, systematic procedure, which may or may not take account of health and safety aspects, which is devised before any work activity is carried out, monitored and reviewed.

See *safe system of work*.

systems framework of analysis is a key component of successful health and safety, in particular *health and safety management*. A simple systems framework, which providing the basic features, i.e. 'input', 'throughput' and 'output', with a 'feedback loop' running from input to output (and return). The feedback loop is essential to monitor and if necessary review, for example, a decision.

T

taxonomy is a classification system (for example of *organisms*) into hierarchical groups.

technical file see *Supply of Machinery (Safety) Regulations 1992*.

temperature, in technical terms, is the measurement of molecular *kinetic energy* of matter and represents the speed at which the molecules in the matter move or vibrate. In simple terms, temperature is the measurement of the warmth or coldness of an object or space.

In the UK, *occupational health*, safety and welfare requirements are for a *minimum* temperature in the workplace of 16°C for sedentary work and 13°C where strenuous movement and/or physical effort is involved. There is no maximum workplace temperature, other than the statutory requirement for *employers* to provide and maintain a safe and healthy place of work, the interpretation of which regarding temperature may devolve to negotiation.

temporary threshold shift see *threshold shift, noise* and *noise induced hearing loss*.

teratogenic substances, agents and preparations are those which, if they are inhaled or ingested or if they penetrate the skin, may cause abnormal development of an embryo, e.g. they may affect the tissues in a developing foetus.

therm is a unit of heat equivalent to 105.5 megajoules. It is now seldom used, having generally been replaced by the megajoule.

threshold limit value or TLV is a term not used any more in the UK but still found in some older UK texts and used in the USA. It is the concentration of an airborne substance which represents the *maximum* exposure to which workers can be exposed day-after-day, it is claimed, without ill effects. The 'values' are for inhalation, in units of milligrams per cubic metre (mgm^{-3}) or parts per million (ppm). Skin absorption figures are denoted by SK. There are different categories of TLV, e.g. *ceiling TLV*, *short term exposure level* and *time weighted average TLV*. *Control limits* which provide the lowest level technically and economically feasible are used in place of TLVs.

threshold shift is a change in the ability to hear. A threshold shift can be permanent or temporary, although a temporary threshold shift may indicate the development of a permanent shift. A regular hearing test may identify that an

269

time weighted average

employee's hearing range is consistently deteriorating. Testing of *employees* should not be conducted within 12-14 hours of any significant exposure to *noise*. This is to minimise the possibility of confusing a temporary shift as a permanent one.

time weighted average see *decibel*.

tinnitus is a form of hearing damage resulting from over stimulation of the hair cells, causing ringing in the ears which can be *acute*, lasting around 24 hours or *chronic*, therefore irreversible. If tinnitus occurs despite, but **only** as a last resort, the wearing of personal protective equipment, it may be because of one or more of the reasons given in *personal hearing protection, limitations of.*

TLV see *threshold limit value.*

toilets see *sanitary conveniences.*

tool-box talk is an informal (regular or intermittent) workplace discussion on health, safety or environmental matters, relevant to that particular *workplace* or small *workgroup*, usually (but not always) led by the foreperson. The speaker often stood on a toolbox to see, be seen and heard, hence the name.

tort is a **civil wrong**, for example whereby a person or *employer* causes injury to another person *because of negligence*, which is a *tort*, and the *injured person* may then *sue for damages* in the civil courts.

total loss control is basically a *systems* based management programme with the objective of achieving the 'the elimination of all incidents which downgrade the system' (Fletcher and Douglas, 1971). It developed from 'loss control' in Canada and the USA and its use in the UK was long strongly advocated by the late James Tye, Director General of the British Safety Council (*not a government body*). It is still in use under its own name but more frequently the techniques of total loss control are found subsumed in various other, newer health and safety management systems. The advocates of total loss control presented the benefits and method in many guises. The emphasis is on the role and contribution of effective management in preventing loss of any kind, not merely health and safety.

The application of the programme is intended to locate errors in judgement, incomplete decision making, bad management and individual practices, operating effectively a 'cost benefit analysis'. The proponents of total loss control advocate that sound advice to management can avoid mistakes. In health and safety such advice could well be from qualified and experienced safety personnel, sometimes requiring the use of professionals from outside the organisation.

total quality management see BS 8800, *risk management, safety management* and *total loss control.*

tower scaffolds are most usually erected from commercial kits, although they can be made 'on site' from steel or aluminium tubing and couplers, to BS 5973. Only *competent persons* may erect tower scaffolds, and check that the structure is sound and constructed to the manufacturer's instructions. Tower scaffolds can be mobile or fixed, suitably braced to avoid twisting. They have a single working platform, constructed of suitable material and appropriately secure and guarded. No ladder or other structure may be placed on the working platform to gain extra height for working. Untied structures should not exceed 9.75 metres, on tied structures the working platform should not exceed 12 metres height from the base.

The base to height ratio is important for stability and should not exceed 1:3 for external use and 1:3.5 for internal use. The base may be extended through the use of out-riggers which, where fitted, must be fully extended and their load bearing capacity never exceeded. A suitable means of *access* must be provided, either through an internal vertical *access* ladder or an integral ladder as part of the commercially designed and manufactured structure. The internal *access* to the working platform should be via a trap door. The wheels on mobile tower scaffolds must be fitted at its corners and should be capable of being locked, to prevent movement while in use. The tower must **never** be moved with persons on it.

toxic substances and preparations (including very toxic substances and preparations) are those which, if they are inhaled or ingested or if they penetrate the skin, may involve serious, *acute* or *chronic* health risks and even death.

See also *toxins.*

toxic shock syndrome (also known as TSS) is a *rare* but possibly fatal illness, which affects women. It is caused when a normally harmless *bacteria* (staphylococcus aureus) found in the vagina and elsewhere in the body, suddenly goes berserk and produces *toxins.* The use of a tampon during menstruation can encourage the rapid growth of the *bacteria* leading to the *toxins* entering the bloodstream. As medical professionals have increasingly become aware of this syndrome, it is now better diagnosed, whereas in the past it may have been unrecognised. Symptoms include: *sudden* onset of a high temperature, vomiting and diarrhoea, sore throat, dizziness, headaches and confusion.

Steps which can be taken to reduce the possibility of TSS include: change tampons every 4-6 hours, handle tampons as little as possible, use external sanitary protection during the night, wash hands thoroughly before and after the use of a tampon. The health and safety legislation which also assists in prevention of TSS includes the **WHSWR** which require *employers* where five or more persons are employed to provide *separate* toilet *facilities* for men and women. The term *toilet facilities* include hot and cold water, sink, towels or hot air dryer and, where women are employed, suitable effective methods for disposal of used sanitary towels or tampons.

toxins are poisons, e.g. of animal, vegetable or chemical origin, or secreted by a micro-organism, which cause a particular disease or ill effect. The effect of toxins cannot always be accurately predicted because the effect is dependent on a variety of factors, including quantity or concentration, duration of exposure, the physical state of the material, its solubility, even variations in resistance between individuals.

Toxins tend to attack a particular organ of the body, for example the lungs or alveoli (and thus enter the bloodstream); sometimes the symptoms only show some time after the invading toxin has gained a foothold. The body provides several natural defence mechanisms against toxins entering it, ranging from cellular defences (e.g. blood clotting, repair of damaged tissue), to defences that are triggered deep in the body, e.g. respiratory tract – coughing and sneezing; ingestion – vomiting or even diarrhoea. Another defence is acquired immunity, where resistance is developed to a specific toxin several days or weeks after exposure.

Several different toxins can produce or contribute to the development of the same ill-health, such as chronic bronchitis which can be caused by mineral dusts (e.g. asbestos, coal, glass fibre, metals and oils), organic dusts, acids or smoke.

trade union representatives are persons who are members of and appointed by a *trade union* after an election, frequently involving the branch membership. Where the rules specify, no election needs to be held (do not confuse with the non-union elected workforce representatives). Some 27 per cent of the labour force in Great Britain are members of 245 *independent trade unions*.

trade unions are basically of two types those listed (in effect, registered) by the *Certification Officer* and those which are not listed. Those listed can be further subdivided into those affiliated to the *Trades Union Congress* (numbering 73, representing approximately 80% of listed trade union membership) and the unaffiliated (160). In June 2000 the total trade union membership was around eight million.

Listed trade unions have a record and reputation of being completely independent of their members' *employers* and all governments (although they may support and identify with the aims and objectives of a particular party). Many listed trade unions are affiliated to the Labour Party, but members can refuse to subscribe that part of their membership fee. Unlisted 'trade unions', often called 'staff associations', are sometimes considered to be closely associated with the aims and objectives of their member's *employers*. However, the **Guinness Staff Association** (membership 55) is certified and affiliated to the **TUC**. Incidentally, there is a Federation of Conservative Trade Unionists.

Affiliated to the **TUC** are the following trade unions that have a membership greater than 100,000 members are. They include:

Amalgamated Engineering and Electrical Union (Tel: 020 8462 7755) (720,000)

Banking Insurance and Finance Union (Tel: 020 8946 9151) (116,000)

Communication Workers Union (Tel: 020 8971 7200) (271,000)

GMB formerly General, Municipal, Boilermakers and Allied Trades Union (Tel: 020 8947 3131) (700,000)

Graphical, Paper and Media Union (Tel: 01234 351521) (216,991)

Manufacturing, Science and Finance Union (Tel: 020 7505 3000) (400,000)

NASWUT National Association of Schoolmasters/Union of Women Teachers (Tel: 020 7379 9499) (172,852)

National Union of Teachers (Tel: 020 7388 6191) (191,800)

Public and Commercial Services Union (Tel: 020 7924 2727) (250,000)

Transport and General Workers Union TGWU (Tel: 020 7828 7788) (882,272)

Union of *Construction*, Allied Trades and Technicians UCATT (Tel: 020 7622 2442) (114,000)

Trades Union Congress (TUC)

Union of Shop, Distributive and Allied Workers USDAW (Tel: 0161 224 2804) (290,170)

UNISON (Tel: 020 7388) (1,300,000)

There is only one *non-affiliated* trade union with membership in excess of 100,000, that is the **Association of Teachers and Lecturers** (Tel: 020 7930 6441) (150,000). However, amalgamations regularly take place and such lists need regular updating.

Trades Union Congress (TUC), founded in 1869, is an independent association of trade unions. The TUC promotes the rights and welfare of those at work, helps the unemployed, carries out research into a variety of labour-related topics, issues reports and publications (e.g. on health, safety and environmental matters), makes representations to government, political parties, *employers* and international bodies such as the European Union. TUC representatives sit on many public bodies (e.g. the **HSC**) at national and international level (e.g. the United Nations body, the *International Labour Organisation*, Geneva).

As an example, education, in the broadest sense (including that for health and safety), is given a very high priority by the TUC and its affiliated unions. Ruskin College, Oxford is a major *training* and education centre for the trade union movement and successful completion of a Diploma at Ruskin can lead directly into a degree course at one of the Oxford University Colleges.

The main telephone number for the TUC is 020 7636 4030 and its web site (e.g. for health and safety information) is accessed through http://www.tuc.org.uk.

trainee is someone who receives *training* as part of his/her *employment*, apprenticeship, student placement, and government *training* schemes. Effectively, such persons are in paid *employment* (including students and pupils on placement and pupils or students on work experience) who are receiving *training* and are thereby covered by Section 2 of the **HSWA 1974** (as amended) and by the *Health and Safety (Training for Employment) Regulations 1990*.

Age may not need to be taken into account, but *employers* must take account of the fact that trainees may act immaturely and are inexperienced.

Parents or guardian of an *employee under* school leaving age must be informed of any identified risks and control measures adopted at the place of work (and their operation) to protect such persons.

Supervision of *high quality* is essential.

All courses which do not fall within the above categories are nevertheless held at educational institutions are covered by Section 3 of the **HSWA 1974** and all other relevant legislation.

training is the *process* of acquiring information, skill, knowledge, *with feedback to ensure it is understood.* The **HSWA** s.2 imposes a general duty on all *employers* to provide *suitable* and *sufficient* health and safety *training* to their *employees*, to ensure, *so far as is reasonably practicable*, the health and safety at work of the *employees*, including the setting out of their *training* provisions in the *safety policy statement.* This requirement to provide *training* may extend to providing *training* to *employees* of other *employers*, who are working in the same premises (see *R v Swan Hunter Shipbuilders Ltd. and another [1981] ICR 831; [1982] 1 AER 264*).

A specific requirement is to provide *comprehensible* (i.e. it must be understood by the trainees) *training* to ALL *employees* as required by **MHSWR** Reg. 11 **and** a requirement for *training* to be considered as part of *assessments* conducted to comply with e.g. **MHSWR** Reg. 3, **HSDSER** Reg. 6; **PUWER** Reg. 9 (which is specifically extended to include supervisors and managers of operators); **PPER**; Reg. 9 and implicit in Schedule 1 in the **MHOR**.

In premises where a *fire certificate* is in force, s.6(2)(c) of the **FPA** requires that persons who regularly work in the premises must be given appropriate *instruction* or *training* in what to do in the event of a fire, with records kept of such *instruction* or *training*.

training needs analysis should always be carried out, on a regular basis and in connection with specific tasks. The needs analysis may itself be specific, e.g. establishing a specific Health and Safety *training* need (e.g. **COSHH**), or general, e.g. identifying the need to re-train *all* staff in new procedures. In both cases the common elements, after initially recognising the need for *training*, would include: what type or level of *training* is required, e.g. induction, organisational development or change, health and safety, etc.; what areas, departments or staff require the *training*; what type of *training* is required, e.g. practical or processual; establishing the educational level of those attending against course demands; and deciding whether internal trainers or outside trainers and/or consultants should carry out the *training*.

The *training* needs analysis must be objective and carried out by a professional, otherwise resources may be wasted and the desired (and required) result may not be achieved. For example, a course designed for managers would possibly not be suitable for rank and file shopfloor staff, partly because of its content and partly due to its tone and thrust. Find out if there are suitable *employees* on site who could carry out the *training*, or would outside trainers be required? If 'outsiders' are used, make sure that professional trainers would include in their *training* programme sufficient reference to the company's organisational and operational demands.

transformer is an electrical device, which usually transforms through electro-magnetic **induction** the voltage of an *alternating* electrical current in a primary winding to another voltage into a secondary winding. Aside from the **auto-transformer** there is no connection between the windings.

Transport of Dangerous Goods (Safety Advisers) Regulations

1999 concern the appointment and vocational qualifications of safety advisers for the transport of *dangerous goods* by road, rail *and* inland waterways. The safety adviser's function is to advise them on health, safety *and environmental matters* relating to the transport of *dangerous goods*. NB These *Regulations* apply to both *self-employed and employers*.

Employers must ensure safety advisers: (i) are appointed in sufficient numbers to carry out their duties effectively; (ii) are provided with adequate informa-tion, time and other resources to fulfil their functions; (iii) hold *vocational training certificates*, achieved after training and examination, renewable every five years and appropriate to the transport and *dangerous goods* carried. Schedule 2 of the *Regulations* lists the duties of Safety Advisers, including: monitoring rules and procedures; implementing verification procedures for documentation, safety equipment and compliance with legislation regarding loading and unloading *dangerous goods*.

transportable pressure containers see various *Carriage of Dangerous Goods Regulations*.

trespassers, according to *common law*, are basically persons who go some-where where they should not or who go 'without invitation', irrespective of their purpose. Even a *visitor* who has in effect or reality been invited becomes a trespasser, if going anywhere other than the area where he/she has been invited. Such persons would be covered by the *Occupiers' Liability Act*. However, a customer in a shop using a staff toilet *without permission* would be trespassing and would lose **some** of the protection of the *Occupiers' Liability Acts*, plus possibly **some** cover from health and safety legislation.

In *occupational health* and safety terms, *employers* and *employees* have a general duty of care to ensure *so far as is reasonably practicable* that their activity at work does not harm others. Trespassers (e.g. burglars), should be protected from harm, such as falling through a fragile roof or from dangerous fumes. (*OLA 1984*).

trichloroethylene, commonly termed 'trike', is a colourless liquid (sometimes dyed blue) with an odour similar to chloroform and of low flammability. Its uses include in dry-cleaning, textile processing, the manufacture of adhesives, paints, plastics, resins and rubber, etc. (see **EH 40**). It is *toxic* by inhalation, ingestion and contact, and highly hazardous to the respiratory system, the heart, liver, kidneys, central nervous system and skin. Symptoms include dermatitis, headaches, visual disturbances, sleepiness, eye irritation and cardiac problems. It is carcinogenic. Call a medical professional. First aid includes: (i) remove from exposure; (ii) rest and keep warm; (iii) if necessary, irrigate eyes *thoroughly*.

trigger finger is where the finger locks, either in a bent or straight position, and requires assistance to unlock. In some cases the affected finger flicks forward.

trike see *trichloroethylene*.

TUC see *Trades Union Congress*.

U

ultra-high frequency is the band of frequency between 300-3000 megahertz in the radio spectrum.

ultrasonic waves are similar to sound waves but have frequencies above the audible range. They are used in industry to clean objects too delicate for other forms of cleaning and for examining, for example pipe-welds.

ultraviolet radiation is high energy, short wave radiation located between visible light and X-rays in the electromagnetic spectrum and form an important part of solar radiation. At 'normal' levels UV radiation acts as a germicide and is essential for the synthesis of Vitamin D in humans; at 'high' levels it causes sunburn, skin cancer and genetic change. Most of the UV radiation that attempts to reach the earth is absorbed in the upper atmosphere by the *ozone layer*.

undertaking is an (business) enterprise.

unfair dismissal see *dismissal*.

Unfair Contract Terms Act 1977, in simple terms, applies where contractual terms attempt to exclude liability, such as liability for personal injury or loss or damage resulting from use of machinery, when such terms are considered unreasonable and/or in breach of legislation.

unsafe acts are caused by failures or faults of persons and may or may not lead to an injury, damage or loss. There are two types of unsafe acts, the *active* and the *passive*. An example of the *active unsafe act* is when an operator removes a safety guard, ostensibly to increase output – assuredly an injury will occur. A *passive unsafe act* is typified by smoking – we are aware of the dangers associated with smoking but still do it and inflict the dangers on others, who may not smoke. Further examples of unsafe acts include horseplay, failing to wear personal protective equipment or trying to work at an unsafe speed.

unsafe conditions are caused by failures or faults of persons and may or may not lead to an injury, damage or loss. Unsafe conditions derive from many sources, including mechanical, physical and environmental, although often they are inter-related and it would be difficult or wrong to 'fit' unsafe conditions into one category. Mechanical unsafe conditions include those due to factors such as poor design, the removal of guards. Physical unsafe conditions include those arising from unsuitable temperature or **noise**. Unsafe environmental conditions can be due to poor lighting or uneven floors.

uranium is a hard grey metal with a number of isotopes. U^{235} is a naturally occurring radioactive metal and the principal element used in production of nuclear energy. One kilo of U^{235} contains the energy equivalent of around 12,000 barrels of oil.

urban waste water is defined as industrial waste water and domestic sewage.

use has various meanings in health and safety legislation, e.g. in **PUWER**, in relation to work equipment, 'use' includes starting, stopping, programming, setting, transporting, repairing, modifying, maintaining, servicing and cleaning.

Use of Transportable Pressure Receptacles Regulations 1996 see (full title) *Carriage of Dangerous Goods (Classification, Packaging and Labelling) and Use of Transportable Pressure Receptacles Regulations 1996.*

users in the DSER are persons employed by the *employer*, including agency-employed temps. See also *Health and Safety (Display Screen Equipment) Regulations 1992.*

V

vacuum is a space that is completely clear of atoms or molecules; in reality, this is impossible to achieve. The term loosely describes any pressure less than atmospheric pressure, e.g. vacuum braking systems or vacuum flask.

vapours are the gaseous form of substances or *preparations*, which are normally in a solid or liquid. Vapours diffuse widely.

ventilation, in *occupational health* terms, is the replacement, removal or substitution of contaminated or unsuitable air by uncontaminated or healthy air through natural methods or with mechanical assistance.

See also *dilution ventilation*.

very high frequency is the band of frequency between 30-300 megahertz in the radio spectrum.

vibration technically is a periodic motion of the particles of a medium in alternatively opposite directions when the equilibrium has been disturbed, e.g. naturally, chemically or mechanically. Vibration can cause *industrial injuries* and/or ill health.

See also *machinery (or mechanical) hazards, sound* and *vibration white finger*.

vibration white finger is where the finger(s) of the hand blanch and therefore look white. It is usually caused by using vibrating hand tools (e.g. chain saws or drills) and exacerbated when working in very cold weather. Prevention includes reducing time exposed, worker *training*.

See also *work related upper limb disorders*.

vicarious liability, in simple health and safety terms, means an *employer* is liable for the *negligent* or unlawful acts of his/her *employee*(s).

vinyl chloride is a colourless gas or vapour, with a sweet odour, used in adhesives, car parts, wall coverings, copolymer products, etc. It is hazardous to the pulmonary system, liver, kidneys, reproductive system, central nervous system, etc., and toxic by inhalation. Symptoms include dizziness, burning sensation on soles of feet, lack of blood clotting, muscle pain, visual and/or hearing deficiencies, etc., birth defects and decreased sexual function.

280

violence to staff is defined by the Health and Safety Executive in the leaflet IND(G)69L as: '*Any incident in which an employee is abused, threatened or assaulted by a member of the public in circumstances arising out of the course of his or her employment.*'

The above definition ranges from verbal abuse through to physical violence, with sexual or racial harassment falling into the same definition, but the latter more relevantly covered by specific legislation (see **Race Relations Act 1976, Sex Discrimination Act 1975/1986** and the **Employment Protection (Consolidation Act 1978)**. However, the above **HSE** definition appears to exclude violence to staff by a member or members of the same staff, such as **bullying in the workplace** (but see reference to **HSWA** s.53 below). What is common to any incident of violence to staff is an aggressor, who may or may not use *physical* violence.

Reference to the **HSWA** shows that s.2, s.40 and s.53 combine in requiring all *employers* to take action*, so far as is reasonably practicable*, to prevent violence to staff. **HSWA** s.53 of **HSWA** requires action to be taken by *employers* in respect of '. . . any impairment of a person's physical or mental condition' as a consequence of activities at work and the work environment. Furthermore, s.22 of the **HSWA** provides for an authorised inspector to prohibit activities which actually *or may* result in violence to staff from a member of the public, e.g., risk of serious personal injury.

The **MHSWR** Reg.3, requires an assessment of all risks to health (as well as safety) to be made of every workplace and system of work, including taking account of the possibility of violence to staff. However, the **MHSWR** Reg. 22 while not allowing civil action (via the **MHSWR**) by *employees* against their *employers* for recompense following violence to staff, cannot prevent action against breach of other relevant statutory duties.

Failure to notify the authorities of violence to staff under the **Reporting of Injuries Diseases and Dangerous Occurrences Regulations 1995** can result in prosecution. Work-related violence to staff, which includes **bullying in the workplace**, whether or not there has been a known injury, requires an entry to be made in the **accident book**, available for inspection by **Safety** or **Elected Representatives.**

virus is a particulate infective agent, smaller than accepted bacterial forms and invisible by light microscopy. Viruses multiply only in susceptible, living cells, and cause many diseases in humans, lower animals and plants, such as foot and mouth disease, poliomyelitis.

visitors are persons who enter land or premises at the invitation, or with the permission, of the occupier, e.g. customer to a shop.

visual fatigue

See also **Occupiers' Liability Acts 1957** and **1984**.

visual fatigue is the partial loss of vision due to prolonged exposure of the eye to high levels of light (e.g. from a **photocopier**) or to light of a dominant colour.

volenti non fit injuria means that a person knew the risk and took it, an assumption by someone of risk – in simple terms, 'if injury follows their activity, their own fault.' Sometimes used as a defence by defendants but it rarely succeeds, because (amongst other things) **adequate supervision** and **suitable and sufficient training** might have prevented the activity, which led to the injury, ill health or damage.

volt is the **SI Unit** of potential difference, electric potential or emf, where the potential difference across a conductor is one volt when one ampere of current in it dissipates one **watt** of power.

W

warning symbols: substances and preparations dangerous for supply see *Chemicals (Hazard Information and Packaging for Supply) Regulations.*

waste is a term with a multiple of meanings and uses; in *occupational health,* safety and environmental matters the term may be defined by legislation to provide a specific meaning. For example, waste can be classified according to:

origin	e.g. clinical, domestic, agricultural, industrial, nuclear;
form	e.g. solid, liquid, gas; or
properties	e.g. carcinogenic, inert, toxic.

Basically, *controlled wastes* are those defined in the **EPA 1990** and the **CPA 1992**, in addition there are *special wastes,* defined in the *Hazardous Waste Directive 1991.* Waste which has been treated or recovered ceases to be defined as waste and it is important to know when the transition occurs because penalties are quite severe (see *Annex* in the former *Department of Environment Circular 11/94 or Welsh Office Circular 26/94, Scottish Office Environment Department 10/94).*

waste auditing are records kept by waste producers of the composition and volumes of wastes produced and the route and manner of its disposal.

See also *environmental audit.*

waste disposal is the storage or destruction of *waste* in such a way that the detrimental impact on the environment and society is minimised. The disposal (as well as mitigation) of *hazardous waste* in most developed countries of the world is subject to legislative requirements and controls. Waste disposal is frequently combined with recycling.

Waste Disposal Licence is a licence required under the **Control of Pollution Act 1974** providing authority granted by a Waste Disposal Authority for sites concerned with the disposal of controlled waste, i.e. household, commercial and industrial waste. The licence also covers all plant and equipment used for waste disposal on the site.

Waste Management Licensing Regulations 1994 cover registers, applications and waste regulation authorities for the recovery and disposal of waste.

Water Industry Act 1991

Water Industry Act 1991 includes the vesting of the *Secretary of State* and the *Minister for Agriculture, Fisheries and Food* with powers of regulation and supervision (*inter alia*) over matters of pollution.

water pollution control is very much subject to EC Directives, emission standards and quality objectives, constantly being updated and changed. For example, there is a framework Directive and ancillary Directives (Drinking Water Directive (80/778)) the requirements of which have to be fully implemented by 2010.

Water Resources Act 1991, amended by the *Environment Act 1995*, includes making it a criminal offence to cause or knowingly permit specified prohibited or restricted discharges into **controlled waters**; provides the *Secretary of State* with powers to establish *Water Protection Zones* with restrictions on polluting activity; gives powers to the **Secretary of State** *or* the relevant minister to designate **Nitrate** *Sensitive Areas* which restrict the entry of nitrates into **controlled waters** from agriculture activity; regulates effluents causing pollution into the sea.

watt is the **SI Unit** of power equal to one *joule* per second, e.g. 1 horsepower = 745.70 watts.

wavelength is the distance between the crests of any two points on consecutive waves.

Weills disease or *leptospirosis* is caught from rat's urine and is a particular hazard in sewers; still ponds (especially found in their water at the banks); warehouses, where rats use 'runs', where persons with ungloved hands may infect themselves. Incubation time is around ten days. It is rarely communicated from person to person.

Symptoms include chills, fever, hepatitis, vomiting and skin rash. A medical professional must be informed by the person who thinks he/she may have contacted the disease that there is a possibility of an occupational induced disease, with a request for a blood test and if positive, **immediate** treatment, since the disease is fatal if untreated. Prevention methods include elimination of rats, workers to wear suitable PPE at all times.

Welfare Regulations see *Workplace (Health, Safety and Welfare) Regulations 1992.*

white finger see *vibration white finger.*

WHO see *World Health Organisation.*

Wiring Regulations see *IEE Wiring Regulations.*

women(s)' health and safety: requirements and cover have relatively minor difference from general requirements and cover – the extent, if any, to which it should differ is a matter still debated. Women make up 44.25% of the UK labour force in *employment*, with 18% of all managers being women. Certain occupations or professions are predominately female (e.g. nursing, shop sales) and 83% of all part-time workers are women.

The major areas where female gender-specific differences are found are generally claimed to be due to physiological and biological differences (e.g. height, possibly raw strength, pregnancy and specifically women's reproductive organs (see also *toxic shock syndrome*). Furthermore unrecognised factors can intrude. For example assessments are often male biased, cultural differences are rarely considered – farm workers in many parts of Africa and Asia are largely female. As examples, ergonomically based assessments of reach, bench and machinery height may reflect male physiological factors; similarly assessments where raw physical strength is involved, e.g. during certain manual handling tasks, may reflect cultural aspects – the 'weak woman' syndrome. Even tools, equipment and personal protective equipment (despite legislation requiring PPE to fit the wearer) may be biased towards considering the male gender. For an assessment to be valid it must take account of the gender composition of the whole workforce in the workplace and/or those carrying out a particular task.

Examples where gender-specific *occupational health* and safety requirements are found include the amended **MHSWR,** which requires women to inform their *employer,* **in writing**, as soon as they know they are pregnant; night workers who are a new or expectant mother are also covered by special *Regulations*; and those who possess a suitable doctor's note, declaring that such work would adversely affect their health and safety, must first be offered suitable alternative *employment,* and the alternatives presented in the immediate above paragraph implemented. Finally, **maternity leave** of 14 weeks is a right for the female gender (as yet, not males), regardless of length of service and number of hours worked.

However, many authorities and authoritative bodies are concerned with the failure to take account of the occupational hazards of particular relevance or unique to women. To fill this gap, various groups and trades unions are carrying out investigations and research into the subject. For example, the GMB union issues a guide to hazards 'women face at work' *Working well together – health and safety for women* (free to GMB Safety Representatives, £10 to non-members). The TUC health and safety unit, also very concerned, carried out research; in April 1999, the TUC issued a (free) report on their findings; *a woman's work is never safe* (copies from TUC Publications Tel: 020 7467 1294).

Woolf Report

The TUC report 'highlights some of the occupational hazards unique to women due to physiological and social differences between the sexes and the way that women's concentration in certain occupations leads to some health and safety hazards having a much greater impact on women'. The researchers involved in the TUC report found that more women than men work in repetitive and monotonous work; young women are more likely than men to be assaulted at work; and the highest rates for work related skin diseases are recorded to be in hairdressing and repetitive assembly, both highly female concentrated occupations. More gender-based *occupational health* and safety research, reports and information are needed.

Woolf Report: the report of a Commission chaired by Lord Woolf, Master of the Rolls, (HMSO 1996) and concerned with reforming civil justice and procedures including personal injury litigation (*not* amounts awarded). In outline the recommendations included:

(i)   making compensation remedies cheaper and easier to use;
(ii)   making litigation the last resort;
(iii) encouraging alternative dispute procedures;
(iv)   judges to act as trial managers, e.g. setting timetables;
(v)   to establish three 'trial tracks',
       (a) small claim courts up to £3,000,
       (b) 'fast track' for up to £10,000, and
       (c) 'multi-track' for bigger and more complex cases;
(vi)   limiting legal fees (suggested £2,500);
(vii) cases to be heard within 30 weeks;
(viii) trial maximum length one day, average to be three hours.

work is defined in Section 52 of the **HSWA 1974** as being 'work as an *employee* or a *self-employed person*' and such a person is considered 'to be *at work* throughout the time he (sic) is in the course of his *employment*, but not otherwise' (S.52(b)).

work environment must satisfy the health, safety **and** welfare requirements and needs of the workforce and includes, where appropriate, those who may be affected by the work activity at that work environment (i.e. visitors, local residents).

The health, safety and welfare requirements and needs for the work environment are, in general, the same as those applicable generally. For example, those covering *lighting* (sufficient for safe working), *smoking* (prioritise non-smoking, consult with all *employees*), *temperature* (minimum, thermometers required), *ventilation* (fresh air of sufficient volume and rate) *workstation* and *sick building syndrome* are those universally applicable.

work equipment is defined at **PUWER** Reg. 2(1) as *any machinery, appliance, apparatus, tool or installation for use at work (whether exclusively or not)*.

work of engineering construction is defined (as is *building operations)* as within the meaning assigned to that phrase by **CDMR** Reg. 2(1). In brief, the term covers any **construction**, alteration, conversion, etc., including site clearance, prior to and after completion of the work.

work related upper limb disorders or *WRULD* is the term used for disorders arising from repetitive work, usually that carried out in an awkward posture and/or constricted working conditions, e.g. forceful and repetitive gripping, twisting, reaching, etc. Many factors common to **WRULD** can be identified, albeit sometimes rather loosely. They include the following:

- involvement of mechanical, physiological and possible psychological processes
- relationship to work intensity and duration
- result in pain and impaired work performance
- increase with the intensity and duration of the work
- may be poorly localised, non-specific and episodic
- are often unreported *
- are 'multifactorial'

It is also possible to identify some of the characterising factors of the disorders and the fatigue:

Factors characterising disorders

- may require periods of hours, weeks, months or years to develop
- may require periods of weeks, months or years for recovery

Factors characterising fatigue

- recovery occurs with cessation, reduction or change of task
- recovery should occur within minutes or hours after cessation of task or, in extreme cases, after a night's rest
- the symptoms . . . (of fatigue) . . . may be confused with those of work related upper limb disorders

There are a number of musculoskeletal disorders that have been shown to be caused or exacerbated by work factors, while others are considered possibly, but less clearly, to be work related. In the early stages of the disorder there may be no indication of the potential **WRULD** long-term symptoms, with little evident bruising or swollen joints.

workforce agreement

The types of disorders or conditions often categorised as **WRULD**s, together with basic explanations, include: muscular pain; separation of surrounding muscle tissue; inflammation of the tendons or the sheath of the tendons; nerve pain caused by inflamed tendons in the wrist; inside palm affected; painful knuckles or joints. Hand-arm vibration syndrome (or HAVS) is another form of **WRULD**, with possibly the most common form being *vibration white finger*.

In summary, work related upper limb disorders or **WRULD** are disorders of the fingers, hands, wrists, elbows shoulders and neck which may be caused or made worse by some work activities. The provision of a safe system and place of work, which are legal duties and requirements placed on *employers* by s.2 of the **HSWA** would significantly reduce, if not totally eliminate, the onset of many WRULDs.

workforce agreement is one made between an *employer* and representatives of its workforce *in the absence of a recognised trade union*. This agreement requires that workforce representatives have been elected.

workforce representatives are persons elected by secret ballot from members of a relevant workforce, for a defined period.

workgroups (psychological term) *form* (e.g. self-form) or are *formed* (e.g. by management) in every work environment, generally to carry out particular tasks. A small workgroup would have up to 20 or so members. Irrespective as to why they are formed, the members of a workgroup adjust to each other and patterns of behaviour develop and become established as the group *norm*, e.g. the expected behaviour or 'custom and practice' of the group as a whole or of each individual member.

These norms can lead to an increase (positive) or reduction (negative) in productivity or positive or negative development of safe working practices. The group leader may be formally or informally 'appointed', with the formally appointed person not necessarily the recognised leader by members of a group. Effectively, workgroups are a social group, with jointly held expectations, loyalties, exchange relationships and compulsory duties.

From a health and safety perspective, workgroups and particularly their leaders, are very important. *Group cohesiveness* can cause the members of a workgroup to unite against what they perceive as a threat to an individual member or the workgroup as a unit. To initiate desired change in behaviour is best achieved through identifying the actual group leader and changing his/her negative beliefs and behaviour regarding health and safety, which will eventually permeate throughout the group and become the group norm.

working at heights is largely covered by four *Regulations*. They are the *Provision and Use of Work Equipment Regulations 1998, Workplace (Health, Safety and Welfare Regulations 1992* and, for all construction sites (including demolition), the *Construction (Design and Management) Regulations 1994* and the *Construction, Health Safety and Welfare Regulations 1996.*

working space should be 'sufficient' in floor area, height and unoccupied space for the health, safety and welfare of *employees.*

See also *Workplace (Health, Safety and Welfare) Regulations 1992.*

Working Time Regulations 1998 (WTR) came into effect on 1 October 1998. The WTR have three main factors within them which, with significant exclusions, otherwise cover all *employees* and in effect straddle both health and safety and *employment* legislation. However, despite publicity, the WTR are often not applied, poorly understood by employers and employees, and seldom enforced. Salient points include:

(i) *employees* have optional agreements and if they are dismissed because they have not agreed to the *employer's* preferred choice, they are *automatically* considered to be unfairly dismissed;

(ii) unlike under *employment* law, the rights provided to *employees* under the **WTR**, as with all health and safety legislation, start immediately, there is no waiting period;

(iii) finally, similar to the **HSWA**, the **WTR** cover *all employees*, subject to the noted exemptions (see below).

In a simplified overview of the **WTR**, the main features are as follows:

agency workers are covered by the **WTR**.

annual leave: after three months' service all *employees*, from 1 October 1998 until 22 November 1999, will be *entitled* (as a right) to three weeks **paid** leave. From 23 November 1999 this *entitlement* goes up to four weeks **paid** leave. (See also **public and/or bank holidays** below).

daily and weekly rest periods: after six hours work an *employee* is entitled to a 20 minutes break period, although if an *employee* wishes to work through a rest break, he/she can do so. Each 24 hours an *employee* is entitled to a minimum of 11 hours rest break and 24 hours continuous rest break each seven days. It is the *employee* who holds the entitlement and the option to work extra or not.

derogation is specified in Regulation 19, and concerns activities such as those affected by *accident*, imminent risk of *accident* or where there are exceptional circumstances beyond the *employer's* control.

excluded from the **Regulations** are those *employees* who work in the following sectors: air, rail, road, sea, inland waterway and lake transport; work at sea; doctors in *training*; armed forces, police and similar services. Partial exceptions apply to domestic servants in *private* households. Length of night work and rest periods and rest breaks do not apply to specified categories of workers (see Reg. 27).

health and safety implications, basically covered by Reg. 28, are mainly concerned with hours of work, monotonous work, rest periods, health assessment, night work and record keeping.

inspection of records by the appropriate authorities means that an accurate copy must be kept and made available for inspection by the relevant inspecting authorities.

maximum working week, averaged over a 17-week period, must not exceed 48 hours *unless or until the employee and employer mutually agree otherwise.* Neither party can *force* the other to agree to work extra hours.

night work is defined in the **Regulations** as a period of at least seven hours which includes the hours between midnight and 05.00. The exact period will be determined by the relevant agreement or, in default, the period between 23.00 and 06.00. According to the **Regulations**, there are two different types of night work, the 'normal' and the 'hazardous'. 'Normal' **night work** broadly follows the standard dictionary definition; 'hazardous' night work is that identified as such by a relevant collective or workforce agreement, or following the findings of the mandatory risk assessment.

penalties for convicted offenders against the **WTR** are similar to those provided for breaches of the **HSWA ss2–7,** with fines of up to £5,000 per offence and/or six months' imprisonment in the *Magistrates' Court* or an unlimited fine per convicted offence and/or up to two years' imprisonment per convicted offence in the higher courts. It is **not** a defence to declare ignorance of the **Regulations'** existence or their content.

public and/or bank holidays are an area of negotiation and debate, *case law* will eventually determine whether they part of an annual holiday entitlement. (See also **annual leave** above).

records must be accurate, regularly maintained and updated, kept for at least three years after the last entry. Records must be readily available for inspection by the appropriate authority (see *inspection* above).

written agreement must be provided to *employees* who wish, or agree, to work over the 48 hours average, with a declaration to that fact. The *employer* must keep a record of the *employees* and number of hours each week the relevant *employee* works.

workplace, according to the **WHSWR** Regulation 2, means 'any *premises* or part of *premises* which are not domestic *premises* and are made available to any person as a *place of work*' and includes rooms, lobbies, corridors, staircase, road *or other place* used as a means of *access* or *egress* from the workplace or where facilities are provided for use in connection with the workplace, other than a public road.

Workplace (Health, Safety and Welfare) Regulations 1992 with **ACOP (WHSWR or 'Welfare Regs')** place duties on *employers* regarding workplaces under their control and controllers of premises in respect of matters within their control, such as owners of buildings responsible for such matters as toilets, stairs, ventilation plant, etc. (see also *HSWA s.4*). The *Regulations* are mandatory, except for temporary sites and agriculture (e.g. fairgrounds, where Regs. 20-25 and for agriculture, Regs. 20-22, apply *so far as is reasonably practicable*). The **WHSWR** generally cannot be used in civil actions.

The **WHSWR** apply to virtually all *workplaces*. Exempted are means of transport (unless stationary or when a vehicle is on a **non**-public road); *mineral* extraction mines and quarries; building or engineering **construction** sites. NB If **construction** work is carried out in a workplace and the area is **not** fenced off, then *both* Construction and **WHSWR** can apply.

The **WHSWR** places duties on *employers* including:

Assessments – **must be carried out,** specifically for the **WHSWR.**

Cleanliness – the workplace and equipment **must** be kept clean. Waste must not be allowed to accumulate, except in suitable receptacles.

Clothing – storage accommodation must be provided at work for *employees'* non-work clothing, their work clothing when kept at the workplace and suitable changing facilities provided.

Doors and gates – must be constructed for safe operation, e.g. two way connecting doors should have visibility panes, powered sliding doors should have devices to prevent them falling off their tracks.

Workplace (Health, Safety and Welfare) Regulations 1992

Drinking water – must be provided, readily accessible for all workers.

Escalators and moving walkways – must be safe in use and fitted with necessary safety devices, e.g. emergency stop controls.

Facilities for rest and meals – must be provided at convenient, accessible places, with protection for non-smokers from tobacco smoke in rest rooms and rest areas. Where meals are normally eaten at work, special facilities must be provided.

Falls – preventive measures should be taken to stop people from falling or being struck by falling objects. Tanks or pits should be covered *or* securely fenced.

Floors – should be kept free from obstruction or spillages which could cause slips or falls. They should **not** be slippery, uneven or holed.

Lighting – 'suitable and sufficient' lighting must be provided, with natural light used wherever possible; where necessary, emergency lighting must be supplied.

Maintenance – workplace and equipment must be maintained in good condition (Reg. 5).

Pregnant women and *nursing mothers* – must be given suitable facilities.

Seating – a suitable seat must be provided for those who sit while working.

Space – there should be sufficient floor area, height and unoccupied space for the health, safety and welfare of *employees.*

Staircases/steps – should be well constructed and maintained, with handrails as required for safety.

Suitable and sufficient toilets – must be provided, the numbers per number of *employees* detailed in a schedule to the *Regulations*, at readily accessible places. The toilets should well ventilated, well lit and kept clean. (See also *sanitary conveniences*.)

Temperature – a reasonable temperature must be provided and maintained. The accompanying **ACOP** declares the temperature should be 16°C minimum where sedentary work is carried out and 13°C where work requiring severe physical effort is being done. **NB** There is no maximum temperature cover, however the **HSWA** s.2 requires a 'safe and healthy place of work' *so far as is reasonably practicable*.

Traffic routes – must allow safe usage by pedestrians and vehicles, with traffic routes clearly indicated, e.g. surface marking and suitable signs. The **ACOP** accompanying the **WHSWR** requires the separation of traffic from pedestrians.

Ventilation – enclosed workplaces must be provided with fresh or purified air (Reg. 7).

Washing facilities – including, if needed, showers must provide hot and cold water, soap and hygienic drying facilities.

Windows – transparent or translucent doors or walls must be made of a safety material *or* protected against breakage and must be clearly marked. Opening windows must be safe to use and all windows and skylights must allow safe cleaning.

Workstations – must be suitable for the *employees* who use them and the work which is done, for which see *ergonomics* and *HSDER*.

World Health Organisation (or **WHO**) is a United Nations agency, formed in 1948, to consider and deal with global health issues. It initiates, funds and is responsible for, research studies. The WHO is particularly effective in developing and underdeveloped countries.

World Resources Institute is an organisation funded by the United Nations, together with some national governments and various private organisations, to study the relationship between developmental strategies and environmental issues.

world wide web, www or **the web** is the leading information retrieval service of the *internet*. Released in 1992 the web facilitates *access* to e.g. health and safety information and documentation from worldwide sources, much of it free of charge. Where available, appropriate and possible, web-site addresses are provided in entries in this reference dictionary.

WRULD see *work related upper limb disorders*.

X

X-rays are electromagnetic ionising radiations travelling at the speed of light but whose wavelength is shorter than light. As ionising radiation penetrates matter it collides with atoms and molecules in its path, thereby giving rise to ions and *free radicals*. X-ray collisions are sparely distributed which means that X-rays can traverse the whole body. The *linear energy transfer* (LET) of X-rays is relatively low (compared with alpha particles).

Prevention of damage to persons caused by X-rays can be through isolation, reducing exposure time, screening or by distancing persons from source.

Y

young persons, for the purposes of *occupational health* and safety legislation, are workers under 18 years of age (see also *child employee*). The *Health and Safety (Young Persons) Regulations 1997* (HSYPR) place certain requirements on *employers*, such as a risk assessment *before* young persons start *employment*.

During the prior-to-*employment* assessment (or for any assessment) to comply with the HSYPR *employers* must take account of young persons: lack of experience; immaturity; lack of awareness of actual or potential risks. During the assessment *employers* must check to see if young persons are prohibited from carrying out certain work. The HSYPR and requirements do **not** apply to young persons undergoing *training* at work, the assumption is that they would be closely supervised and any risks reduced to the lowest practical level.

The outcome of the prior-to-*employment* assessment and details of control measures introduced must be passed on to parents or those who have parental responsibilities over the young person(s).

Z

zinc works are where zinc is extracted from ore or from any residue containing zinc, by the application of heat, and/or works in which compounds of zinc are made by methods producing dust or fumes. The *Health and Safety (Emissions into the Atmosphere) Regulations 1983* as amended by the *Health and Safety (Emissions into the Atmosphere) (Amendment) Regulations 1989* cover some of the activities at such places.

zoonoses include: *anthrax* which can be contacted through stripping plaster containing cow-hair (often foreign sourced), included to strengthen the plaster used in 'old' buildings; brucellosis which can be caught by cow herdpersons; leptospirosis **(Weills disease)**; and rabies.